"SURPRISE," 1261 TONS, BUILT AT EAST BOSTON, IN 1850

Before the Mast in the Clippers

The Diaries of Charles A. Abbey
1856 to 1860

Harpur Allen Gosnell

DOVER PUBLICATIONS, INC.
NEW YORK

Published in Canada by General Publishing Company, Ltd., 30 Lesmill Road, Don Mills, Toronto, Ontario.

Published in the United Kingdom by Constable and Company, Ltd., 10 Orange Street, London WC2H 7EG.

This Dover edition, first published in 1989, is an unabridged republication of the work originally published by The Derrydale Press, New York, in 1937, in an edition limited to 950 copies. Some of the illustrations have been moved from their original positions in the book. The frontispiece, originally in color, is here reproduced in black and white.

Manufactured in the United States of America
Dover Publications, Inc., 31 East 2nd Street, Mineola, N.Y. 11501

Library of Congress Cataloging-in-Publication Data

Abbey, Charles A. (Charles Augustus), 1841–1919.
    Before the mast in the clippers.

    "Consists of chapters comprising parts of the diaries, interspersed with short chapters written by [H.A. Gosnell]"—Introd.
    Reprint. Originally published: New York : Derrydale Press, 1937.
    1. Seafaring life. 2. Voyages and travels.
3. Clipper-ships. 4. Abbey, Charles A. (Charles Augustus), 1841–1919—Diaries. I. Gosnell, Harpur Allen, b. 1890. II. Title.
G540.A25 1989   910.4'5   88-31086
ISBN 0-486-25937-4

TABLE OF CONTENTS

(Italicized chapters are diaries)

LIST OF ILLUSTRATIONS

INTRODUCTION

THE clipper ship lore that has come down to us is all too deficient in volume; and now it is fading too fast from the memory of living man. It is hoped that the diaries which form the main body of this book will do their part toward filling a gap in the records of the life lived in those finest days of sail. The manuscripts were written first-hand and on the spot; accordingly they are presented here exactly as written, with no corrections or omissions. When a reader peruses writings of this period he should bear in mind that quotation marks and underlines are often used with meanings the reverse of those to which we are accustomed.

A chart is provided for each voyage, and several also for parts of voyages. Every locality mentioned in any important connection is shown on the pertinent chart. In using any chart, it is convenient to remember that a degree of latitude, 60 minutes, is approximately equal to 60 sea miles—"a mile a minute."

In the diaries there may be some words and terms the meanings of which will not be clear to the uninitiated. It is believed, however, that the enjoyment and the essential understanding of the text are impaired in only a negligible number of places. Therefore no definitions of words, etc., are given in the footnotes.

The reader will find that this volume consists of chapters comprising parts of the diaries, interspersed with short chapters written by the undersigned. The first line or two of each one will show unfailingly in which category that particular chapter belongs. In the Table of Contents each chapter that consists of part of a diary is given in italics. In the chapters which complement the diaries, an attempt has been made to confine the words and phraseology to expressions which cannot fail to be clear to all. If this procedure seems to lead to the use of unnautical terms, a plea for forbearance is hereby made to the more "salty" readers of these pages.

H. A. GOSNELL.

LIEUTENANT COMMANDER
U.S. NAVAL RESERVE

*Princeton, N. J.,
July 15th, 1936.*

BEFORE THE MAST IN THE CLIPPERS

My Johnny was a shoemaker
But now he,s gone away from me
For to reef the topsail he has gone
And sail upon the rolling sea-ea-ea

CHAPTER I

THE CLIPPER AND HER ERA

Of all the ships in which man has ventured upon the waters, probably none is surrounded by the aura possessed by the wooden clipper. She is synonymous with the greatest days of sail. Even the names of the most noted clipper ships tarry in our minds— *Comet, Red Jacket, Flying Cloud, Surprise, Great Republic, James Baines, Challenge, Intrepid, Sovereign of the Seas,* and many, many others. Their era was brief; unfortunately it is fast being forgotten. May these pages serve a little to keep alive the fading memories.

What, then, was a clipper ship? And, first, what was a clipper? Not any old square-rigged "windjammer." Nothing could be farther from the truth, though such belief is widely held. The designation of "clipper" has reference to the lines of the hull of a vessel and, to a slight degree, to the area of canvas carried. It means that the hull was long and sharp and narrow compared with that of the average ship; she was designed for speed at a sacrifice of carrying capacity. Hence a clipper might be a clipper schooner or a clipper bark, etc., or finally a clipper ship. Her complete designation depends upon her rig. It is the clipper *ship* with which we are most intimately concerned.

As has already been intimated, the clipper came into being as a result of a desire for speed. This quality, strangely enough, seems to have been considered of little consequence prior to the 19th century. At any rate the designers seemed either undesirous or incapable of turning out vessels of especially great speed. In the War of 1812, however, the American privateersmen naturally desired, and also required, speed. Consequently a number of sharp fast vessels were built. These were mostly small and many were schooners; a large number of them were built in and near Baltimore, Md. Upon the arrival of peace it became a business proposition from that time on. This must never be forgotten; and it should be further explained at the outset that the fast, small-capacity vessel was a poor investment unless speed was a prime asset. The extremely sharp vessel was still not fast enough to transport the same amount of goods per year as the vessel which had fuller lines and fair speed. And for speed: along with the sharp hulls came the lofty masts and great sail area. This meant larger and hence more costly crews; however, the rig and crew could be reduced, in a measure, in times when speed was at a smaller premium. The 1812 privateers turned to trading after the War, but the vogue for sharp fast ships did not live after them.

One or two decades passed, and in their course a ship was built now and then with sharp concave bows and the long fine lines aft, which meant speed. Notable among these few was the Baltimore clipper *Anne McKim*. But there had to be some real call for speed to bring forth many such vessels. The next demand arose as a result of the opium trade from India to China. Speed was a requisite here for three main purposes: to smuggle successfully, to escape from pirates, and to make progress in the China Sea when the winds and the currents were not right. Here again, however, not so very many fast vessels were constructed, few were very large, and few were ship-rigged.

Next came the desire for speed in the China tea trade. It became quite profitable to transport tea from the Far East—to England particularly—and to get it to its destination in good condition; and the first cargoes to reach port, each season, commanded the best prices. This was a good, long, ocean haul and it brought into being the first *big* clippers—the first big clipper *ships*. Clippers may be denominated in degree as "extreme" and "medium." The year 1845 marks the launch of the *Rainbow* which was probably the first large extreme clipper ship. It might be pointed out here that fast passages could be and were made by several fine ships which were not even medium clippers; for, fast times could be made by full-bodied ships if they had heavy spars and a great spread of sail, if they were driven hard, and if they had good luck with the wind. However, any vessel mentioned in this volume may be taken to be a clipper ship unless otherwise designated.

Thus far, we have seen no great demand for any considerable number of fast large ships. But marine architecture was advancing fast, and also it was enabling the sailing ship to keep ahead of the steamer. So the stage was set for the first real call for the clipper ship. This was the stupendous news of the discovery of gold in California in 1848. A journey across the continent was a terrible undertaking. An Isthmian canal was still nearly seventy years in the future. The route by sea to Panama and then up the Pacific to California had the impediment of a trip across the Isthmus. This part of the journey was only about fifty miles in length but it was a fearful experience. The best way to get from the East Coast to San Francisco was to sail around Cape Horn. And a big strong clipper ship was about the only vessel able to do this with any sort of speed. So the American shipyards began to turn out magnificent ships as plentifully as they could. These could be seen sailing for San Francisco only a few months after their keels were laid.

Thus did the clipper ship era come into being, an era that was to flourish for not more than ten years. The impetus of the gold rush can best be described by pointing out that 4 vessels had reached San Francisco from the East Coast in the twelve months preceding April 1, 1848; and 775 cleared for San Francisco in 1849 (though some never arrived). In 1849 over 90,000 passengers landed at San Francisco from various parts of the world. Then in 1851, strangely enough, came the discovery of gold in Australia. Here was another tremendous boom which the clipper ships helped to make great. In the boom years one-third of a million people landed in Australia annually. The California trade was an affair restricted to the U. S. flag. And as to Australia, too, the American ships had a great advantage for a period. Due to unfortunate shipping laws in effect till 1849, English merchant ships were far behind those of the United States at this time. So, American shipyards constructed and sold to the British nearly all of the finest ships in this trade. They carried the army of gold-seekers and immigrants to Australia and brought the tons of gold dust back. The clipper ship era is truly an American saga.

 Instead of coming home empty, the California clippers soon began to cross the Pacific to China and carry tea from there to the North Atlantic. This made a splendid lucrative combination, and the Yankee ships ran off with the cream of the business which the British had held. A little later some of the ships found profitable cargoes of grain, etc., to take home direct from California. The perfection of the clipper brought many of these fast vessels into the transatlantic trade. When the Australia boom became less frenzied, some of the British-owned speeders entered the England-India trade. Ships which sailed from the North Atlantic to Australia (around the Cape of Good Hope) returned via Cape Horn. Thus were all the leading trade routes of the world covered by flying sails.

The China tea trade, which was the first important clipper ship venture, was also the last one on which the clippers maintained their hold. It has been mentioned how it received its first real spur from the advent of the California ships. This group was augmented later by a few ships from the Australia trade; also by American vessels sailing direct to China from the North Atlantic after the California gold rush was over. The early 'Fifties saw the high-water mark of the clippers, a period when the U. S. merchant marine was for a time ahead of them all. In the later 'Fifties the clipper era had passed its peak but was still strong. The extreme clipper was no longer profitable and the medium clipper was more favored. Soon the drop in trade was such that few new ships of any sharpness could be justified by a demand for speed.

The end of the 'Fifties and the 'Sixties were marked by two great factors: first, the turn of America away from the sea to the winning of the West; and, second, internal strife. Thus ended the dominance of the American clipper ship. The palmy days of the 'Fifties were followed by the continuation of the tea trade carried on with increased vigor on the part of the British. Relieved from the stagnating effects of their former shipping laws, and relieved in large part from American competition, the English went ahead and built some fine clippers of their own. Most of these ships were built for not quite such hard driving and high speed, and were a good deal smaller than the American clippers. The latter had been built for the violent Cape Horn route. The voyage to China and back was a much milder affair. The Britishers were built with an eye toward skimming across the broad tropic areas of calms and faint breezes; and were designed also for beating against the unfavorable though moderate northeast trades to be encountered when almost home.

In these two decades, the 'Fifties and the 'Sixties, the steamship had been developing slowly but surely. It was to be a long time yet before a steamer surpassed the best day's run of a sailing vessel— 449 miles. But the average passage time of the steamer was getting shorter and shorter. The Suez Canal was opened in 1869. Therefore the year 1870 may be taken as the end of the supremacy of the clipper in the tea trade, and the end of the glorious career of the clipper ship forever. Even so, when all is said and done, the sailing records of the clippers still stand unbeaten.

CHAPTER II

A LITTLE SEAMANSHIP

It is hoped that this volume may be acceptable to the average lay reader. Accordingly no attempt will be made here or later to explain in any complete detail the operations involved in sailing a full-rigged ship. A few elementary matters are constantly recurring, however, and it is believed that the diaries can be more fully enjoyed if a few minutes are spent considering these things. There follow at this point, therefore, what may be considered "guides to memory" on a few subjects such as bells, watches, compass directions, masts and sails, etc.

The Ship's Bell

Commencing with the simplest—the bells—we have the system of keeping time aboard ship. All of us are familiar with the scheme used ashore which has a 12-hour cycle of time-keeping where the number of strokes denotes the number of hours elapsed since 12 o'clock. Thus 5 strokes of the clock denote 5 o'clock. On a ship, each cycle is 4 hours in length, and the cycles begin at 4, 8 and 12 o'clock. The passage of time in each 4-hour cycle is announced by the striking of the ship's bell, and the number of strokes signifies the number of *half* hours elapsed since the start of the cycle. Thus, 10:30 o'clock is 5 bells. Four o'clock is 8 bells, as are 8 and 12 o'clock. A complete 4-hour cycle is as follows.

4:00	o'clock	8	bells
4:30	"	1	"
5:00	"	2	"
5:30	"	3	"
6:00	"	4	"
6:30	"	5	"
7:00	"	6	"
7:30	"	7	"
8:00	"	8	"

Ashore, there being just two cycles in the 24 hours, the time is designated as such-and-such an hour A. M. or P. M. At sea there are six cycles, and it is all the more necessary to specify the cycle in order to locate the hour exactly. So, a time is spoken of as a certain number of bells in a certain *watch*. This is the kind of a watch taken up second in order, in the following section.

Watches

The seamen were divided into two approximately equal groups called the starboard and port "watches," each one being under the supervision of one of the Mates, i.e., officers. The starboard watch was berthed in the starboard or right-hand side of the ship, and the port watch in the left side. The crew space was up forward, "before the mast." These two watches were on duty alternately. Their periods of duty also are called "watches," and the duration of these is usually four hours. The watches bear the following names.

12 P. M.– 4 A. M.	Mid watch
4 A. M.– 8 A. M.	Morning watch
8 A. M.– 12 M.	Forenoon watch
12 M.– 4 P. M.	Afternoon watch
4 P. M.– 8 P. M.	Dog watch
8 P. M.–12 P. M.	First watch

In order to remember the names correctly one must bear in mind that the "morning" watch runs from 4 to 8 A. M., *not* from 8 A. M. to 12 M. Incidentally, the "first" watch (8 to 12 P. M.) is the first *night* watch, just as the "mid" watch is the watch in the middle of the night.

Now then, it must be realized that, with the above arrangement of watches, the same group of men would have the same hours on duty, day after day. In order to avoid this circumstance, the dog watch is often divided into two parts, the "first dog" and the "second dog" watch. This makes a total of seven watches a day instead of six; and with two (or more) groups alternating on duty, the times of the watches will change every day. The name "dog" is a corruption of "dock," a "dock watch" being one that is "docked" or shortened. If the men off duty have supper at 6 P. M. and relieve the watch after supper, the first dog watch will be longer than the second. With such a set-up they are often called the "big dog" and the "little dog." Similarly, when midday dinner comes at noon, the forenoon watch is of approximately 4½ hours' duration and the afternoon watch only 3½.

Severe as was this duty of "4 hours on and 4 hours off," it was quite often necessary, in addition, to "call all hands" (i.e., both watches) to shorten sail or perform other duties, no matter what the hour of day or night. Furthermore, the amount of ship's work to be done, frequently required the watch off duty from 8 A. M. to 12 M. or from 12 M. to 4 P. M. to work along with the watch that had the duty. All in all, it was a heavy schedule, and it was frequently difficult or impossible for a man to get enough sleep every 24 hours, let alone have time to attend to any of his own affairs.

The Compass

A brief inspection of the compass card reveals nothing appalling in the way of terms. There are 32 "points" altogether; a point, or the distance between two points, is equal to 11¼°. It would be difficult to memorize all these 32 directions in a cold-blooded manner. In these paragraphs an attempt will be made to furnish a few simple guides which can be remembered easily, and will enable a person to figure out any direction named, and to name correctly any direction desired.

First we have N, E, S and W. That is easy. In between these directions come NE, SE, SW and NW; and the eight, in clockwise order, are N, NE, E, SE, S, SW, W, NW, and N again. In between these eight come eight others: NNE, ENE, ESE, SSE, SSW, WSW, WNW and NNW. That is almost as easy; for it is seen that, in each case, the name of the intermediate direction is simply the combination of the two names of the adjacent directions. It is believed that one will naturally combine the names correctly and not, for instance, say NEN instead of NNE, or NEE for ENE. Incidentally, whenever "north" or "south" is used in conjunction, the pronunciation is *nor'* and *sou'* respectively. Thus *sou'sou'east*, a *nor'wester*, etc.

We have now sixteen directions designated: N, NNE, NE, ENE, E, ESE, SE, SSE, S, SSW, SW, WSW, W, WNW, NW, NNW, and N again. As our list is now getting a little long, let us cut it down so as to include only those directions between N and E: N, NNE, NE, ENE and E. With the next step, the system becomes just a bit complicated. The direction between N and NNE is called N by E (N x E); the direction between NNE and NE is called NE by N; that between NE and ENE is called NE by E; and between ENE and E it is E by N. Offhand there would seem to be no regularity among these designations. Fortunately, however, it is very simple. For instance, it has been pointed out that the direction between NE and ENE is called NE by E. The same direction *could* be called ENE by N. In this class of cases, however, the rule is simply to *call the direction by the briefer name;* thus the direction between NNE and NE is always called NE by N and not NNE by E. This holds all around the compass. We have now covered the last subdivision of points. So, if one remembers this one guide, he can recall and name every one of the thirty-two points of the compass.

COMPASS CARD
From *The Bluejacket's Manual*, U.S. Navy

Almost every direction mentioned in the diaries is the direction according to the magnetic compass, and not the true direction. A compass needle lies parallel to the earth's lines of magnetic force as they exist in the locality in question. (This disregards local conditions whose effect is in fact negligible on a ship built of wood and carrying a cargo including no iron or other magnetic material.) Except in very few places on the earth's surface, these lines of magnetic force do not lie in a north and south direction. The angle by which their direction diverges from true north and south is called the "variation." Tables showing the variation in all important parts of the earth's surface are used to obtain the true direction.

Masts and Sails

No doubt the average lay reader is appalled by any proposal to learn the names of all the sails and spars on a full-rigged ship. As an actual fact, however, it is a simple matter, at least in the case of all the principal ones. This is because each sail, spar, stay, etc., bears the same name as its mast. We shall take a three-masted, square-rigged ship, which is the kind of a vessel we are concerned with throughout the diaries.

Let us, then, consider the masts. First of all each *mast* as casually thought of, consists of a number of sections, one above the other, forming a series of "masts." The names of these masts in each case are as follows, starting at the bottom: *lower* mast, *top*mast, *topgallant* mast, *royal* mast, and *skysail* mast. Each complete mast has a name, the first one being the *fore*mast, the next the *main*mast, and the last the *mizzen*mast. Thus we have the *main topmast, mizzen royal mast*, etc. Every sail and everything else belonging to any section of any mast bears its name, and that is what makes the whole system an easy one. Topgallant is pronounced "t-gallant"; and in every case where "-sail" finishes a compound word, it is slurred as though spelled "-sul"; thus, main *t-gallantsul*. As for the exceptions to the above rule for naming the sails: the particular lower sails, or *courses*, do not bear the complete names of *fore lower sail, main lower sail* and *mizzen lower sail;* their names are *foresail, mainsail* and *crossjack*, pronounced *crow-jick*. Topsail sail area is sometimes divided into upper and lower topsails to facilitate handling.

So then, by learning seven or eight words, the location of all the square sails can be determined. Thus, the fore topsail is the second sail from the bottom on the first mast; the main royal is the fourth sail up, on the second mast; and the mizzen topgallant sail is the third sail from the bottom on the third mast; etc. On certain occasions the square sail area may be extended on one or both sides by the addition of *studding* sails ("scudding" sails), pronounced and often spelled *stunsails*. The system of naming them follows the same rules. Thus the *port main topmast stunsail* is the sail which comprises a left-hand extension of the second lowest sail on the second mast.

The spars to which the tops of the sails are fastened bear the same system of names as their sails and masts. These spars are called *yards* in the case of all the sails just mentioned, except the spars belonging to the stunsails; these are called *booms*. As in the case of the spars and sails, all other gear associated with a mast, bears the name of that mast.

So much for the principal sails and spars of a ship. In order to complete the story it might be well to mention the rest of the sails, giving the few guides necessary for remembering them. These other sails are rigged in a fore-and-aft direction contrary to the square sails which are approximately at right angles to the ship. Now, the top of each section of mast is supported from forward by a *stay*. (The other mast supports do not concern us here.) On some ships, sails are rigged on many of these stays. As before, the names of the stays and of the *staysails* conform to the rules already laid down—for instance, *mizzen topgallant staysail*. As to the fore-and-aft sails which are rigged forward of the first mast, not all conform exactly. These are the sails, *all* of which the average person thinks of as *jibs*. Their actual names are as follows, starting forward from the foremast: *fore topmast staysail, jib,* and *flying jib*. The stays on which they are rigged are secured at the bottom to a series of booms which extend out from the bow. These are known as *bowsprit, jibboom* and *flying jibboom.*

One more group of sails and we are done. Some square-rigged ships carry also a fore-and-aft sail rigged abaft each mast, similar to the principal sails of a schooner. Each has a spar at the top called a gaff. There is a spar at the bottom of the third sail only, however, and it is called a boom. These three sails bear the following names, starting from forward: *fore spencer, main spencer,* and *spanker*. The spanker is really one of the principal sails of a full-rigged ship, as important and as universal as the three jibs just listed. A triangular sail rigged above the gaff of a spencer or spanker is called either a *gaff topsail* or a *club topsail.*

When all is said and done the only terms out of all the foregoing that need to be memorized are: *fore, main, mizzen; lower, top, topgallant, royal,* and *sky*. Crossjack, spanker and stunsail are additional miscellaneous names worth remembering.

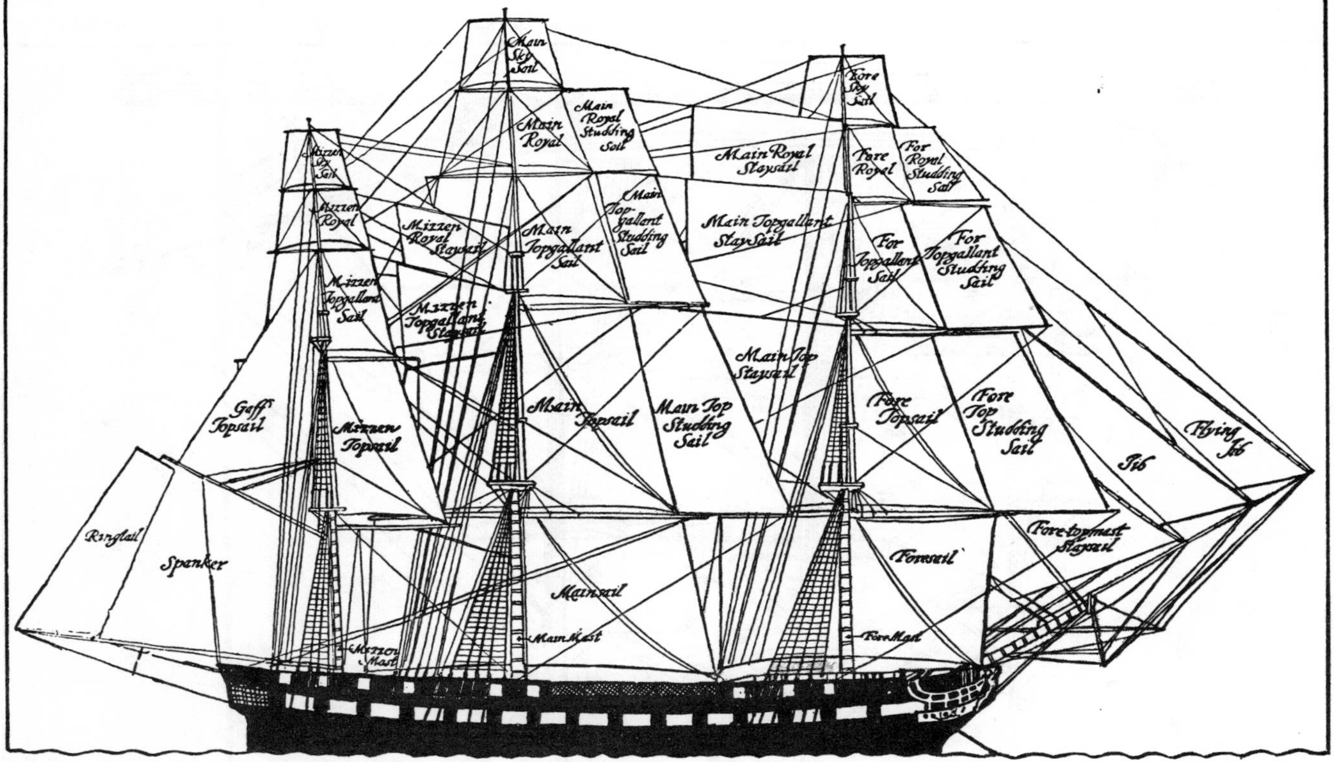
Main Sky Sail
Main Royal
Main Royal Studding Soil
Main Royal Staysail
Fore Sky Sail
Fore Royal
For Royal Studding Sail
Mizzen Sky Sail
Mizzen Royal
Mizzen Royal Staysail
Main Topgallant Sail
Main Topgallant Studding Sail
Main Topgallant Stay Sail
For Topgallant Sail
For Topgallant Studding Sail
Mizzen Topgallant Sail
Mizzen Topgallant Staysail
Main Top Staysail
Gaff Topsail
Mizzen Topsail
Main Topsail
Main Top Studding Sail
Fore Topsail
Fore Top Studding Sail
Flying Jib
Jib
Ringtail
Spanker
Mainsail
Foresail
Fore-topmast Staysail
Mizzen Mast
Main Mast
Fore Mast

From Snow and Gosnell's "On the Decks of 'Old Ironsides' *"*

SAIL PLAN OF A FULL-RIGGED SHIP

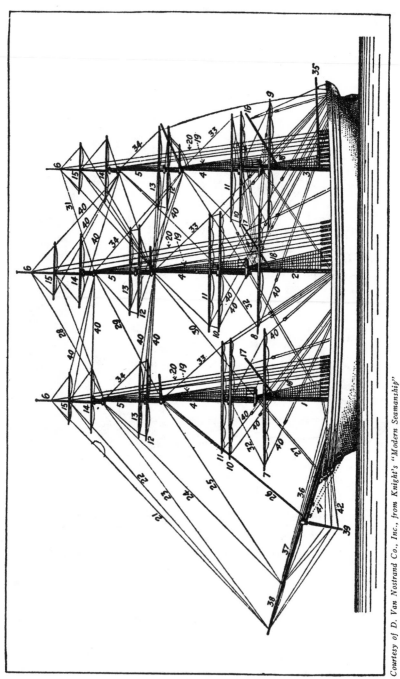

Courtesy of D. Van Nostrand Co., Inc., from Knight's "Modern Seamanship"

RIGGING OF A SHIP

[12]

RIGGING OF A SHIP

1. Foremast.
2. Mainmast.
3. Mizzenmast.
4. Topmasts; fore, main and mizzen.
5. Topgallant masts; fore, main and mizzen.
6. Royal and skysail masts; fore, main and mizzen.
7. Fore yard.
8. Main yard.
9. Crossjack yard.
10. Lower topsail yards; fore, main and mizzen.
11. Upper topsail yards; fore, main and mizzen.
12. Lower topgallant yards; fore, main and mizzen.
13. Upper topgallant yards; fore, main and mizzen.
14. Royal yards; fore, main and mizzen.
15. Skysail yards; fore, main and mizzen.
16. Spanker gaff.
17. Spencer gaff, fore and main.
18. Lower shrouds.
19. Topmast shrouds.
20. Back stays.
21. Fore skysail stay.
22. Fore royal stay.
23. Flying-jib stay.
24. Fore topgallant stay.
25. Jib stay.
26. Fore topmast stays.
27. Fore stays.
28. Main skysail stay.
29. Main topgallant stay.
30. Main topmast stay.
31. Mizzen skysail stay.
32. Fore and main lifts.
33. Topsail lifts.
34. Topgallant lifts.
35. Spanker boom.
36. Bowsprit.
37. Jib boom.
38. Flying jib boom.
39. Dolphin striker.
40. Braces (named from the yard to which they belong).
41. Bobstays.
42. Back-ropes.

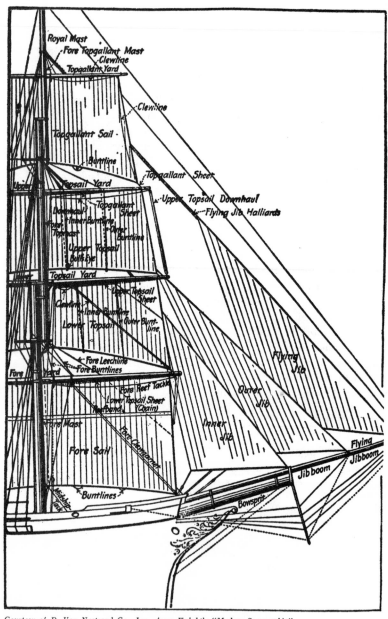

Royal Mast
Fore Topgallant Mast
Clewline
Topgallant Yard
Clewline
Topgallant Sail
Buntline
Topsail Yard
Topgallant Sheet
Upper Topsail Downhaul
Topgallant Sheet
Flying Jib Halliards
Downhaul
Inner Buntline
Fore Topmast
Outer Buntline
Upper Topsail
Bulls Eye
Topsail Yard
Upper Topsail Sheet
Center Inner Buntline
Lower Topsail
Outer Buntline
Fore Leechline
Fore Buntlines
Flying Jib
Fore Yard
Outer Jib
Fore Reef Tackle
Lower Topsail Sheet (Chain)
Reefbands
Inner Jib
Fore Mast
Fore Clewgarnet
Flying Jibboom
Fore Sail
Jibboom
Flying Jibboom
Middle Yard
Buntlines
Bowsprit

FOREMAST AND HEAD-BOOMS OF A SHIP, SAILS SET

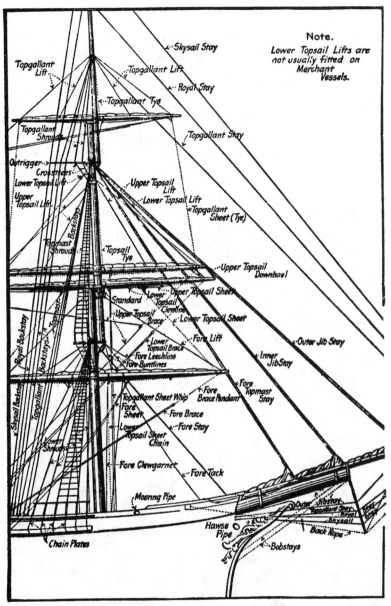

Note.
Lower Topsail Lifts are
not usually fitted on
Merchant
Vessels.

Skysail Stay
Topgallant Lift
Topgallant Lift
Royal Stay
Topgallant Tye
Topgallant Stay
Topgallant Shrouds
Outrigger
Crosstrees
Lower Topsail Lift
Upper Topsail Lift
Upper Topsail Lift
Lower Topsail Lift
Topgallant Sheet (Tye)
Backstays
Topmast Shrouds
Topsail Tye
Upper Topsail Downhaul
Standard
Upper Topsail Sheet
Lower Topsail Clewline
Upper Topsail Brace
Lower Topsail Sheet
Royal Backstay
Backstays
Topmast
Lower Topsail Brace
Fore Lift
Outer Jib Stay
Fore Leechline
Fore Buntlines
Inner Jib Stay
Topgallant Backstay
Topgallant Sheet Whip
Fore Brace Pendant
Fore Topmast Stay
Skysail Backstay
Fore Sheet
Fore Brace
Lower Topsail Sheet Chain
Fore Stay
Lower Shrouds
Fore Clewgarnet
Fore Tack
Mooring Pipe
Outer Jibstay
Topgallant Stay
Royal
Skysail
Back Rope
Hawse Pipe
Chain Plates
Bobstays

Courtesy of D. Van Nostrand Co., Inc., from Knight's "Modern Seamanship"

FOREMAST AND HEAD-BOOMS OF A SHIP

[15]

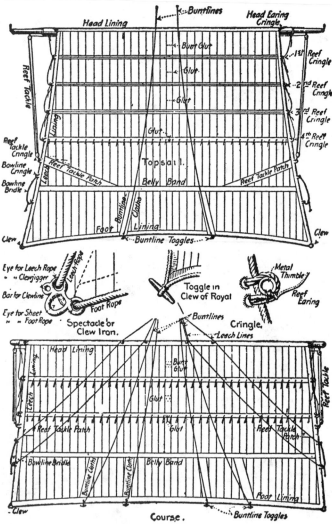

TOPSAIL AND COURSE, FORWARD SIDE

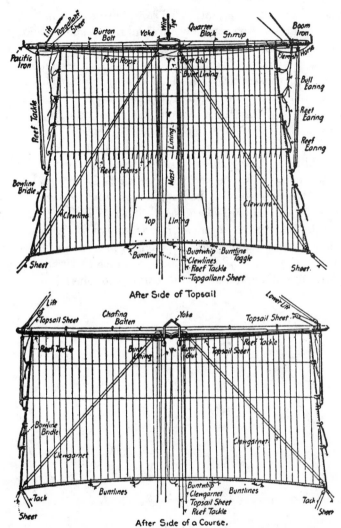

Courtesy of D. Van Nostrand Co., Inc., from Knight's "Modern Seamanship"

TOPSAIL AND COURSE, AFTER SIDE

Sails as high as skysails were not exactly the usual thing, nor stunsails higher than topgallant stunsails. However, the American-built flyer *James Baines* once boasted skysail stunsails and a sail above the main skysail! The sail above a skysail is called a moonsail and was an extremely rare sight. A romantic mate of the lofty clipper ship *John Stuart*, in describing how his ship carried sail, said that above the main skysail she carried a moonsail and above that, consecutively, a cloud-cleaner, a stargazer, a sky-scraper and an angel's footstool; the last, however, was set only in dead calms, and then the watch on deck were not allowed to cough or sneeze for fear of carrying it away.

In addition to the pronunciations already given, the following few also should be borne in mind. Forecastle is *foke-sul*; tackle—*take-ul*; bowline—*bo-lin*; boatswain—*bo-sun*; leeward—*lew-erd*. If "northward" is used in the sense of *north* rather than *toward the north*, it is pronounced *northerd*; similarly with southward, which is pronounced *sutherd*. Keeping in mind the various nautical pronunciations will enable the lay reader to "read" correctly the following diaries even though reading to himself.

CHARLES A. ABBEY AT THE AGE OF FIFTEEN
From an old daguerreotype.

SAIL LOFT

SHIP
CHANDLER

SOUTH STREET, NEW YORK CITY, IN THE 1850's
From a photograph of the miniature group in the Museum of the City of New York.

CHAPTER III

CHARLES A. ABBEY, "BOULD AMERICAN"

Thus does our diarist entitle himself at one point in his writings. This is the youngster who wrote of his life at sea and whose words we are about to read. At the start it is well to study a page or two of his early life and background; this will enable us to appreciate the things he writes and thinks, and to realize in part why he feels and sees various things as he does.

His full name is Charles Augustus Abbey and he was born in Brooklyn, N. Y., April 28, 1841, the son of Horatio Gates Abbey and Maria Young Abbey. The two parents were of pre-Revolutionary stock, of English and Scottish descent. Both were well educated; and in addition each was a musician of no mean report. The mother had been Principal of the Castle Street High School at Geneva, N. Y. The father, an A.B., could well be termed a "scholar." In 1845 he founded and became the head of the Columbia Institute at 61 Hicks Street, Brooklyn. To take care of increased enrollment this academy "for the education of boys" was moved in 1848 to 75 Columbia Street. Here young Abbey received the first four years of his schooling, from the age of six to the age of ten. His parents were identified with Plymouth Church and so he was brought up in the parish of Henry Ward Beecher.

In 1851 Abbey's parents separated and he went to live with a paternal aunt and her husband at Rondout, N. Y. This is a small community about 90 miles up the Hudson River, close to Kingston. Here young Abbey attended the local public school for three years. His uncle, George North, was a prosperous landowner, merchant, and building contractor. Before and after school Abbey worked at all kinds of odd jobs for him while he was living at Rondout. Although little more than a child he covered a milk route for a while, and served virtually as a timekeeper over a number of laborers on other occasions. In 1854 he went to the Peekskill Military Academy at Peekskill, N. Y. As for his future, his uncle wanted him to enter business; his father wanted him to study and to train himself to be an educated and talented scholar. Abbey decided that he wanted to be a sailor; and so he went to sea.

Always a restless youngster, he left home against the advice of all relatives and friends, but not without family consent finally. In pursuance of his decision he left the Peekskill Military Academy in the early spring of 1856, before finishing his second year there.

Abbey's schooling and background have been outlined here in a certain amount of detail; for it is believed that the reader of his diaries will be impressed with the quality of writing and the soundness of views of this mere boy, only 14 years old when he started out. Perhaps it is an indication of superior soundness in the basic primary schooling received by boys of that day. An additional item of interest that will be noted is the manner in which Abbey's viewpoint on many matters alters and matures as the years pass. One more point: among the songs and poems which Abbey included in his diaries (most of which are omitted from this book through lack of space), one is struck with the apparently undue number of melancholy, not to say morbid subjects. This should not be taken as an indication of a gloomy streak in Abbey's make-up; for some reason, any number of sailors on many occasions show this predilection for sad songs, poetry, music, etc. In most cases, however, these same fellows are ordinarily as natural and cheerful as any of the ship's company, both at sea and ashore.

In addition to the songs and poems themselves, are a few lists of song and poem titles and a few lists of book titles. One of these book lists takes the form of a series of one-word "book reviews" which read either "Good" or "Bad." What could be simpler!

Many readers no doubt will be led by these diaries to recall Richard H. Dana's *Two Years Before the Mast*. It is hoped that Abbey's writings may furnish a picture of going to sea in sail in the 'Fifties of the last century, as did Dana's book for the 'Thirties. As will be seen, there was an immense change—and advance —in these twenty intervening years. The chief difference in the two publications is that Dana's experiences were written some time later and were in the form of a narrative. The material in this volume was recorded on the spot and, in most cases, only a few hours after the events described. Each method has its recommendations. It is believed that the reader will find that each presentation furnishes a vivid portrayal of the scene.

CHAPTER IV

THE SHIP *SURPRISE*

ABBEY first went to sea in the *Surprise*. Although he appears not to have realized it, he was starting off in one of the most famous clipper ships of them all. She was built by Samuel Hall in East Boston, the first clipper ship to be constructed there. In fact she was the first large clipper to be built anywhere outside of New York. She was 183′ 3″ in length, 38′ 8″ in breadth, and 22′ in depth of hold. She was designed by Samuel H. Pook, already famous though only 23 years old at the time. Her construction was supervised by the man who was to be her first commander—Captain Philip Dumaresque (pronounced *Du-merrick*). The lengths of the different sections of her mainmast were as follows, starting with the lower mast: 84′, 49′, 28′, 17′ and 13′. Her main (lower) yard was 78′ in length. The bowsprit was 30″ in diameter and extended 35′ from the bow. The reader will be aided in his appreciation of the lengths of masts, etc., if he bears in mind that the height of one story of an average building is roughly 10′.

The tonnage of the *Surprise* was 1,261 as calculated by the method in use prior to 1854. The method used since that date rates her as 1,006. In the earlier days the tonnage was obtained by a complicated series of measurements and arithmetical calculations based upon various dimensions of the ship. The result, however, had little if any real significance, due to the presence in the formulas of arbitrary steps and empirical constants. But, since 1854, the "tonnage" has been at least a true measurement of the interior *volume* of the ship, for it equals the number of cubic feet enclosed by the hull, divided by 100. It is evident that even this "tonnage" has little to do with weight. Where freight rates are mentioned, a "ton" usually means 40 cubic feet unless a ton weight is specified.

The launching of the *Surprise* was a gala affair. A pavilion had been erected from which the ladies might witness the event. The ship was launched not only complete but fully rigged; even her skysail yards were in place. On October 5, 1850, she slid down the ways in perfect style, despite some misgivings. There were those who thought she might be too topheavy for launching if rigged fully and without ballast aboard. After the launch, a grand banquet was held in the gaily decorated mold loft, where the molds or patterns of the ship had been laid out. This feast was given in honor of the families of those men who had actually built the ship. A splendid gilded eagle adorned the bow of the vessel, and the coat of arms of New York was blazoned on the stern. Though built not so sharp as some of her contemporaries, she was nevertheless a sharp clipper. Her owners, A. A. Low and Bro., of New York, were so well pleased with the ship that they donated a bonus of $2,500 to the builders.

With only part of her cargo aboard, the *Surprise* was towed to New York by the *R. B. Forbes*, a noted tug of the period. In the metropolis the beauty of the new clipper was remarked upon widely. She shipped her crew for San Francisco. Her normal complement consisted of 4 mates, 2 boatswains, carpenter, sailmaker, steward, 2 cooks, 30 able bodied seamen ("A. B.'s"), 6 ordinary seamen and 4 boys. This provided 15 A. B.'s, 3 ordinary seamen and 2 boys for each watch. It will be seen that there were only 8 A. B.'s, 2 boys and 4 Chinamen per watch when Abbey sailed in her. Her career opened with a great bang. Her first cargo weighed 1,800 tons, was valued at $200,000, and the manifest was 25 feet long! She was away on December 13, 1850, less than 10 weeks after she had been launched. She anchored in San Francisco Bay 96 days and 15 hours after passing Sandy Hook. Thus, on her very first voyage she cracked the existing record which was held by the *Sea Witch*. A certain native son of California had wagered that she would do so, but the days went by and she did not put in an appearance at her destination. As the limit of time was drawing near, this sportsman rode over the hills to search the horizon. A fog shortened his vision and he returned. The *Surprise* was inside before he got back to his office! On this voyage the topsails were reefed only twice. The ship covered 16,308 miles. A smaller clipper, the *Sea Nymph*, had left New York two days ahead of the *Surprise* but arrived 59 days after her. Only seven ships ever surpassed this time of 96 days. Strangely enough Captain Dumaresque came within three hours of the *Surprise's* time when he was master of the *Romance of the Seas* later on.

From San Francisco the *Surprise* sailed to Hong Kong in 46 days. There she loaded tea for London and she commanded £6 per ton for her freight. This was double what the English ships were getting. The *Surprise* was the second American vessel to enter the China–England tea trade. She reached London in 107 days and, when accounts were reckoned up, an astounding result was apparent. To date, she had *netted* her owners $50,000 profit over and above all expenses and costs *including the cost of the ship herself!* She continued throughout her career to be one of the best money-makers of all the clipper ships.

The *Surprise* returned to Hong Kong in 123 days, requiring 42 from Anjer to destination. Also on the return trip she was delayed in the China Sea by the monsoon, taking 30 days to Anjer but only 76 from there to Deal and one more to London. At last she returned to New York, the crossing taking 42 days against continuous westerly winds. Here Captain Dumaresque left her and Captain Charles A. Ranlett took her. As before, she headed for San Francisco when she left New York, and another interesting voyage followed, though no record breaker. She passed Sandy Hook just before noon on March 15, 1853. She was drifting along outside when the *Express* came out a few hours later and a fine race started then and there. The *Surprise* was 5 days ahead at the Atlantic equator and 4 upon reaching the Horn. There the *Express* regained 2 more days when the *Surprise* was balked for a long time by westerly gales. She had a bad time. Captain Ranlett logs on May 7, off the Horn: "Everything wet and cold   men almost ready to give up, in fact 2nd mate and Botswain & some 6 or 7 men have given out—two men for want of clothes." The *Surprise* sailed into San Francisco Bay late in the afternoon of July 9, beating the *Express* in by 2 days. Just outside the Golden Gate she overhauled and passed the clipper ship *Sirocco*. The *Sirocco* was 147 days from Sandy Hook, the *Surprise* 117 from New York. The latter consumed 24 days sailing from 50° S. in the Atlantic Ocean to 50° S. in the Pacific Ocean—i.e., rounding the Horn. When it is considered that the record for this comparatively short stretch is 6 days (*Young America*), it can be seen that the *Surprise* turned in another good performance for the voyage as a whole.

This time the *Surprise* went from San Francisco to Shanghai and then returned to New York. The passage home required 98 days, but she arrived in company with the *Stag Hound*. This latter vessel had started her shorter voyage from Whampoa only a day after the *Surprise*. Next came the third and last passage which the *Surprise* made from New York to San Francisco. The time was 118 days, 18 being consumed this time in doubling the Horn. In spite of the fact that these were the only three runs she ever made over this course, only seven other ships ever surpassed her average of 110 days for three trips. Incidentally, four of these seven ships are included in the lone seven that have surpassed her single-trip performance. Again the *Surprise* went from San Francisco to Shanghai and again set sail from that port for New York. She breezed along to the Atlantic equator in 68 days which put her in sight, at least, of the all-time record. The *Surprise*, however, after getting all the way past Bermuda in good style, encountered 20 days of head gales; and so a good performance was spoiled.

A round trip to Shanghai brings her back to New York in 1856 when 14-year-old Charles Abbey goes in her as a "boy." We find Captain Ranlett still commanding her and his son is the Chief Mate. Abbey kept the diary for his first trip in a quaint old ledger 14″ high and with lined pages only 5″ wide. We find blazoned on the flyleaf: "The DAILY JOURNAL for 1856 Published Annually by Francis & Loutrel, Manufacturing Stationers, 77 Maiden Lane, Between William and Gold Streets, New York." On each page is printed the month, date, and day, one page to a day. As Abbey used the January, 1856, pages for his January, 1857, notes, the printed day of the week was two days off. These accordingly were made correct. The manuscript is in pencil but the writing is not bad for a youngster.

Abbey is bound for Georgetown, on Penang Island, which lies off the Malay Peninsula; thence to Singapore, Hong Kong, and Whampoa (Canton). The route lies around the Cape of Good Hope. For some time at the start of the voyage, it will be noted that the course of the *Surprise* is east. Although the Cape is about southeast of New York it was necessary to get to the eastward up in the latitudes where the westerly winds prevail, since the easterly trade winds were to be expected farther south. Should the reader desire to know in greater detail the wind conditions likely to be encountered throughout a China voyage, he may find it expedient to study at this point the accompanying chart.

So now let us, ourselves, embark on the clipper ship *Surprise* for the Far East, and carry with us sympathy and understanding for the boy leaving home so early in life for the hard occupation of "going to sea in sail."

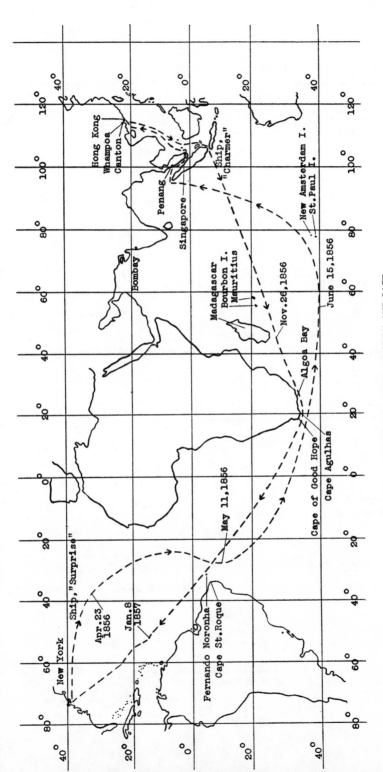

TRACK OF ABBEY'S FIRST VOYAGE TO CHINA AND BACK

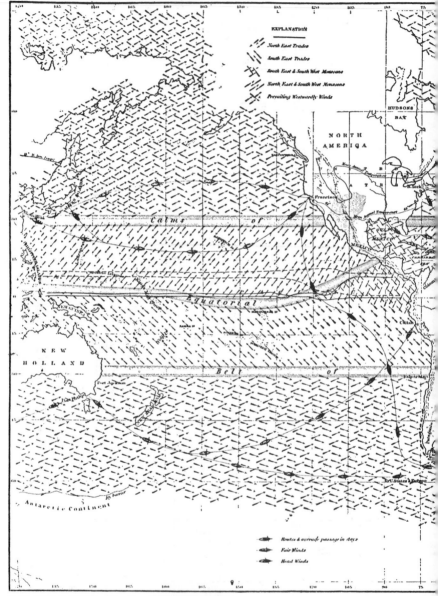

WINDS AND ROUTES

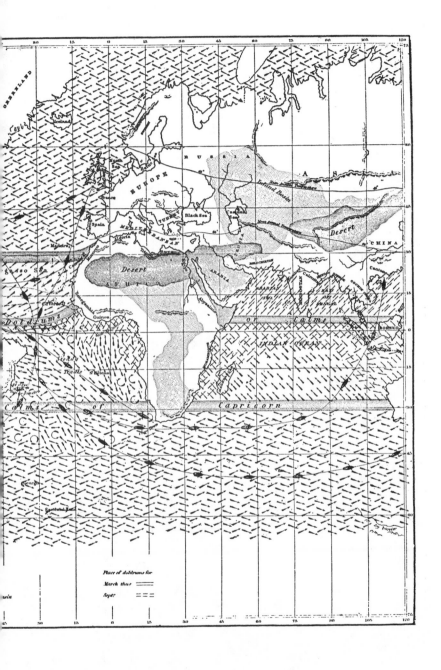

CHAPTER V

THE DAILY JOURNAL FOR 1856

kept by C. A. Abbey on board the ships Surprise & Charmer
to China & Back

Officers of Ship Surprise

Captain

Charles A. Ranlett

Chief Mate

Charles A. Ranlett Jr

2^{d} Mate

J—— Dow

3^{d} Mate

Arthur Brown

Passengers

John Hilliard

Harry Price

of Wilmington Del

April 12 Saturday

I went on board the Ship Surprise & sailed that day for Penang,
East Indies. A very fresh breeze & a heavy sea with the ship in
ballast soon made me "*cast up my acc/*," which I think my father
(who was in the steamtug ahead of us) saw me do.

April 13 Sunday

This day I was too sick to notice anything in particular except
that the cheif mate & captains son was turned off duty by his

father for swearing at one of the sailors   wind blowing quite
fresh & the ship rolling heavily
Course due East. Saw a bark

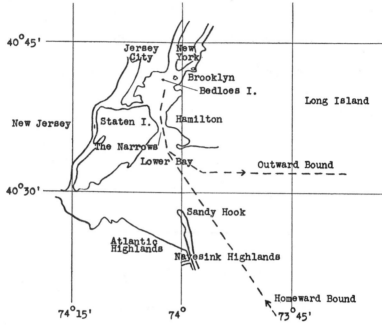

NEW YORK HARBOR AND VICINITY

April 14 Monday

Sea sick still but had to go to work. Reef topsail breeze all the
while because the ship being so light she would not carry any more
Course due East   saw a Hmd^{te} brig

April 15 Tuesday

Sea sick still. This morn went to washing off the quarter deck in a
rain storm So weak that I could not work very well (which the 2^d
mate in whose watch I am) did not like nor would he make any
allowance for sicknefs. Shook the reefs out of the topsail (main)
but not the fore & mizzen
Course East by a little South

April 16 Wednesday

Sea sick still in a measure This morning while taking in the fore
top Gallant Sail the second mate threw a length of rope (at the

crowd in general & me in particular), (I suspect) which struck me
on the back of the head. Repeated the operation twice and all because we did not hurry faster than our legs would carry us, to the
lee rigging
Course East by a little South.
The mate got struck in the head accidentally a few days before we
sailed, by a piece of wood (which was partly the cause of his going
below) & this morning the captain had to lock him in his room as
he was crazy

April 17 Thursday

Quite thick headed yet. This morning we shook the reef out of the
maintopsail & having only the watch on deck took the topsail halyards to the capstan to hoist the yard   got the turns around &
the bars in in their holes but still the word to heave did not come so
we leaned up against our bars & waited. bye & bye the last man
came down from the yard & the 2ᵈ mate met him as soon as his
feet touched the deck with a *"thumper"* right in the mouth & nose
& then asked him what he meant by leaving the earings flying
the man maddened by the unexpected blow, growled out some un-
intelligible words at which the mate got mad & ran "aft," to get
a belaying pin with which he struck the man & ordered him to the
capstan. He did so but words were constantly passing between
them & at last the man spoke out loud enough to be heard by all
around & said, That, "If he struck him again he was as able as
the next man to strike him back & he would do so," at which the
mate made a spring for a belaying pin again & the man ran forward, aft the foremast & soon came walking or rather running
back with a capstan bar   the mate met him & ordered him to put
it down   he would not do it & the mate then struck him a quick
blow on the knuckles which made him drop his weapon & run with
the mate after him striking him on the back & head   he got to the
capstan & we *"mast headed"* the yard & then he went aloft & made
fast the ———— troublesome earings   set the main royal.
Course East by a little South

April 18 Friday

Sea sicknefs all gone feel *"tip top"* all but a little Homesick. This
morn all the watch went aloft to furl the *"crofsjack"*   when we got
through I came down & on reaching the deck the 2ᵈ mate ordered
one of the men to slack some rope which I knew nothing about &

I was a little bewildered but started just as he repeated the order to me & struck me on the back of the neck & head twice & swore at me   Quite a fine breeze

Course due East

Saw a sail & had all hands on deck in the aft^n making "Sennet,"

April 19 Saturday

Do not feel well have been very weak ever since we sailed. Our forenoon watch below today, so I *"bunked in"* & had a snooze. Made "sennet" this aftn. Had "watch & watch" today.

Course East, with a good breeze. Getting quite warm   Sent up the main "skysail" yard this evening

April 20 Sunday

Feel quite unwell today   had watch & watch & nothing to do. Washed & drefsed ourselves   overhauled my chest.

Course SouthEast by South   getting very warm.

Tonight about 11 oclock Mr Dow the 2^d mate set the watch at work getting the topmast studding sail boom aloft. He told me to take the boom Brace up on the fore yard to the men & gave me the end of it. It was coiled away on some other rigging & I not knowing any thing about the work commenced to clear it away to take it on my arm   one of the other boys (Wm Scott by name) stood behind me & commenced to take it up   I had rather have gone aloft a great deal than stay on deck & was on the point of telling Scott to stop, when the 2^d mate struck me with all his force in the back of the head & said. *"G–d, d—n you will you let that boy take it aloft, will you, will you"* at the same time knocking me down on the deck & springing upon me & striking me on the back & head with both hands & pounded me with his heel on the head all the time swearing fearfully,   as soon as I could get up I started to go up aloft & he took out a belaying pin & would have struck me had he not found it to be iron instead of wood. I could not come out on the next watch my head was so sore. That he inwardly injured me I am confident for I find great difficulty in breathing. It was more than 12 times that he struck me

April 21 Monday

Dont feel very well. Have had a very light breeze with every thing set that we had up. About noon we descried something about 1½ miles off, The mate with one of the quarter boats started for it. It resembled from the ship a man clinging to a spar with his head ontop the water It proved to be a cotton wood stump. Saw some *"Portugese men of war."* a very hot day for our latitude which was 37° 24' North

Course SouthEast by South

April 22 Tuesday

About as well as usual. The 2^d mate set me alone at work to make "Sennet," which I in my state of feeling just then liked very well. Have had a fine wind all the morning & at noon set the starboard Lower *"studding"* sail. Had the fore & main topmast and main top gallant studding sail set all night. Quite cool to what it was yesterday.

Course South by East

April 23 Wednesday

About as usual today. Had a pretty good breeze all day with everything set that would draw. In the night watch from 12 till 4 it came on squally with a little rain & we had to take in the studding sails but soon set them again. The sailors say they never were in such a ship because they dont give us anything fit to eat over 2 or 3 times a week The usual fare is for breakfast salt *"junk"* or beef. For dinner one day bean soup, the next rice the next *"Duff"* & repeat. We had all hands this aft^n cleaning up the *"between Decks"*, All hands are pretty well set against the 2^d mates tyrany Today he for some trifling accident took a large club & beat a sailor most awfully swearing terribly the captain stood by & said to him. "Hey Hey Hey, stop swearing if you cant get along without swearing & knocking the men so, you may quit, I will not have it, I have gone through & knocked down 15 or 20 men but it's no use & I never got so much work done after it." Since that the mate has not sworn so much. Our course today is South & the latitude about 35°

April 24 Thursday

About as usual today. Had all hands in the aft^n. The mate shifted me today from the 2^d mates watch to his an occurrence at which I rejoice greatly. Have been employed "puttying" the cracks between decks all day. The 3^d mate told me last night that our longitude was about 38 West, & the latitude 34°

Course South by East with a good wind

April 25 Friday

Feel pretty well today. Had all hands & finished puttying one side of the between decks   nothing happened in particular

Course South by East with a light wind

I find no time, *"I may as well here note"*, to study or read or take the sun or anything else, & my father will not like it I suppose as He was told by the mate that I would have plenty of time whereas I have none excepting four hours in the night when of course I cant do anything

April 26 Saturday

I am very weak today. Went at my old employment that of puttying the between decks. Nothing of note happened except that Mr Brown 3ᵈ mate (upon my inquiring of him) told me that he thought the *"Skipper"* would have no objections to my coming home in any ship I can find upon our arrival out which would lessen the time of my imprisonment at least 4 months.

Course South with good breeze   averaging about 6 knots

April 27 Sunday

I got some Salts from the 3ᵈ mate (who is very kind to me) & took some & I guess they will help me. My ilnefs is caused by indigestion & entire change of life. One of the boys who is in the 2ᵈ mates watch told me that he told him, he did not know that it was me whom he struck on last Sunday night. But he could not have mistaken me for one of the young men whom he said he thought it was. About noon today the Captain spied a bale of Bombay cotton floating about a mile off & sent a boat & got it but the mark being torn off. He also saw several more.

Course South with a good wind going about 10 knots.

I have this day made up my mind that if I ever get to the good port of New York Again & find my father alive I will go at anything he may set me to & pursue it with as much dilligence as possible

April 28 Monday

I *"Laid up"* last night sick & could not observe anything that passed on deck.

Course South with a good wind.

Really a very fine commencement for my birthday.   The last one

I was sick   the one before that had a bad cut on my knee, & four years ago broke my middle finger on my right hand, in fact not a birthday to my rememberance has passed (of mine) but something has been the matter of me

April 29 Tuesday

Sick as I well could be   the steward made me some Gruel which was the only thing I could eat
Course South

April 30 Wednesday

Sick yet. The Chinese steward brought me some biscuit with butter on them & a cup of green tea sweetened with sugar the greatest luxury I have tasted since we sailed
Course South & by East with fair trades

May 1 Thursday

Quite sick but better than I was yesterday. Got some *"Curry"* from the cabin table today. It was neither more nor lefs than *"boiled" "Chicken"* highly seasoned & mixed with boiled rice & plenty of Gravy.
Course South & by East with fair trades.
The sailors all have a kind word for me & one of them asked me if I wanted any washing or mending done saying that if I did he would do it

May 2 Friday

Sick yet & very weak. I firmly believe that the cause of my sicknefs & weaknefs was caused by the pounding the 2^d mate gave me on the night of the 20th. Signalized a large ship showing English colors, homeward bound
Course South & by East with light winds
Latitude 8° 44′ North
Long — — —

May 3 Saturday

I feel very weak today but I *"turned to"* this evening   I furled a skysail for the first time & I thought I should fall before I got to the yard I was so weak. One of the boys in the 2^d mates watch had to furl & unfurl the skysail 11 times & come to the deck every time the other morning for not turning out when the morning watch was called   we saw five sail today & spoke the French bark *"Tigre"* from Bourbon isle for Havre

Course South by East with light airs

May 4 Sunday

Getting better at last I think   Today the wind is very light & we all sit round ready for anything or something to turn up, every once in a while the officer of the watch gets up & looks to windward if there is any such place & then at the Yards in a dubious manner & the sailors then say, "Now cant you scare up a breeze", & sure enough at that moment the order comes, "Lay aft here the watch & square the Yards" which done in about 5 min. comes the order again "Lay aft here & brace the yards", & repeat.   At about 2 bells in the evening watch came the order take in the *"flying kites,"*   & from that moment we commenced taking in sail as fast as we could down to doublereefed topsails & the rain drenching us through   "Ah thought I this is indeed sailors comfort". While hauling on the reef tackle there came a noise like a clap of thunder & every one thought the fore top Gallant mast was about to go but looking forward by the light of the signal lantern we saw the flying jib blown & split to ribbons & then came the job of taking in & stowing the remains which was quickly done. The wind blew very hard for about 20 minutes & in the next watch we set the *"flying kites"* once more. One of the sailors had a *"Bonita"* on his hook today but before anyone could put the *"Grainse"* into him he worked himself loose.

Course Every way & no way with light catspaws every once in a while from all directions. Latitude about 6° N

Signalized a vessel from Calcutta for N.Y. & saw several sail. Her name was the North America 105 days out. I have since heard that she reported us at New York

May 5 Monday

I feel very well today. We have had light airs & puffs of wind all day, but I was in the between decks & so had nothing to do with the sails but it was hot unto suffocation   now here I sit & cant think of anything to write so Ill stop & mend my clothes

Course South Sou west ½ west

May 6 Tuesday

I am quite unwell today & my head pains me. Nothing in particular happened. I was making sennet all the aft^{n}
Course South Southwest ½ west with light wind

May 7 Wednesday

About as I was yesterday   We moved the spars on the port side & lashed them anew
Course South Southwest with fine trades

May 8 Thursday

Quite sick today & likely to be. Instead of washing decks this morning, we moved all the boats but one & made quite a change in the looks of things. Was employed making *"sennet"*
Course South & by west with good wind
We crofsed the Line last night

May 9 Friday

I am quite well today. Was employed making *"sennet"* as usual all my watch on deck. I cannot find anything to write & so I have to leave a blank space on every leaf   I have been on the Quarter deck once since we came out to take the sun but no one offered to show me anything about it more than I knew or even asked me anything about navigation since we sailed. So as I shall never go to sea again I guess I will keep my Quadrant as nice as I can & when I get ashore I can sell it again. It is indeed a dog's life that I am leading & it makes me mad to think that I should have come when all my friends were against it & I could do so much better & be improving my time ashore. As to having any spare time here it is all nonsense for what with sleeping of which I dont have half enough & washing & mending & taking care of my things I dont have any time left   The greatest comfort I take is in thinking of the time when I shall set foot in New York again & laying plans for the future, But it is no use to groan over it, here I am & here I must stay till we get to some port or another, but my mind is made up that when I can find a ship for New York I shall go home in her if possible
Course South Southwest with light wind

May 10 Saturday

A very fine day. Have been employed making *"Sennet"* as usual &

trimming sail   Today is the anniversary of our sailing & my leaving home if I may use that expression. I should like (oh how much) to be in New York today, & I am sure that if I was I never would come to sea again the longest day I live

Course South South west with fair wind

The captain took a lunar observation today & made the longitude 28° & some minutes

Lat 8° south.

MAY 11 Sunday

I am quite well today. Of course we have nothing to do but trim sail & read. The Captn distributed some tracts among the crew which they most of them read. A great many of them ask me if I cant take them up into the country when we come back, saying they would be willing to work for their board alone, if they could get away from the sea. Very few would follow it at all if they could once get clear of the boarding masters when they get ashore

Course South Southwest by West

We have 41 persons on board all told & the steward is sick & two Chinamen & one sailor has had the scurvy ever since he has been aboard, & some say so bad that he wont live to see the end of this voyage. And besides all this we are very shorthanded for a vessel of this class there being but 8 able seamen 2 boys & 4 Chinamen in each watch making 14 to the watch when there should be not lefs than 20

Latitude 10° 8′ South (at noon)

Longitude 28 West

one month out   MAY 12 Monday

Very well today. The usual routine of sea life. Have got so used to "Duff" that I dont *"hail it with joy"* any more but eat my allowance of molasses with broken crackers

Course South & Southwest with a breeze averaging 9 knots

MAY 13 Tuesday

Another fine day   now we are out of the rainy "Lats." I am now quite used to my duty & sea life & in my watch everything (that is in fine weather) is left to me about furling or loosing the Sky sails or Royals   If a Skysail wants loosing it is "Abbey loose the Main Skysail" or "Abbey furl the Mizzen Skysail" & I tell you *"Abbeys" "shins"* are pretty tough now from constant practice of such things. The 2^d mates watch sent the fore Royal & Skysail yards down yesterday in consequence of the fore topmast head being very rotten & I should not wonder if we loose the upper spars altogather going round the Cape though I hope not   If we do the men say they will take me for the main topgallant mast because I am so tall & long but I guess there aint much danger of such a thing happening

Course Southwest with fair wind

MAY 14 Wednesday

Fine day as usual. While I was eating my ("apology for a breakfast") this morn I heard a noise forward & jumping up I ran along on top of the house to see what was the matter when the 2^d mate came running aft & up to the carpenters bench from which he took the 1st article he could lay hands on (which happened to be a broad axe) with which he ran forward again & one of the men (a young fellow whom the officer has beaten at every opportunity since we sailed) yelled out "Oh you bring an axe here to me you "*Son of a B———h*" at the same time casting about him for some weapon of defence, at which the 2^d mate handed the axe to one of the boys & stepped up to the fellow who retreated as fast, & jumped upon the top gallant forecastle,   the mate telling him to stop which he would not do "then says the officer Ill butcher you now mind", "well butcher away heres a heart that can stand it", says the man, let go those halyards said the mate cooling down at once, the man looked at the ropes & jumping down let go the rope, Now said the mate I want that knife from you   I am using it said the man & you cant have it was the reply. Come aft said the mate which the man did & they went to the captain. The upshot of the matter was that the sailor had his knife taken away from him & was "*hazed*" all day in mid air pounding the rust from the fore topsail halyards. It seems that the cause of the trouble was this. The 2^d mate ordered Bill (the mans name) to let go a tripping line & by mistake he got hold of some halyards, the mate struck him twice at which Bill drew his knife & made two stabs at the officers breast & then it was that he got the axe   the rest you have above

Course South Southwest with light breeze   Saw 2 or 3 sail

MAY 15 Thursday

We have now got a good wind & are standing on our course averaging about 9 knots an hour*   Have been employed picking cotton oakum all day. Every once in a while there comes a little rain squall & of course a little puff of wind; but we dont have to take in any sail so that makes no difference

Course South SouthEast with a very fair wind almost too fair

MAY 16 Friday

The same as usual, an old story of sea life. Picking Oakum all the while I was on deck to caulk the cabin the carpenters have been building ever since we came out. I cant find anything more to add now but when I get ashore (if I ever do) I may have some leisure time in which I think I shall take pleasure in reading these pages over & filling them up with remarks & explanations of a good many things which will interest my friends who may wish to see this book

Course S. S. E. with the same breeze good as yet

MAY 17 Saturday

This morning I had my first hard job, (one which sailors hate) which was reeveing royal studdingsail gear. I had got up on the top gallant yard when I had to go right down again & take a line (the Halyards) up. The way I managed it was thus, I made a "*bowline*" on one end & put it over my shoulder (so that I could use both hands) & then shinned about 30 feet on 2 ropes & rove it through a block at the royal mast head & then, I had to take the bare end & creep out on the yard (a ticklish place) & laid flat holding on with my feet & rove it through another block as far out as it possibly could have been hung. When done I had barely strength to hold on to the rigging. But the worst of it was that we took it all down in about 2 hours & took in all but the topsails

Course SouthEast by East

MAY 18 Sunday

Today we have been under reefed topsails all the time & one reef in the spanker. Crofsjack hauled up. We are just—in fact this is our first touch of the cape   Saturday night there came on an unexpected squall & one sea (an extra one) knocked a poor coolie slap dab out of the weather gangway (where he was on the look-

* The knot is now a unit of speed only, not of distance, and equals one sea mile per hour. A sea mile equals 1.15 land miles.

out) to the deck & wet him through, Ever since then there has been a heavy sea on
Course S. Ea. & by E. ½ E. & there about according to the shifts of the wind

MAY 19 Monday

Topsails reefed as yet. Wind quite strong with very heavy sea The waves averaging about 20 ft in height & frequently higher I have for a part of my regular duty to hold the glafs when the log is hove. This is done twice every watch, viz: at 4 bells & at 8 both night & day. Often will the man at the wheel strike 8 Bells, & our watch go below & get well into our (or my) dinner when, "hold the reel," sings the officer & down has to go the pot, pan, or spoon, as the case may be for that plaguey old glafs. The operation is performed thus, One Chinaman holds the reel, & another stands by ready to catch the line, I have the sand glafs to hold. The officer takes the line & heaves it over the stern at the same time saying to me clear glafs which I repeat he then says, watch, which I also repeat, & watch the glafs closely by this time a small portion of the line has run off & he sings out to me, turn, which I repeat after him at the same time turning the glafs over & watching it till the sand has all run out when I say stop! & he immediately stops the line & looks at the number of knots on the place he caught it up which when he has counted he knows how fast the ship is going each knot denoting two miles*
Course S. W. by S. & thereabouts

MAY 20 Tuesday

Whole topsails now & topgallant sails too with an indifferent breeze. In getting into the mates watch I was lucky for I have to stand no lookout whatever unless to stand by the halyards in squally weather, from the time I come on deck till I go below I can sit or lay down or do as I please so long as I am on hand at 4 & 8 bells to hold the glafs when the log is hove, While the 2d mate makes the two boys in his watch stand a lookout on the forecastle 2

---

* This "knot" is not the unit of velocity, or "sea mile per hour," to which reference has already been made. One was derived from the other, however. The distance between knots on a log line is 47′ 4″. Therefore if a 28-second glass, or "long glass," is used, each knot run out on the log line will denote 1 mile per hour. Since each knot on the log line of the *Surprise* denoted *two* miles (per hour), a 14-second glass, or "short" glass, was used.

hours apiece & walk the quarter deck (lee side) the other time. One of them a Washingtonian (& a fair specimen of the inhabitants of that place) gets *"hazed"* considerable on a/c of his carelefsnefs & nonsense. Many a time when he is called will he turn over & go to sleep again & then the 2^d mate comes in & pulls him out by the heels & sends him up to the mizzen skysail & back, & one night he made him ride the topsail halyard block when it blew a perfect *"Paddys"* hurricane.* Last night when our watch went below, we heard him (*"this boy"*) singing out a peculiarly long strain & upon inquiry found that he had gone to sleep the night before on his lookout for which he has to stand his 2 hours on the forecastle on top of the capstan & at every bell instead of singing out *"Starboard Cathead"* he has to say *"I am standing on the capstan for going to sleep on my lookout"* but he being a regular scapegrace dont care a snap & says he is bound to go to sea anyhow & means to stay in this ship as long as he can

Course, no way in particular & every way in general

MAY 21 Wednesday

We are at last under royals & skysails again. This morning our watch unbent the mizzen topsail & the new mainsail & bent two others in their places which occupied us the whole morning. This aft^n the weather came on squally & with some rain & we were under the top gallant sails the rest of the day. The man who had the scurvy has become somewhat crazy & we have put him into the house over the main hatch where I sat with him the whole of the evening watch & read the bible to him, He would start up & say "what do they want to tie that black dog there to frighten me for I know them, they are going to set him on me" & then he would lay down awhile, then he would tell us to call the captain that he was going to die & when the captain came & asked what he wanted he would say *"nothing"* but his principle horror was *"that black dog"* but no black dog was aboard, so we had to humor him & tell him there was no dog there   He told me that he was a native of Halifax & he could neither read nor write which he regretted greatly. He is in the prime of life & one of the best sailors aboard & it would be a pity to loose him

Course S E by S & thereabouts

* Our chronicler evidently meant that it was blowing very hard. A "Paddy's hurricane," however, is slang for no wind at all. Sometimes called an "Irish gale."

MAY 22 Thursday

Was awaked from a good nap this morning by being hove on my *"beam ends"* to leward in my bunk & starting up found the vessel pitching like one mad & from the noise on deck knew the watch were taking in sail. Now thought I, here is a very pleasant prospect of being turned out of my warm bunk & called on the cold wet decks. Just at that moment I heard the mate go past my door & say to the 2ᵈ mate *"Call the watch"* & without more ado I tumbled out, & in less than 5 minutes was *"laying"* over the foretopsail yard *"hauling out to leward,"* & knotting reef points, in a drenching rain. (I found upon reaching the deck that we had been struck by a very heavy squall). We manned the Halyards & *"Old Tom"* gave us a good song (*"A Whiskey Johnny"*) & we soon had the yards up. The weather continued squally all day & we reefed the main top gallant sail which was as much as we dared to carry. We now can set down to do nothing with a will, for the next minute we have to let go all the topgallant halyards & in 2 or 3 more set the sails again The weather is very squally.
Course South East
Lat 24° 52′ South

MAY 23 Friday

The wind holds pretty good. The sea is pretty (yes very) rough. The usual routine of sea duty, letting go & hoisting the yards & reefing topsails all the while We have to be resigned to our food which is enough to turn ones stomach & would ours were we not so hungry. And to make the matter worse we are on allowance of 5 biscuit a day. The food is of the poorest quality & was (I suppose) bought as cheap as possible. Many is the time I go to sleep & am so hungry that I commence dreaming about the best of dinners & eatables of all sorts & just as I am ready to eat am called out to help reef a (confounded) topsail or some other such work. My greatest comfort is to plan what I will do ashore (if I ever get there) & think what I would eat if I was there now, & what I would do first upon getting back to New York. But that is all foolishnefs you may say & that my thoughts are of my stomach more than my work. Let me beg of you to try it & see where your thoughts will run. Besides it cheers me up & I feel all the better for doing it. But when I think what I must go through before that good time of reaching home I get the *"downs"* again But I must *"grin & bear it*" for my own foolish waywardnefs has brought it all upon me & I blame no one but myself. It will be the making of me though I think, for when I get back I shall go at something in earnest & attend to it. I have laid out plans which if followed up will suit me & cannot fail to suit my friends also. But I shall not introduce them here of course

Course S. E.

May 24 Saturday

Last night while lying in the House over the main hatch, I was alone & as usual thinking of home when all at once (I was half asleep & half awake & so was taken off my guard) There came a *tremendous* sea (a huge roller) & the next I knew I found myself bang to leeward among a medley of boards old canvas, tarpaulins, & what not & had it not been for the combings of the hatchway, (which prevented the house itself from going over) I might easily enough have been smashed up & killed. I picked up my legs & being fully awake to my dangerous position, had sense enough to know that the receding of the swell would send things back as far to windward as they had gone the other way, I sprang out upon deck just in time to keep out of the way of the return of the house   I found the state of things on deck as bad as they were in the house for the boats on the beams had shifted & the "*wash deck*" (blasted be the term) pump had gont over & lay flat on deck. Here was an hours work for our watch thought I, but the mate with more generosity than he ever displayed before only kept us about half the time.

Course S. E. with good breeze

May 25 Sunday

This is the 3ᵈ uncomfortable Sunday we have had in succefsion We tacked ship 3 times today & of course had to "*roust out*" all hands to perform the operation   For a description of all the orders you must look at "*Two years before the mast*" where the operation is all very minutely described. My station is at the Lee crofs jack braces which it is my duty to haul round assisted by the other boys. We have nothing to do of course but trim sail today & have "*duff*" for dinner. Oh with what significance does that word "*duff*" ring on my ears. Ever after I shall remember it in connexion with the hardest spots in my life   It is simply flour &

water with dried apples mixed in & the whole boiled down hard & heavy as lead in a canvas bag. When first taken out of the bag it looks like a loaf of white sugar as much as can be   Two months ago I would have turned from it with disgust but now I am glad enough to get it. I have made *"scouse"* for the last two days out of my allowance by breaking up some biscuit & soaking it in water a few minutes & cutting in bits of beef, then put in some *"slush"* or grease of any sort & let the cook bake it for me   It is better than nothing though, how ever bad it may be. But *"Starvation reigns supreme"* in reality here

Course No way in Particular & every way in general.

MAY 26 Monday

This has been a very fine day taken altogather,   Have been under topgallant sails all day with a light wind the ship going about 6 knots on an average. Was employed making *"sennet"*   nothing of note transpired besides

Course S. S. W. & thereabouts

MAY 27 Tuesday

This day comes in squally with some rain, which state of things continued till about 6 bells in the morning watch,   when it commenced to rain, & breezed up untill it got to be a *"fair wind"* & the Captain says it will hold for 3 weeks. I only hope it does for it will take us clear of the *"Cape"* which is the *"bugbear"* of the crew. It is now my businefs on the night watch to stand by the mizzen royal or topgallant halyards & I regularly get my back soaked with rain water but "there I am & there I must stay" stiff as a dock spile till 8 bells & *"relief"* by one of the other boys. We set the foretop & main top gallant studding sails today for the first time in a good while.

Course SE by S. & S.S.E. going about 8 knots

MAY 28 Wednesday

We have been pulling & hauling this way & that all day long & to crown all rove a lot of studdingsail gear (which is some of the hardest of sailors duty) which we have not used at all & have fair Prospect of having to take it in tomorrow

Course S. E. by South

May 29 Thursday

Today has been a very uncomfortable day out of doors but it was bright enough inside for we have had *"Sea Pie"* for dinner & that (for us poor half starved wretches) was enough to make anything bright. I went to the galley for my mefs & got an enormous quantity, but my stomach was not to be beat & naught but an empty pan went back. I forgot to say that we killed a pig yesterday which furnished us with fresh meat for the *"Sea Pie"*. We are now just in the Latitude of the Cape though we have no very bad weather yet. The "Magellan Clouds" & *"Southern Crofs"* have been in sight for a long time which I have before forgotten to state. There are also plenty of *"Gulls" "Boobys" "Stormy Petrels"* or as the sailors call them *"Mother Carys Chickens"* & they also say that each one of them is a dead sailors soul which of course is nonsense
Course S. S. W & S. W.

May 30 Friday

Our watch has the forenoon watch below today & I having written a letter or commenced one, set myself to work to make a "Thrum Mat" to take home with me. I can not read so I got a small block & commenced a boat. It may be foolish but every man & boy on board is commencing something for a memento of *"hard times"* & I must do so too.
Course S & thereabouts
Lat 34° —′

May 31 Saturday

When I went on deck this morn I went to the locker & proceeded to get some *"sennet"* out to go to work at when the men, some of them, said what are you doing *"Abbey"* there is no work today (it was stormy) put that back. I did so & went into the house to change my pants when Mr B———n 3ᵈ mate called me out & made me & 2 other hands go to slushing down,   And of all the dirtyest, nastiest, stickiest, hardest, work I ever done that was the *"cap sheaf"* & to make it still worse I had the main top & top gallant mast & never having done such work before I made an awful job of it. But as *"Dana"* in "two years before the mast," says, I knew it could not last always so I stuck it out & finished it.
Course S. & thereabouts, with light wind

June 1 Sunday

This is a beautiful day & a morning watch below*   makes it all the more agreeable to me. I employ my time in reading & writing & sleeping   The captain & cabin passengers are trying to catch Albatrosses & Cape Pigeons but cant make it out   We have not seen a sail for some time, but I hope in a day or two we shall head off for the North & East & as soon as we are clear of this *"buggered"* ("Cape,") we shall see plenty of them
Course S. E. by E. ½E.

June 2 Monday

When called at 7 bells this morn to take the deck one of the boys said, Oh you didn't turn out in time to see the whale, & there is a large ship astern too. But if I didnt see the whale I saw the ship & if the *"Old Man"* want in a stew for fear she would overhaul us then nobody ever was. A pretty set of officers we have at any rate both the 1ˢᵗ & 3ᵈ mates go to sleep in their night watch & If they wake up & find me or the other boys doing the same, Why they are pretty sure to stir us up with a capstan bar & make us shoulder it & keep sentry along the ¼ deck   I have had it done to me twice but I shant again if I can help it. Last night the 3ᵈ mate went up on the poop & sat down by the mate & went to sleep while talking with him but the 1ˢᵗ mate is not much better & so he said nothing. The men in the forcastle say to me, "You keep a journal, why dont you put all these things down & when you get back make a *"bloody show"* of these fellows, say you got 5 biscuit a day for an allowance & generally 1 & sometimes 2 & 3 of those were rotten & mouldy so that you could not eat them"   which is in fact the case. But as I cant help it I sing, *"Hurrah for Hard times"* & *"Good time coming"* *"Wait a little Longer"* & grin & bear it, But though hard is our or my lot, I have friends in the sailors forward (who not being on allowance as we boys are), have plenty of biscuit & beef & they always say *"Charley"* got enough grub for ten if not come forward I'll give you some. And many is the time I avail myself of their aid for which they consider themselves well paid with the loan of a book, or, the waking of them up to take their wheel at night when they are asleep in the *"Hatch House"* or Sailors Lodge as we call it. I must not forget to state that we

* Probably the "forenoon," or 8 A. M. to 12 M., watch is meant. The morning, or 4 to 8 A. M., watch would be spent below anyway by the men not on watch, especially on Sunday.

soon had the ship we saw this morn "Hull Down" & finally out of sight.

Course E. S. E. ½S & thereabouts

It was one evening in the month of June 1856, that the good ship Surprise was off the Cape of Good Hope. I was standing by the mizzen royal halyards & the mate was pacing the poop in expectation of a change in the wind very soon, as the sky was dark & lowering & banks of mist kept rising incessantly Just as 1 bell struck he stopped & looked steadily to windward. At this junction the captain came on deck & cast a hurried glance around till his eye rested in the same spot as the mates, he looked no longer but sang out at the top of his lungs, "*Clew up the royals.*" In one instant I had let go the mizzen which I had all ready & ran up to the topgallant mast head & furled it. Before I was done I heard the topgallant yards rattle down, & I lent a hand to furl one. Then I went down on deck & laid up the ropes. By this time it was blowing & raining quite hard. All hands then stood by for a call. At 4 bells the mate sang out, "*Call the Watch*" & soon they came tumbling up from below to lend us a hand in reefing down, which operation was performed in about 50 minutes. Then being under snug sail the watch went below. Shortly after it struck 8 bells & I went below. When I came on deck again the sky was clear, the stars were shining & we were under skysails once more.

Chas A. Abbey

*
———*———

Galley Talk

Cook give us that "'*orse*" & the "spuds" "just ask the old man when I shall come & dine with him," "*clar* de kitchen dar" I got my "*reg,lar beef,*" wheres my pot, Tom lend us your spoon & dont cut all the fat off that meat, — Al———l hands shorten sail there

Confound you & your Sails

JUNE 3 Tuesday

I went out on the flying jibboom this morning to loose a couple of jibs & while there espied a sail on the Starboard or Lee bow. This was about daylight & as soon as the mate saw her, he commenced to "*pile on*" sail but much to his & the "*Skippers*" Chagrin she kept along at an even pace with us & continued to do so all day

continually *"luffing"* & we running free once in a while till about
4 oclock in the aftn when we were within ¼ of a mile of her. She
was the *"Skimmer of the Seas"* belonging to & from London for
"Algoa" bay 600 miles north of the Cape. She is one of the
"crack" English craft & is quite celebrated in London for her
speed but she got most awfully *"Surprised"* & beaten too.* We
had scarce passed her when we spied the *Royals* of another craft
just at the horizon on the weather beam. Not long after I went up
to reeve the royal studding sail halyards, & such a job I never had
before nor never want or will have again if I once get home again.
Our Skysail yards being on deck there was nothing to hold on to
but the yard arm & what with a dull heavy sea which sent the yard
1st one side then the other with a jerk hard enough of itself to send
you off the yard if you didnt dig your finger nails into the wood
& my shoes having just been Greased I could not manage to do
anything for a long time   At last one of the sailors looking up
from the yard under me saw my predicament & said, "Sling one
leg over the royal brace Abbey, then hook your block on"   I
thanked him in my heart a thousand times & did so but even then
I was so near tired out with my previous exertions that it took me
a long time to hook it on & mouse it with rope yarns. But he
kindly *"lit up"* the halyards to me & took them down a ways too.
Being in the highest spot on the ships spars I took a seat on the
yard & looked at the last mentioned vessel we saw. From the deck
she was but a speck, but from here I could see the whole of her &
full 10 miles beyond. She carried a main Royal & nothing higher,
but didnt she look insignificant on that broad waste   a mere *"pin
point"* in a mill pond as it were
Course South East by E

JUNE 4 Wednesday
In one month from today it will be the "Glorious 4th & then what
a rejoicing there will be in the States   How queer it seems to be to
talk about the States as a foreign country but it is so neverthelefs. I am now off the Cape in pretty cool weather   I wonder where
I will be then   most probably near the coast of Sumatra in a
burning heat. *"So mote it be."* On that day my friends as well as
myself will be thinking & wondering where *"Carelefs Charley"* is,

* In justice to the *Skimmer* it should be pointed out that the *Surprise* was a
good distance to windward at the start and got in front by giving up this distance.
See also the "race" on June 6.

& whether he is overboard or not & when he will be back if safe
But of one thing I am certain & that is, they cant be more anxious
to have me get back than I am to do so myself. A pretty fine day,
made sennet all the watch
Course S E by E. with "fair wind"

JUNE 5 Thursday

I made "*sennet*" all day today & wrote all my watch below. Now I
cant think of anything to add here so I ll close & fill it up some
other time when I can
Course S. E. by E.
One of the boys is the Captains nephew & has been a voyage before in the ship & he thinks he can do as he pleases in the house, &
being the largest & oldest & strongest he wants to "*bully*" over us
& say & talk as he pleases about us & friends & relations. I have
borne with him a long time & he has struck me twice though I did
not say anything or offer to strike him back. But if he goes on
much longer I shall take "*all aback*" & if I work it right I think
I can whip him. I shall try hard for it anyhow if I do

JUNE 6 Friday

Went on deck this morning & saw a large Clipper Ship about 10
miles to leward & somewhat ahead. We had our topgallant sails
furled but seeing she was carrying hers we of course set ours but
she still continued to haul ahead & soon loosed her royals. But our
"*Old Man*" wouldn't trust to his "*Sticks*" any higher while the
wind continued so strong. Presently the order came "*Abbey*"
loose the Main Royal & I started up the Rigging   when I got upon
the Yard, looking round I espied a "*Chinaman*" lumbering along
up to loose the Mizzen Royal   These once set we were soon skimming along on her heels & finally passed her, & had her out of
sight in 2 hours   She proved to be (another crack John Bull) the
English Cliper Ship "*Mireage*" 3000 tons burthen of & from
London for Bombay. She is considered the crack of the British
Merchantmen in point of sailing but I think she got pretty well
"*Surprised*". The 1st mate C. A. Ranlett Jr is the most boyish
Human being that ever I saw he has two dogs aboard & he plays
with them from morning till night. I do believe that in the most
exciting moment when reefing topsails he would stop & fondle the
dogs if they came in his way. Yesterday he got the cat, (the only
one we have aboard) & put her up in the boats. She being very

wild ran under a grating in the bows of one of them, (the boats being upside down on beams amidships) & he proceeded to set both dogs to teasing her. There they were he & the dogs tormenting a poor half starved cat. They kept it up over ½ an hour & she seeing a chance suddenly started & ran flying over the poop right aft & making a flying leap over the taffrail fell into the water astern & of course was drowned. We are overun with Rats & of course will be worse now she is gone The captain blew the mate Sky High for it but he didnt care. He is no more fit to go mate of this ship than I am for he goes to sleep on his night watch quite often. Course S E by E with good wind

June 7 Saturday

Forenoon watch below today & when ever that is the case I cant note what passes on deck much. Any how I wont forget that we have been put on an allowance of water today for the 1st time. All we get for 24 hours is 3 quarts & from this take 1 qt for tea & 1 qt for coffee & it leaves only 1 qt to drink in 24 hours which is little enough. I never knew or had any Idea what it was to have an allowance of water & food & be so situated that you could get no more, and if ever I get back to N. Y. I never will again. The owners & Captain are very much to blame for sending this ship to sea before she was ready as we now find they did. Why the day we left N. Y. everything was flying & everything down between decks went adrift & upset tar lumber & everything else. And to crown all not more than 2/3 enough water, which is inexcusable. For dinner today I expected to get our usual mefs of codfish & Rice but I was glad to find it Potatoes & Fish instead for a wonder. I suppose that the captain finding them rotting concluded to let the crew eat them up instead
Course S E by E with a "*Paddy's Hurricane*"

June 8 Sunday

It has rained all day or at least all the forenoon watch The mate & captain have caught 2 "*gooneys*" & 5 "Cape hens" this morn both of the 1st measured 7 ft from tip to tip & they have a most beautiful head. As a matter of course as soon as he got the hook out of the birds mouth the mate had both dogs set upon him & tormented the poor thing all the forenoon The "Cape hens" are a little larger than our pigeons but are not uncommon handsome A couple of the sailors & myself secured one of the "*Gooneys*" &

[47]

cleaned him & had him cooked for supper & I must say he was "*good*". We took the remaining one & one of the "*hens*" & after tying a piece of lead to each of their legs with the longitude name of the ship & day of month let them go.

Course S E by E with another "*fair wind*"

JUNE 9 Monday

This was a very fine day & continued to be so till about 5 bells in the middle watch when it commenced to lighten very sharp on the Port Quarter & then every one was watching the horizon on the Starboard Quarter which soon loomed up as black as ink, then what a scrabble to take in sail which the increasing breeze made neccesary. All this I got clear of by standing by the Main Topgallant halyards, In the midst of the muss it struck 8 bells & up came the other watch We now expected to hear the welcome cry of "That will do the Watch" but instead we heard "Lay along here the Port watch & reef the fore topsail. We now gave it up for if the fore topsail was reefed the mizzen we knew would be too & the main topgallant sail furled But we did it in a hurry & got below about 4 bells, & had 1½ hours sleep. We made a beautiful run from 12 oclock yesterday till the same time today. Over 354 miles clear.* We are now well to the Eastward of the Cape & clear of it & its gales, & Ploughing the Indian Ocean

Course E by S. with good wind

JUNE 10 Tuesday

When I was waked this morning at 7 bells for my ½ hour for breakfast (As it is termed) I would not turn out, for the ½ hrs sleep was more enticing than the "*Biscuit & Junk*" so I turned over & slept it out.

Course E S E & S E by E

JUNE 11 Wednesday

This is a very fine day. Sent up the main Skysail Yard, & set every "*bloody*" studding sail in the ship except the 2 main top mast ones. The evening was as beautiful as the day & Mr Price (a young man in the cabin, a passenger) got out his Guitar & collected all the boys in the waist, on the spars & all the sailors who wanted to & we had some very good music. The sails would

* This is a better 24-hour run than had ever been made by a steamer up to that time; the average speed is almost 15 knots.

back & fill every minute & kept up an idle flapping noise all the while & we were in the middle of a song, when, "Crash mash, Bang," & down came the starboard fore topmast & Lower studding sails the boom having carried away. Here was an end to all our music & the commencement of our work for we took in all the studding sails & about 4 oclock in the morning double reefed the mizzen topsail. But that is the way in sea life nothing to depend on but your watchfulnefs & care to look out to windward. The ship shows good time most of the while averaging 12 knots Course E by S.

2 months out   JUNE 12 Thursday
It is blowing 40 horse Power today & the ship is ploughing through the water at the rate of 14 knots I am so hungry that I would eat anything I could get hold of & so are all the rest of the crew Being on allowance of water we cannot have our Rice beans or codfish in fact all we have is "*Duff*" 3 times a week & all the other time 5 seabiscuit & a piece of Salt Junk. All this time they live like princes in the cabin, I only hope I may have a chance some time of serving out old "*Bully Ranletts*" rations, I would starve him as sure as I live He finds the ship in provisions under a contract & he starves the crew. Not one will stop by the ship & come home in her
Course E. S. E. & E by S.

JUNE 13 Friday
Oh dear me I am tired out & cant think of anything to write, so as it is almost 4 bells & I have to go on deck at 8 I will turn in & sleep a couple of hours Besides I have 8 hours on deck to night & the "*bloody*" decks to wash down in the morning.
Course E. S. E. with Light Air & some Studding sails set

JUNE 14 Saturday
I no sooner got on deck this morn than Mr B———n told me to take a grease bucket & slush the Main mast from the skysail mast head down. I got up on the royal yard & from there I could reach high enough. Just then the mate sang out, "Abbey get up on the skysail Yard & grease the pole." This I knew was only for spite for there is no necefsity for doing it & It made me mad so instead of getting upon the Yard I climbed chock up the pole & ontop of the truck the very highest pinnacle on the ship. I then proceeded

to Give the ship a blessing by taking a handful of slush from my
bucket & putting it in a nice little heap on the truck   I then came
on down the rigging & managed to make 4 bells of it for having
to grease the pole. We have got a splendid wind & are averaging
12 knots almost all the while
Course S E by E & E. S. E.

As usual, this a rough stormy rainy day & quite uncomfortable
withal, The only thing to cheer us being a splendid 14 knot wind
& a "*DUFF*" dinner but our short allowance of water almost
stops that   We shipped 2 quite considerable seas today for the 1st
time & once when I came down from the main topsail Yard I took
hold of some of the running rigging & swung myself from the rail
to the deck which were so wet & slippery that I slid at once from
the Weather rail to the lee scuppers*   leaving a heavy track behind me on the deck
Course S E by E & E S E
Longitude about 55° East, Latitude 39° or 40° S.

JUNE 16 Monday

The wind continues fine & the ship is ploughing along splendidly
If we could have this for 20 days we would be at Penang. But tonight in the first watch   we double reefed the topsails & furled
the spanker   Until we got this done it was bright moonlight &
blowing a perfect hurricane. Then it commenced to rain & rained
all night. I was sent to the Lee wheel   for the 1st time & got pretty
well wet. The ship rolls awfully at times & many a poor unlucky
chap is seen sliding from the weather rail to the Lee scuppers on
his stern   I have had one turn at it & suppose I shall have another
when I least expect it. My water was all gone this morning at 9
oclock & I had to go without till 4 oclock in the aftn during which
time I was almost crazy for a drink but could not get it. I never
will go away from fresh water again when once I get home you can
bet high on that
Course S. E. by E. & E. S. E.

JUNE 17 Tuesday

We went from Double Reefed Top sails, fore & aft, to the Main
Skysail in lefs than 2½ hours this morn & the rain stopped & it

* The lee *waterways* (gutters) are meant here—a common error. The scuppers
are the pipes draining the waterways.

cleared up beautiful. Saturday night I paid my first contribution
to old Neptune & Davy Jones by losing my cap overboard. I was
on the mizzen topgallant yard loosing the sail & had let go my
bunt Gasket & was singing out "*Sheet Home*" when "*up*" flew the
sail & took my cap as slick as could be & the last I saw of it, It
was flying over the foot rope off to leward. The next day I got an
English Man of War cap of the Captain. The other night I saw
a pretty sight, a school of Porpoises under the Lee bows* It was
just moonlight enough to see them plainly & every once in a while
they would plunge ahead of us (and the ship going 14 knots) &
run to get out of our way "*scart*" as could be. I saw a plenty more
afterwards from the poop.
Course S E by S & E S E
We are near St Pauls & Amsterdam the Captain says

June 18 Wednesday

This is an awful uncomfortable day & we have bean soup for
dinner, which makes It all the worse. I can write no more now for
the ship rolls awfully & I have all I can do to keep my seat, & it
has been blowing a gale for 2 or 3 days. Split the fore topsail all
to Ribbons at 8 bells this morning.
Course S E by E & E by S.

June 19 Thursday

Reefed Topsails fore & aft & the wind blowing "blue blazes"
While pulling on the main brace this evening there came an unlucky sea & took me for one on the back. The ship gave a lurch
to L'eward at the same time & I caught hold of a door to save
myself which happened to be fastened with a single ropeyarn
which parted & away I went to the Lee Scuppers covered with
water & my hat gone somewhere or another I didnt know where.
I jumped up & got out of the wet as quick as I could & found that
a Chinaman had gone (at the same time I did) over the capstan &
carpenters bench head first & jammed his head under a spar which
knocked his senses out of him. They Lugged him away forward &
nobody knew whether he was dead or not. Oh my this is going to
sea though & I cant expect anything better
Course E. by N.
Long. 75° E

* "Lee bow," more properly, there being only one on each side. In addition, of
course, the forward part of the ship is "the bow."

[51]

June 20 Friday

The gale has finally subsided & we have now got the wind on the Starboard quarter from the south'ard & west'ard & the ship tearing along at the rate of 11 & 12 knots. We have not done any work but trim sail for 3 or 4 days. Heading as much north as possible

Course N E by E &c*

June 21 Saturday

All studding sails set on the starboard side & the ship "Full & by" the SouthEast trades; Sent up the fore royal & mizzen Sky sail yards. We are to have the 3 Skysail yards aloft all the while we are in Penang & there will be a fine job at sunrise & sunset to send down & send up all 3 of those yards every day. A great change has taken place in the temperature of the air from quite cold to quite warm. If the wind holds good we may reach Penang in 2 weeks

Course N. N E, & N E by N

June 22 Sunday

A beautiful day & the 1st one for a Sunday we have had in a good while. Employed my time in reading & putting on a button here & there. I have been appointed Mizzen Skysail boy & have to loose, furl, & bend the sail, send the yard up or down as the case may be & in fact have the entire charge of the yard during my watch on deck   one of the boys in the other watch tends to it the rest of the time. It is an awful job when the ship is pitching to go up & loose or furl it for being so high up & the foot ropes too short   the halyards loose on deck & the mast in the same state as the British left the old flag staff on the battery N. Y. upon evacuating it,† you can get nothing but your finger nails & eyelids to hold on'to. Many a time I have been *"almost"* gone when another lurch would bring me back only to have the operation repeated   When one gets up there he is well tired with the exertion of climbing so high & then to have to balance himself upon his stomach on the yard & "pick up" 44 yards of canvass   stow it & pass his gaskets make them fast & get down on deck in about 5

* The various directions mentioned under June 20 do not check up with each other.

† They left it greased, thus giving the Americans a difficult job to climb it and remove the British flag.

[52]

minutes & then perhaps be told he must do it quicker, it is hard. But all this is comprised in *"Going to Sea"* & any one who is fool enough to go must take his share of it. One of the passengers has a guitar & I often hear him play in the dog watch on moonlight nights & then my thoughts wander home & I wish & wish & wish again that I was there or could hear from there either but all to no account

Northerly Course

JUNE 23 Monday

Another fine day & by the way the days ought to be fine now for we are going to the Northward at a fine rate. Had a forenoon watch below & *"duff"* for dinner in the bargain. "Why, what luck:" fine day   forenoon watch below & "duff" for dinner in the bargain. You may laugh but go to sea & have such luck yourself & see what you will say then. Took 4 Coolies & went between decks in the aftn & pounded the rust off the water tank. We are continually carrying away something or another splitting a sail &c, & we find plenty to do at that alone. The 2ᵈ mate had another set'to last night with a Mexican sailor in which neither gained the advantage & both used belaying pins freely. Our Main top mast Staysail has been patched & mended till it looks like a *"Sand barges Main Sail"* & now it is gone again.

Latitude 24° 41′ South

Course N by E

JUNE 24 Tuesday

Ripped the main topgallant sail all to smash last night & sent the sail down in the middle watch. Nothing in particular occurred. Weather somewhat squally

Course North E by N

JUNE 25 Wednesday

A beautiful day. Had all hands in the aftn for the 1ˢᵗ time in a great while. It is awful hot & we are in about 18 South & should this breeze hold will be at Penang in 5 days

Northerly Course of course

JUNE 26 Thursday

Oh how hot! hot! hot! but no *"Skeeters."* I have been puttying nail heads in the cabin & scraping the main chains   Yesterday the mate ordered me to serve out 4 qts of water an occurrence at which I rejoice exceedingly

Course N ½ E.

JUNE 27 Friday

"*Watch & watch*" again, for a wonder, after having had "*all hands*" 2 days & nothing more than usual going on, I dont see what the idea was. Slowly & gradually the good old steady South-East trades left us last night after having cordially shaken hands with every sail in the ship for about 10 hours & we are now in the Latitudes where it rains 5 minutes then blows 5 minutes then comes dead calm 5 minutes & repeat

N E by E

JUNE 28 Saturday

Copious showers all day & of course we caught plenty of water. Toward evening there came one of the heaviest ones I ever saw & then what a time; every one in the ship almost was in the Lee Scuppers where the water was almost 1 foot deep washing clothes. The rain continuing till every thing on deck was caught full we rigged the hose & pump & filled a lot of casks in the hold which may be of a good deal of use.

Course N E by E

JUNE 29 Sunday

A beautiful day & very hot too   One of the boys went in swimming & hung on to a rope quite a while till letting go he struck out & swam a little, when a "*Shark*" appeared swimming leisurely along within about 10 feet of him. He concluded it was about time he "*vamosed*" which he did without delay. We got out the shark line but could not catch him. We have been almost totally becalmed for 2 days with plenty of rain

Course Every way & Any way

JUNE 30 Monday

For 3 days have we been becalmed with every now & then a puff of wind always from a different quarter which keeps us bracing the yards all the while. Early in the forenoon the "*Old Man*" (who always sees a sail before they come in sight) sang out "*Sail ho*" from the Poop Deck & rushed forward with his glass to the top gallant forecastle. I jumped into the Starboard Gangway &

looked in the direction he was looking but for a long time could see naught but a plain straight horizon. All at once a small spick caught my eye & was out of sight in a minute I looked again & there it was sure enough. She proved to be a bark with the *"Blood & Guts"* of "Old England" at her peak She was steering acrofs our bows homeward bound. We tried hard to come up within signalizing or hailing distance but before we could do so it came on dark & so we lost her. In the aftⁿ while I was busy sewing there came a great "Hue & cry" from the Poop Deck which we understood as, *"Come aft here & haul in this shark"* I was there very quick for I had never seen one before we got a Bowline around him & after breaking the line with the hook on we managed to haul him in over the taffrail & then all hands got hold of the rope & ran forward with him he got hold of every coil of rope within his reach & bit like everything but we killed him & when cutting him open out tumbled 8 young sharks all alive & kicking we cut their tails & threw them overboard but they soon died. 9 sharks at one hand is quite considerable I think
Every Course

July 1 Tuesday

All day we were becalmed but in the evening there came a breeze which made us take in our skysails & bids fair to hold Employed scraping the Mizzen Chain Plates sitting on a *"Boatswains Chair"*
Course N. E. by N.

July 2 Wednesday

Morning watch on deck & all out of sorts with myself the ship & everything else, except the breeze we have now under which we can just carry topgallant sails fore & aft. To cap it all I had to sit under the Lee Quarter almost into the water with a bowline hitched around me scraping Chain Plates. We expect to be in Penang by Saturday so as that we can have a fine time working all day Sunday. Never mind I shall have a *"Blow' out"* on sleep then anyhow & no sail to trim & nothing but an hour anchor watch to keep every night.
Course N. N. E.

July 3 Thursday

Oh my back! Instead of washing decks this morning we got one of the anchors over the bows. It is daylight at 2 bells in the morning watch now & what was my surprise at that time this morning (when I heard the old cry of "*Lay the Ropes up*") to find upon trying to get up that one of my legs had taken a sort of "*bowline*" in it & as fast as I straitened it out it flew back at last with a good deal of kicking & pulling I managed to stump up on the Poop & do my share of "Laying the ropes up". But when I had done I went forward & found them getting the fish tackle rove to "*take out*" the anchors & we have had one of the hardest days work as yet though lightened somewhat by several good "*shantys*" or songs as we pulled on the ropes

July 4 Friday

This is the "*Glorious 4th*" in the States but oh how far from that was it with us. It rained all the forenoon, as it never rained before, & then instead of having (as we expected we should) something different for dinner than usual there was nothing but that ("I cant give it a name bad enough") apology for "bean soup." We had an old torn & tattered "*Stars & Stripes*" at the spanker gaff & the captain & mate tormented the dogs with a few fire crackers, & thus we celebrated the forenoon but in the aftn it cleared up beautiful & what made it more enlivening was the cry of "*Land Ho*" from the main truck. Where away? said the mate. "About 2 points on the Lee bow sir;" then again Sail ho 2 points on the weather bow & shortly after "Land all along ahead sir" & before 4 bells in the first night watch we had "Acheen head" the Northernmost point of Sumatra well on the weather beam At 6 bells we sighted the rock of "*Pulo Rondo*" which is in the middle of the Straits of Malacca* & passed within 4 miles of it & now have the way clear to Penang where we expect to arrive hourly if the wind holds. At 8 bells sighted the Main Land†
Course N E by E.

July 5 Saturday

The fine breeze has fallen off considerable & in fact it was almost a dead calm till evening when there came on a squall of wind & rain which lasted about 2 or 3 hours. When ist we began to take in sail I went with one of the men up in the main top & helped him

* Rather the *Pass* of Malacca, a narrow passage just north of Sumatra. Pulo Rondo (Rondo I.) is a bit to the north of it. The *Straits* of Malacca comprise the large body of water between Sumatra and the Malay Peninsula.

† Something wrong here. Pulo Rondo is 230 sea miles from the mainland —the Malay Peninsula—and 320 from Penang.

to take in the main top gallant "stunsail" then down on deck & up alone & furled the mizzen royal then down again & up with a sailor & furled the fore royal, then down & lent a hand at the fore top gallantsail. By this time it struck 8 bells & I went below wet as a drowned rat but I had 8 hours below that night so I didnt care. Land in sight all the while   the Malay Peninsula
Any course to keep clear of a savage coast

July 6 Sunday

A beautiful day with the Northern part of Sumatra on the weather side & in sight. The only thing bad was Lack of wind & we were bracing the yards from starboard to port & back again all day. I made out a sail from the foretopsail yard & the captain said it was a pirates "*prahus*" & we stood off as much as possible on the other tack & kept a bright lookout all night. Hove the Lead in the morning & got soundings at 80 Fathoms
Course E. by S.

July 7 Monday

Becalmed all day. In the dog watch I went up on the fore topsail yard & sat down to watch the birds that were tormenting the sharks ahead, & before I came down I had seen all of 20. The water is covered literaly with sponges & sunfish, & here & there a snake is seen. We are continually passing bannana peals cocoa nut shells & various other fruits   The 3ᵈ mate saw an island ahead & a sail on the Lee bow, from the main topgallant yard   The mate took one of the quarter boats   & rowed off around the ship
No course at all

July 8 Tuesday

This morning at daybreak we sighted some boats out fishing & passed several logs covered with birds. In the aftⁿ saw two junks & a clipper brig to leeward, besides a small island. At two bells in the first night watch the junks passed within hailing distance almost, but did not try to board us. A light breeze sprang up in the evening
Course E by S.

July 9 Wednesday

This morning at daybreak we sighted the island of Porto Penang the long desired place & had the satisfaction of getting becalmed

within 6 or 8 miles of it & knocking about all night again. We have been "humbugging" about within 2 days sail of Port for a week. The smell of spices bananas & fruits of all kinds is delicious, & I kept snuffing & snuffing all my lookout to get enough
Course East & thereabouts   Tacked ship 3 or 4 times

July 10 Thursday
This day we were all the while in sight of Port with Light wind while eating breakfast we heard a noise & running out saw a handsome boat manned by about 12 Malays with a pilot for us. Met a bark coming out & passed a brig coming in with Main top gallant mast gone & fore royal also   with stunsail booms for topsail yards Let go the anchor & in the night I stood my 1st anchor watch from 3 to 4

July 11 Friday
This day we had two bumboats alongside with Bananas Plantains Pineapples &c & I laid into them deep. We were employed heaving up the anchor & furling the sails &c all the while

July 12 Saturday
We have at last got somewhere near the town & I must say it looks like a pleasant place but to morrow I suppose we shall see on liberty

"INDIA INK"

It is a tarry sailor man
  Doth shift his quid & sigh
And musing oer his "Injun Ink"
  He spits & pipes his eye

    In all his queer variety
      Perusing one by one
    Spars anchors ensigns binnacles
      His "fokesal" chums have done

Around his arms all down his back
  Betwixt his shoulder blades
Are Peg & Moll & July Ann
  And "Mer" & other maids

    And just below his collar bane
      Amidship on his chest
    He has a sun in blue & red
      A-rising in the west

A bit abaft a pirate craft
  Upon his starboard side
There is a thing he made himself
  The day his Nancy died

    Mayhap it be a lock of hair
      Mayhap a "kile o' rope"
    He says it is a true love knot
      And so it is I hope

Naught recks that gentle foremast hand
  What shape it wear to you
With soul elate' & hand expert
  He pricked it — so he knew

    To "Ed,ard Cuttle" mariner
      His sugar tongs & spoons
    Not dearer than that rose pink heart
      Transfixed with two harpoons

And underneath a grave in blue
   A gravestone all in red
Here lies alright, poor Toms "delight"
   God save the mark — shes dead

     Permit that tarry mariner
       To shift his quid & sigh
     Nor chide him, if he sometimes swear
       — For piping of his eye

Few sadder emblems are the hearts
   Than traced at first in Pink
And pricked till all the picture smarts
   Are fixed with "Injin Ink"

"THE DAILY JOURNAL FOR 1856"

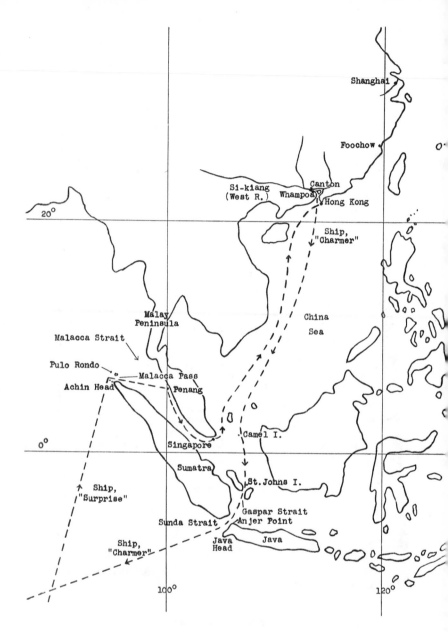

TRACK OF ABBEY'S TRAVELS IN THE FAR EAST, 1856

CHAPTER VI

IN THE FAR EAST

July 13 Sunday

One half of each watch went ashore today & I for one was with
them. I shall not try to describe the place any more than to say
that the streets are narrow & you seem to be walking between 2
walls all the while you are in them   there are more Chinamen than
Malays at least you see more. We got a carriage (another of the
boys & myself) & went to the water fall about 4½ miles from the
town & had a good swim in fresh water   we cannot go in the bay
the sharks are so thick   We got our dinner & a plenty of fruit &
as we were to be off at sundown I thought it was time to go aboard
but my comrade was so drunk that he swore he would not go
aboard before 8 bells & so coming across some of my shipmates
they tried to get him but could not & we had to leave him. About
11 oclock at night he came aboard making considerable noise

July 14 Monday

Hove the anchor up today & drifted up to the town among the
other vessels. Of these there are quite a number but only one
American besides ourselves & she sails tomorrow for Salem Mass.
I went aboard of her & tried to get a chance to go home in her but
could not. About 6 oclock there came an East India Company ship
in & she made 5 tacks, let go the anchor & clewed up her sails in
fine style   We are the finest looking vessel here & of course must
do everything up brown. We hoist & strike our colors all at once
send the Skysail Yards up & down all at once & everything is done
Man of War style as near as possible   The british mail steamer
arrived here today & brought us the news that England & America
were about to have a war & we will be in a pretty fix if they do
with the prospect of a prison till it is finished & settled

July 15 Tuesday

I was at work cleaning the wheel all day, & I left a mark on it to
show when I come back to New York   a Bark & a Brig or 2 Barks
came in toward evening

July 16 Wednesday

Old routine of Port life with the exception of 600 Bags of Beetle nut for Singapore I had an all day job clearing out the Boatswains locker of which I have charge as well as the Boatswains mates which is forward. This is aft under the cabin. Our Chinamen came off Sunday night chewing Beetle nut & have done so ever since till now they have to Holy Stone the spit out of the decks where they have deposited it. The Malays do not allow the young men to chew it till they are married

July 17 Thursday

We have taken in some 200 or 300 bags more of "*betel nut*" & if we get it as quick & fast (this & any thing else we may carry) as we have got this we will get home in good time

July 18 Friday

Took in 210 bags of betel nut today. I was cleaning brafs all day. The mate took the sail boat & went over to the main land some 4 miles off. While he was gone it fell calm & pretty soon it came on to blow & a head wind for him to come back & he did not arrive at the ship till after 6 bells in the aft^n & the captain blew him up.

July 19 Saturday

We got the cannons down from the poop to the quarter deck & scraped & painted them. Nothing of much account has happened.

July 20 Sunday

The rest of the men went ashore today & I went in one of the boys place For want of better company I went with the men & stayed till they were all drunk but "*Long Jack*" (as we call him or Jack Williams) & we walked about the town till we met the 2^d mate & he had the ships cutter down at the wharf & invited us to take a sail over to the main land. We raced a Sampan over & when near shore 3 of us "*off dudds*" & dove overboard We went ashore & all we could see was cocoa nuts & the beach I never expected to see so many in my life. I can say I have been ashore in Penang & Malacca

July 21 Monday

Old routine of Port life. I have not time to write any more for it is "*turn to*"

BURNING OF THE CLIPPER *JACOB BELL* BY THE CONFEDERATE RAIDER *FLORIDA*

From Harper's Weekly, March 21, 1863.

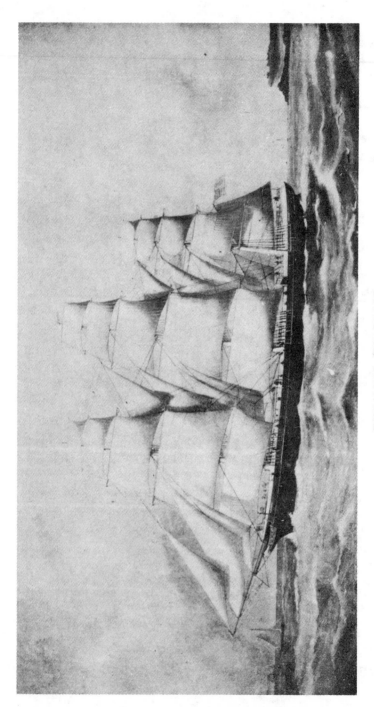

THE SHIP *SURPRISE*

From a painting in the Macpherson collection.

JULY 22 Tuesday

An American Screw Steamer came in from Singapore & she made a fine mefs which spoke but poorly for us Americans. He came up splendidly ran alongside the Landing   Let go a mudhook but it did not hold, so he up steam & went ahead again Let go another & 30 fathom of chain in 9 fathom of water & the anchor dragged & let him drift into a Dundee Bark (Scottland) the Heathpark carried away the Spritsail yard, smashed the figurehead, & shortly after the flying jibboom, & finally left with a bill of about $500.00 on his back

JULY 23 Wednesday

A splendid shower last night & a splendid job today to loose & furl the sails. I was along with *"Old Tom" "Passing Ball"* for him to serve the flying jib foot ropes

JULY 24 Thursday

Usual routine of port life

JULY 25 Friday

I was taken with pains & cramps all over my body last night & today am laid up   The Captain told the Steward to give me a dose of calomel & jalap & let me eat rice for a couple of days. Commenced taking out ballast today having got 5,500 tierces of rice as freight for Hong Kong
American Clipper Ship Jacob Bell* came in today & left in the night

* The *Jacob Bell* was an "extreme clipper" ship less than four years old at this time. She was described as being "of faultless model and exquisite symmetry, everywhere attracting admiration as being a perfect specimen of naval architecture and the foremost production of" the shipyard of Jacob Bell himself. Her helmsman's platform was built in the shape of a heart and was made of brass.

She reached Penang on this occasion following a very fast passage of 77 days from New York to Bombay. In the first stage of this voyage she performed the noteworthy feat of running from New York to the equator in 18 days and 1 hour, logging 3,703 miles. For this period, therefore, she maintained the high average speed of 8.55 knots.

In 1863 she was homeward bound from Foo Chow with a cargo valued at a million and a half dollars. Captain Frisbie reports as of February 12, the ship being about 400 miles north of Puerto Rico:

"About noon discovered a steamer in pursuit under full head of steam and all sail set. After a chase of over four hours she fired a shot which struck about twice a ship's length astern and we hove to; the steamer, carrying the Federal flag, sailed around the *Bell* three times, presented her broadside, ran up the rebel flag and sent a boat aboard. Our officers, crew and passengers, including Mrs. Frisbie and child and another lady, were allowed half an hour to collect a

July 26 Saturday

Laid up still. The crew & a crowd of malays still at work taking out the ballast. The malays brought their cooking utensils aboard & I had a chance to see them eat curry & rice. The curry was made of fish & was in one kettle   the rice of which there was about a ton was in another   they took 1st some rice & put it on a large tin plate & then the cook dipped his ladle into the curry & distributed it about (there being 4 plates)   Then 6 men got around one dish & mixing it up with their fingers went to eating
British Man of War "*Spartan*" came in today

July 27 Sunday

Some of the men went ashore but I (though I turned to) had had enough of the shore & staid aboard. A couple staid ashore all night & of course were uselefs the next day

July 28 Monday

Took out ballast & took in rice all day. I have nothing to do but sit on deck   slate in hand & keep tally of the bags as they come in the port

July 29 Tuesday

Tallying rice today

July 30 Wednesday

Tallying rice & Beetel Nut & loosing & furling sails.

July 31 Thursday

Employed tallying rice &c

August 1 Friday

Employed as usual

few necessities, the prize crew appropriating what remained. All our people were then taken aboard the *Florida,* which set off in pursuit of a schooner, after leaving instructions as to the *Bell's* course during the night. The next morning the *Florida's* crew were so busily engaged in transferring plunder as to neglect the management of the ship and the *Bell,* with sails set, bore down on the *Florida,* the rigging of which had to be manned to shove the *Bell* off. She was then set afire and burned to the water's edge. Four days later all the *Bell* people were transferred to the Danish brig *Morning Star,* which landed them at St. Thomas, Feb. 19, 1863."

J. T. Scharf in his *History of the Confederate Navy* states that "This vessel, and her cargo of tea, silks, etc., was.....the most valuable single prize taken by any Confederate cruiser."

August 2 Saturday
The old story again

August 3 Sunday
Of course we did nothing after 8 bells, so I "laid to" with a book & my "Monkey" by my side

August 4 Monday
Taking in cargo again among which was some opium & sharks fins & tails

August 5 Tuesday
Cargo ! Cargo ! Cargo !

August 6 Wednesday
Ditto ! Ditto ! Ditto !

August 7 Thursday
All e same

August 8 Friday
Almost full & filling up rice

August 9 Saturday
A small piece to fill up in the between decks

August 10 Sunday
I went ashore this aft^n with the 3^d mate met one of the boys & we got some horses & rode out to a place called the waterfall & when nearly back it commenced to rain & wet us through

August 11 Monday
Crew employed getting the ship ready for sea

August 12 Tuesday
Got our passengers (who are 12 Chinamen for Macao & an English Missionarys wife & 3 children) aboard, hove short in the forenoon, tripped our anchor & set sail about 4 P. M. The Malay Christmas

August 13 Wednesday
This day we kept "bobbing around" Penang not being able to get any where at all

August 14 Thursday

Passengers getting sea sick & the wind getting "noisy". Came down to the top gallant sails & at last furled them. While on the Mizzen topgallant yard I saw a Water Spout ahead. The sea under it was one caldron of spray. Came down just in time to see a little brig ahead of us go out of sight altogether in a whirlwind which soon struck us but not very forcibly we let go the top sail halyards "*fore & aft*" & hauled out the reef tackles in a drenching rain. We finally got out of the mefs & made sail & spied a ship following us with "*every stitch*" set

August 15 Friday

Spoke the Englifh Ship Princefs Royal & made the light ship 180 m from Singapore

August 16 Saturday

Arrived at Singapore & anchored

August 17 Sunday

Nothing to do after 8 bells. In the evening the mate came on board & gave me two letters from home which I devoured eagerly as might be expected. I sent one home by the mail steamer the next day

August 18 Monday

We expected to be up and away but were not at noon so we did not go this day

August 19 Tuesday

Today we received news that 40 tons of rice were to be taken in here so we shall be ready to race with the Jacob Bell.

August 20 Wednesday

All day in that sweltering rat hole the "*lower hold*" stowing rice

August 21 Thursday

Came down from furling the mainsail today & found a juggler aboard & of all the deeds of darkness I ever saw done he beat the lot. After going through a numberlefs amount of tricks he actually forced his entrails (or a portion of them) up & out of his mouth & wound up by cramming a sword 3 feet long down his throat 2/3 of the way or rather its length

August 22 Friday
Got ready for sea & hove short on the anchor

August 23 Saturday
Left Singapore at daylight for China & at 2 oclock were out of
sight of land in the China Sea
Course N E by N with a roaring breeze
Took 6 more Chinamen aboard here from Mauritius

August 24 Sunday
I intended to have cleaned up & drefsed myself today but as soon
as I made my appearance forward "Abbey you & Frank go up
forward & take the lee topgallant studding sail gear & reeve it for
the weather royal. The ropes being likely to be too large to reeve
in the blocks & moreover it being Sunday I was almost enraged at
such an order. I took the halyards & got out on the end of the royal
yard & the rope would not reeve. "wont reeve hey! says I then
Ill blamed soon make you" So I out knife & whittled it down till
it would. Now thinks I when you see that rope you wont send me
to reeve topgallant fore royal gear again I'm thinking
Course N E by N & tearing along furiously

August 25 Monday
Have almost every stitch set today & are going along finely. Some
how or other we got cheated out of our duff today but as it has
never happened before we didnt grumble
Holystoned the poop. I got hold of a "Family Bible" which I
preferred to a *"Prayer Book"*

August 26 Tuesday
Oh my! I cant remember, what did happen today
Holystoned the quarterdeck

August 27 Wednesday
Every thing went smooth today till the latter part of the first
dog watch when it commenced to breeze up & continued to do so
till we had taken in sail from Royal stun sails to the fore & main
topsails the mizzen being lowered down. All that night I was wet
through
Course N E by N

[67]

August 28 Thursday

Got under royals again today but toward night it commenced to rain & blow & in came every thing & down went the topsail yards & out flew the reef tackles

Course N E by N

Sent the skysail yards down & the royal & topgallant stun sail booms also

August 29 Friday

Holystoned the main deck and when most done the 2ᵈ mate came forward & said, "knock off" & go to work at lashing every movable thing & I heard him say to the 3ᵈ mate he wants to send the yards down too. This was because the captain found the barometer falling and was afraid of a Hurricane   All night it has been dark & lowering

August 30 Saturday

We did not get our hurricane after all. But we got a top gallant sail breeze & I never saw the Old box ship so much water before as she does now. It has evidently been blowing tremendous somewhere near for there is a terrible heavy sea on & a cross one at that

August 31 Sunday

Heavy sea & strong wind as yet. Today we got our regular "duff" or *"Clagger"* as we call it. But we have got some molasses from Pinang & it is so strong that ½ a pint will make one drunk & it almost spoils the duff

September 1 Monday

We did not do anything today but trim sail & the wind has hauled around ahead so that we cant get in tonight for Hong Kong is almost in sight & the land to the southard & west'ard of it is right away on the weather beam

September 2 Tuesday

The wind continued ahead till toward evening when we got a fair wind & stood on our course

September 3 Wednesday

Rose the land again & kept in for the shore *"cracking on"* to her hard

September 4 Thursday
Ran into the harbor at Hong Kong & came to an anchor in splendid style

September 5 Friday
Got a pilot & hove up the anchor & started for Whampoa. As soon as we get this cargo out we are going to take 5 or 6 hundred *"Coolies"* to Melbourne & that will be awful I shant go in the ship if I can possibly avoid it for we shall be at least 3 months going & coming back & then shall lay 2 months more in Shanghai. The *"Charmer"* is in Whampoa almost ready for home & I shall ask Captain Ranlett to let me try & get a chance to go in her Clipper Ship Alfred Hill came in today

September 6 Saturday
Of all the Pulling & hauling I ever experienced this beats it all we are in an archipelago with a China Pilot & have the wind dead ahead, & of course have to beat dead to windward in a river so narrow that we have to tack ship every 5 minutes & no exaggeration this we did all day & ½ of the night (the Sunday ½) Once in going about (the captain was doing it) she would not work because he chose his time bad & we had the after yards braced up & were standing by the head braces, when *"Let go & haul"* shouted the captain. Off we went with the braces, but twas no'go, the after yards were all aback. "Port fore brace quick" said the *"Skip"* & *"box"* her off, but no she got all *"buggered"* up main sail & all the courses full & topsails & all the rest aback. The old man rushed down onto the main deck & commenced a tirade. "He had had this ship worked well & it should be done now. We were all a set of loafers & might leave him as soon as we pleased, &c & soon & I mean to take him at his word as do all the rest. With him we are none of us worth our salt, but when we want to leave, "Oh no" that will never go down

September 7 Sunday
Laid at anchor ½ the day & toward evening "tripped up" to within 8 miles of Whampoa where we anchored again

September 8 Monday
Up anchor at 4 o clock for Whampoa or Old *"Bamboo town"* where we anchored at 7 o clock furled the sails & thats about all

September 9 Tuesday

Raining like Blackballs   Crew employed in trying to moor ship.
We came in under top gallant sails & the confounded old China
pilot would not take in a stitch till about 3 minutes before we let
go the anchor so you can imagine what sort of a come to we made
of it, bearing in mind that we were not 30 feet from an old hulk
of a storeship

September 10 Wednesday

Raining yet   last night we were rousted out to unship the spanker
boom for it had gone spang through the stern of the old hulk &
come out again with a blanket on its end having gone through a
bed. Never mind thats *"all serene"*

September 11 Thursday

Raining yet. We got the ship moored at last.

September 12 Friday

Unbent the sails & prepared for sending the foretop mast down

September 13 Saturday

Commenced discharging cargo   At night the captain gave one of
the other boys & myself leave to go up to *"Canton"* & we started at
9 oclock & went sailing along up the Si Kiang River by moonlight
singing at the top of our voices*

September 14 Sunday

Arrived in Canton 2, o'clock last night   Slept in the sampan till
daylight & went ashore. Went straight ahead till we had to turn
when we continued on so till we arrived at "Acows" hotel where
we *"put up"* with due ceremony & proceeded to our breakfast at
75 cts apiece. We then took a survey of the city & the China wall
spent all our money & started for the ship where we arrived at 4
o clock in the aft^n
All the men received $5.00 per piece & liberty ashore from where
they returned all drunk of course between the two days
We stopped at a large Pagoda about ½ way down the river &
took a look at it. I guess it was about 160 or 80 feet high about 40
in diameter at the base & 20 at the top   there were about 10 corri-

---

* Whampoa is below Canton on the Canton River, not on the Si-kiang, strictly
speaking. The Si-kiang, or "West River," is one of the branches of the Canton
River which flows in above Canton. Whampoa is the Canton anchorage.

dors around it at intervals & it was surmounted by a large black crofs It stood about 100 feet from the river on a small hillock. The color on the outside was a dingy brown but the inside was snow white. I was the first to reach it & ran up a small pair of stone stairs "*full dig*" calculating to get some where near the top before my companion got inside, & I had like to have got my neck broke for my haste, for the stairs broke short off & I chanced to see it or I might have gone headfirst to the bottom amongst the "*Joshes*" & "*Chin Chin*" arrangements which had been in use the night before, it being full moon. We went in the lower part took a look at the arrangements   inscribed our names & places of residence on the wall & left

How I Saw Canton

The ship was lying in "Whampoa Reach" opposite "old Bamboo Town," slowly discharging her cargo of rice, betel nut, pepper, rattan, &c, which had been taken in at Penang & Singapore a month or so previous.

I had been hard at work with the rest of the crew getting it out, and on the saturday night when my story opens, was pretty tired and glad of the prospect of a days respite, for the weather was fearfully hot, even upon deck, and in the breeze, while down in the hold among the monstrous piles of pepper bags and sacks of rice, the thermometer ranged as high as 120°

It was a little after six o'clock, & having eaten my supper of tea, salt beef, and hard bread,—very hard bread in more than one sense, and beef, and tea too, for that matter,—I was lounging about the "waist," or center of the ships decks near the mainmast, exchanging a few comments with a messmate, upon the scene surrounding us; the passing boats, filled with their curious looking crews, or laden with tea, cinnamon, or fire crackers, for some "homeward bound" vessel, and wondering how long it would be ere *we* could expect to see some of them bringing our homeward cargo alongside, and wishing that we were a grade or two higher than mere "boys" before the mast, that we might be enabled to go on shore and obtain a glimpse of the many wonderful sights which our boyish imaginations conjured up as to be seen there.

"Its only ten or twelve miles up to Canton from here! Dont you wish we could go up there and see the city?" said Bill,

"Yes!" I exclaimed, "I guess I do! How did you know it was so near? I thought it much farther away,"

"Oh, I heard the captain talking to the mate about it, and telling him that he had better go up there before we left port" returned Bill.

(*Eventually the two boys hailed a sampan man and*—)

As soon as safely off, we began to bargain with him to carry us to Canton, and he finally agreed to take us up at once, and bring us down the next night, for the sum of four dollars, we to advance one quarter of the amount as an earnest of our good intentions.

We were not so wise about Chinese boatmen then, as we have since become, or we would not have made any advance at all, and thereby tempted him to run ashore at the nearest point and leave us to our own devices; but, as this one did not shew any disposition to serve us so, it's just as well, now.

The boat was about twenty feet long, and six feet wide in the middle. Amidships was a permanent, arched, bamboo roof, some three feet high in the center, and under which, was a comfortable cushioned seat upon which we reclined and slept with lots of room to spread our legs about and be comfortable. On top of the roof were several extra sections which could be quickly pulled forward & aft, and the boat would have a complete canopy over her. These were not used now of course the weather being fine and the boat pulling along the river.

Except where we sat, she was completely fitted with a movable deck, upon which the crew, consisting of the sampan man, his two sons, and his wife, sat and pulled at the oars.

That is,—the three men sat and pulled, while the woman stood up on the stern of the boat and *pushed* at one oar, and steered with another, merely touching it from time to time with her leg.

Just back of our seat was the little "Joss House," or altar, at which they worshiped; a little box, about eighteen inches square, with much gilt paper and tinsel fixtures inside a small quantity of "chow chow," (food,) to appease the Gods appetite, should he wax hungry, and a few tallow dips, about the size of lead pencils and colored red, which were blazing away, while a faint smoke arose from the slowly smouldering "Joss stick," (the "punk" which all American boys use on the 4th of July to light their fire crackers with.)

Before this flimsy little arrangement of nothings, this man and his family,—for they all lived, ate, drank, and slept, in this boat, —were in the daily habit of prostrating themselves, and going through their forms of worship, which they term, "Chin-chining."

With so little awe did the shrine inspire us, that we came near pulling everything out for inspection, before the boatman could explain to us, in his "pidgin English," what it was that we were so unceremoniously investigating; but as soon as we knew, we of course desisted, much to his satisfaction, and betook ourselves to smoking some Manila Cheroots, which he provided from some unseen store in the depths of the boat.

The tide had turned favourable, and we were rapidly flying up the river; past hamlets and villages, fishing stations and fleets of boats,—all, or the most of them, moored for the night under either bank; thro paddy (rice) fields and marshes, past temples and pagodas upon occasional hills, and rapidly nearing the city.

What time we got there, we never knew, as we had no watches, and furthermore, were asleep.

The boatman, thinking us well enough situated, did not disturb our rest, but made the craft fast amid a crowd of her species, wrapped himself up in a rug, and followed our lead; so that the first intimation we had of our having arrived, was the jangling of gongs, & beating of "tom toms" (a sort of native drum, as resonant as a barrel head) as the multitude about us paid their morning devoirs to "Joss."

Springing up & calling to Bill, I pushed away the sliding cover above us and gazed out upon the scene.

We were close to the "Factory," so Sam said, (all Whampoa boatmen are Sams) and surrounded by, I'm afraid to say how many thousand other sampans; on both sides of the river the city lay about us for,—we couldnt tell how far, but, to judge from the noises, I should have said, many miles. It was one continual cry, from the mouths of boatmen, coolies, venders of all descriptions of stuff, children, & dogs, while now and then the melodious bray of some forlorn Jackass, reminded me of an immense well sweep upon a rusty hinge.

While we were staring about us, Sam arranged a basin and towel, and, taking turns, we performed our ablutions.

We then ascertained that we were hungry, and Sam said that we could have breakfast, and, in fact, all our meals, on board the boat. Thinking this a "big thing" we told him to provide for us at once, and he soon brought on board fowls, eggs, bread, butter, and various other things which his wife speedily prepared and cooked, and within half an hour we sat down to a very fair breakfast; a much fairer one than we knew was cooked for us on board the ship down the river.

The meal over, we engaged the ever ready and obliging Sam, to guide us about and shew us the sights, and stepped across numerous boats to the "jetty" (or wharf) close by, from which we emerged upon a large open quadrangle surrounded by goodly warehouses belonging to foreign residents.

Thrusting aside the hundreds of garrulous beggars, coolies, would-be guides, and children, that at once encompassed our path proffering their services, or extending their hands for "cash," (as the brass money, of which it takes ten pieces to make one of our cents, is termed,) we passed across the square, up a street, and found ourselves at once in Canton.

One could scarcely call it a street either, where only two or three can walk abreast, but it was as wide as any we saw there. The houses were from two to three stories high, and the upper portions, if they did not project over the lower, had balconies, or bow windows, which overhung us as we passed, tending, with the numerous signs, and clothes lines adorned with the weeks washing, to make it dark even in midday.

The stores were small, having a face upon the street of ten feet, and generally shallow, tho' not always. All kinds of business seemed to be represented, and all looked odd and strange to us as we sauntered along, our eyes wide open with interest.

Sam soon led us into a shop where he said they sold silks and after a few words with an old party in a dark fur edged jacket, silk hose, and small round felt hat, about which his cue was neatly wound, numerous packages of the article were placed before us. We turned them over and admired them, which seemed to please him, altho we told Sam to say that we did not want to buy any. A nice old fellow he seemed to be and one willing to take a little trouble for the amusement of a couple of boys like us, and I could not help drawing a comparison and asking Bill what he supposed they would say at "Stewarts," or "Arnold & Constables," if a couple of Chinese boys should happen in and desire to pull their stock over as we were this mans?

One of Bills greatest desires was, to be shewn the "great wall" of China of which he had read, and no argument of mine could convince him but that it passed near Canton so he must needs "bone" Sam about it.

"Wall? Yesee, hab got wall! Can makee shew, sposee wanchee see!"

We "wanted to see" of course, that was exactly what we came for, and so off we started up one street, down another, round a corner, thro an alley, up against one man and over against another, dodging coolies with their loads suspended at the ends of a stout stick and the centre resting upon their shoulders, kicking at dogs and staring at everything; talk of crowds why Broadway never knew what it was to have such a jam in proportion to its width. Now and then we stopped, hailing Sam to "hold on" & come back & talk for us, as we saw things especially interesting.

Once when Sam was well ahead we stopped at a fruit stand and tried to buy some splendid persimmons, but the keeper of the shop couldnt, or wouldnt, understand us; he seemed sullen and looked very unfavourably upon us; and we, not imagining him unwilling to sell, endeavoured to be more lucid shewing him money, touching the fruit with our hands, and then pointing down our throats and nodding at him, rather an expressive pantomime it would have been anywhere else, but it was no go; he seemed to think at last that we wanted to eat *him*, and began to pull in his wares, shut up his shop, and call out for assistance.

Quite a crowd of eager and interested "Celestials" of all grades of society had assembled about us, all of whom seemed to partake of the fruit venders alarm and indignation, and turning about in search of Sam or some intelligent looking one to clear up the difficulty, we were struck by their malicious looks and apparent willingness to "light on" us with their bamboos.

"Bill," said I, "these yellow bellied rascals mean mischief, just see what a bustle there is among them and how they look at us, lets get out of the way while we can," and we moved slowly along, looking for our guide, but nowhere was he to be found. The mob began to advance toward us and some of them to hoot, while one or two athletic, pockmarked, carriers, slipped by us with their staves, evidently intending to cut off our advance.

We both wore the ordinary garb of sailors, and had the usual belt sheath and knife about our waists and, taking this as an overt act, we whipped out our only weapons and turned to face our assailants.

At once, the hooting ceased, the turmoil subsided, and the mass appeared to "simmer down" and each and every one to betake himself to his business, which, it clearly seemed was, *not* to molest us.

We looked at each other in blank amaze; "What, are they such cowards as all that?" said I to Bill, "Seems so"! was his laconic response, "Good gracious!" said I we could capture the whole city I believe, with a popgun & a big drum"

"I say," said Bill, "lets find out where their biggest bank is, and take all the money, we might as well make hay while the sun shines this once for us; like as not we'll never get such another chance"

But there was no bank, and so we couldn't exercise our bravado any more, but walked quickly on in search of Sam whom we soon met He exhibited some anxiety to get us away from that quarter, and quickened his steps; all the time talking about the wall to engage our attention and prevent our stopping along the way.

I did not relish being hauled thro' the town in this manner but as Bill was full of the subject and wanted to see it above all other things I had to give in and follow on as best I could.

We "caromed" along for some time thus, when Sam informed us that we were now close to this great wall and the next turning would reveal it to us, and sure enough it did.

A thick mass of brick work some twenty feet high, by eight or ten through; all covered with dank green mould and moss, and directly in front of us pierced by a gate, through which we passed as we surveyed the locality.

It was city on both sides, and I asked Sam what might be the use of this barrier, as it was evident that the gates were never closed, and if they had been it would have been a trifling feat to scale it entirely.

He told a long story about the antiquity of the thing and the growth of the city meantime, but as his English was inferior at best I could make little out of it when he went into nice historical matters, and so after waiting until Bill had swallowed himself full of the sight I proposed that we should find some more interesting subject for contemplation.

How far from the boat we had got I had no idea; we had walked several miles but I could not keep the run of our direction and was to all intents lost, so I stuck close by Sam.

Wandering along, I caught sight of an English sign, "Acow's Hotel." "Hurrah! Bill," said I, "we can get some milk in that place anyway, lets go in"

But Sam hung fire; "didnt want to"; "knew a better place" &c.

We pumped at him awhile and at last found out that it was a place frequented by Captains and Mates only and he feared getting into trouble if he took us in.

Our dignity was so offended at this that we made a lunge at the doorway and up the stairs at once, and dragged the unlucky Sam after us.

The house seemed deserted tho'; we found a sort of office & reading room and in a few moments a reticent and suspicious servant—we thought; he may have been Acow himself tho'; further research developed a billiard room, and we at once determined to play, though neither of us understood the game at all; but after selecting cues, chalking up &c we came to a dead lock for want of balls.

We demanded them of the servant, who followed and watched us all the time, very much as a New York hotel porter would a couple of playful young grizzly bears, that chance, or some unfortunate showman, had dropped in the house—he directed Sam to show us a placard upon the wall wherein we saw it set forth in very concise terms, that, "This table is for the use of Captains and mates alone, and must not be played on by any others," here was a bluff for us, but Bill scaled it at once by pompously ordering Sam to inform the fellow that "HE was a *Captain*" & I was "his *mate*"

The fellow looked skeptical, but, as he couldnt prove the contrary, he produced the balls and we knocked them about the table and off on the floor just long enough to shew our thorough ignorance of their uses, when he coolly took them away and invited us to leave the place.

But we were in no humor for going and demanded dinner; whereat his eyes sparkled and he demanded a sight of our money.

We shewed him three or four dollars where he at once became subservient and he hastened to order us a meal. We sat down and overhauled some large volumes of statistics about something and passed half an hour or so when he came and called us to our meal.

It was a nice one better than we had seen since leaving our own country. First came some vegetable soup, then some fish; next he brought on some roast beef Macao potatoes beets turnips &c, and then a roast chicken, after which came a pudding, some walnuts, nankin dates & Lychees (a fruit tasting like a raisin)

We filled up with everything but the chicken; he was roasted, claws head, comb and all and we didnt like the looks of him; he seemed too fresh, much as if the sun had caught him at some accidental focus and frizzled him up.

[77]

We imparted our suspicions to Sam, who assured us that it was the style of the country and all right, but our prejudices were not to be so easily overcome and we satisfied ourselves with looking at the fowl, while I made a mental memoranda for home rehearsal—when I should get there. We filled our pockets with nuts &c,—we wouldn't see any more for one while probably, and having satisfied Mr "Acow" took to the street again.

Presently we came to a large gate leading into a stone flagged court, across which we saw a large stone and brick building in & out of which many people were going and coming.

Ascertaining from Sam that it was a temple, or "Joss House," and that we could investigate it, we went in. The court was flanked by beggars & cripples all the way across, to relieve whose importunate clatter we had to exchange some silver for "cash" and distribute.

Such misery & filth I never before saw; such sores; such deformity; it was awful; and when a mass of living rags, from which there protruded what had once been,—but no longer was, a foot, and from whence emanated a moan, which alone established its claim to humanity, I could bear it no longer but pulled Bill away and hastened through the door into the building.

A short vestibule ushered us at once into the centre room, at the back of which, behind a railing, and elevated upon a sort of dais sat Joss in all his glory; at least a wooden image of him did. Upon either side was a female figure, his wives, we thought, tho we did not know, and Sam, like most Chinamen in like circumstances, was all at once very obscure and reticent, and we could not ascertain, for certain.

There were a great many more figures, all gilt & vermillion, like "Joss" himself, but nowhere near as large; stuck around him inside the railing, all looking very wise & stupid, while at the corners of the dais or platform the "punk," or "joss stick," was burning away, emitting a thin white spire of smoke from the stone receptacles in which it was placed

In front of the railing, and at different distances away—according to caste we imagined when surveying their clothes, were numerous worshippers bowing and kneeling, clasping their hands together & raising & lowering them, placing their foreheads upon the flagstones of the pavement and altogether keeping up a ridiculous "bob-bobbing" that amused Bill and me up to laughter.

This shocked Sam, (and us too when we considered it) and he

took us through a passage by the altar into a room adorned with plaster casts representing almost every imaginable manner of torture; doubtless placed there that the wicked might see what they had to expect if they did not mend their ways.

It would take a long time for me to describe what I recollect of these, and then I should not be half done, but one herculean black figure with hideous face walking around a circle at the end of a huge lever which carried a monstrous millstone around on top of another, in the centre of which was a cavity where evil doers were being flung in, never more to emerge alive, but to ooze out in a jelly from between the vast rocks, I shall never forget while I live.

Passing around to the other side of the altar we saw a large cash metal bell, hung very low and apparently of great antiquity. It was badly chipped at the edge, but had no cracks in it and we stopped over ten minutes, snapping it with our fingers & with dollars and listening to the sweet tones as the vibrations grew weaker and fainter; once when I struck it a light tap with a dollar I counted 300 before the sound ceased! I never heard so rich a tone in any other bell before or since.

A shaven priest in a coarse woolen mantle tied with a rope, joined us here, and told us, thro' Sam, that it was—as we understood him, "over three thousand years old, and a great curiosity" whereat we gave it another inspection to see if perhaps we couldnt find "Noahs" name on it, or some trace of its having been hung on the "Ark," but in vain, so, giving the man a "mace" (ten cents) for the light which he had thrown upon the matter we departed & were soon in the jam upon the street again.

It was getting late in the afternoon and we told Sam to work around to the "Factory," that we might get our boat and return to the ship, and, to our astonishment he brought us out upon the landing place opposite the sampan so quickly, that we concluded we had not been far from there at any time during the day.

However we had no cause to grumble, for we had seen more than we could remember as it was so stepping into the boat we lit a cigar apiece, and disposed ourselves for a sail down the river.

We were soon off, and with the strong ebb tide were borne swiftly along through the rice marshes, and past all the scenes of our trip the night before. We puffed away in silence for a while watching Sam and his sons as they bent to their oars.

Presently we neared a Pagoda and I proposed stopping to examine it, so Sam ran the "sampan" ashore close by and we started up the hill upon which the structure stood,—all Chinese Pagodas seem to be upon hills, tho' why, I never learned.

After a few minutes climbing we reached the foot of the tower, and after walking around it, and ascertaining that the distance was thirty five steps we began to ascend by the steps around the outside and through the centre of the shaft. That is—first we mounted about ten or twelve steps, going in at the base and coming out at the opposite side some fourteen feet higher up. Emerging upon a narrow ledge which extended all around the tower, we walked one quarter way around, and entering another stairway, mounted about a dozen steps, came out upon the next ledge, followed it around one quarter of the way again, and entered another stairway, and so on to the top, where we found that we had been preceded by so many name cutting Europeans as to put us to the blush, and cause us to leave the place unblemished by *our* hands.

The view was very pretty to any one who liked the looks of paddy fields intersected by creeks with a few moderate hills in the distance, but it had few charms for us; all we cared was to see the Pagoda, and go through it from top to bottom, so as to have it to say that we had done so.

Bill pulled some plaster out of the cracks and tried to throw into the river beneath us; it was just a trifle more than he could do and contrary to Sams wishes he kept pulling down the mortar and pegging away at the river. I tried it myself once or twice, but being unable to throw so far I failed to see any fun in laming my arm in such vain endeavours, and stopped.

Just back of us, and across a pond, was a small hamlet, whose denizens were closely watching our movements, and it became evident that this pulling down the Pagoda was highly offensive to them, for they began to shout and gesticulate at us, whereat Sam redoubled his efforts to get Bill away, and I seconded him.

But it had become a point of honor, in some sense, with him, to throw a piece of stone into the river from the top of the pagoda, and all expostulation was in vain; he vowed he would, "pull the house down piecemeal, but he would do it"

The Chinamen finding shouts and gestures useless determined to take more active measures, and ten or twelve betook themselves to a boat and started to cross the pond and get to us.

We shewed this to Bill, and threatened to leave him, if he did not stop, and come away; he would not do it, and seeing the crowd increasing, and more boats coming, Sam & I started down, thinking that Bill would follow us.

It took but a moment to run down, and another to reach our boat. The fellows were shouting and rowing as if mad, and we trembled for Bill should his foolishness keep him there too long. They reached the shore & sprang up the hill towards the Pagoda. Just as they did so Bill started down, and as he emerged from the bottom door he was assailed by a shower of sticks, stones, mud, and "Tu-le-ah-ma's" (a native execration) which sent him flying down the slope at railroad speed.

In less time than it takes to write it he was on the bank and as he sprang for the boat, we shoved quickly off and pulled for dear life.

The next moment a perfect hailstorm of missiles came down upon the bamboo roof but did no damage save to dirty it some; the next instant we were out of range of everything but their tongues, which were wagging freely about us.

Springing out from beneath the shelter then, Bill pulled a big chunk of mortar from his pocket and holding it between finger and thumb he shook it derisively at them and shouted

"Ha, ha! I said Id throw a piece of the pagoda into the river, and here it goes!" and he tossed it in.

They couldnt understand the language of course, but the action told all, and as we floated away down the current a fruitless volley of stones was rained after us and a mad howl came over the waters. Of course we had a laugh over the matter,—now that the danger was over, and then, as evening closed in, we ate some supper,—provided by Mrs Sam while we were in the Pagoda—and lay down to rest awhile and talk.

We fell asleep, and the next thing we knew Sam called us saying "Hi yah! come! have catchee Whampoa! mus go board shipee"

We roused us, and, sure enough, there we were, close to the vessel.

SEPTEMBER 15 Monday

Everything went smooth in the forenoon & we got the fore topgallant mast ½ way down. But after dinner the 2^d mate came aft & told the mate (in my presence) that some of the men had made a *"moonlight beat"* (I.E.) cleared out & we found 5 men & one boy among the missing. However the officers are glad of it for we have got a regular *"Guffy"* crew.

[81]

September 16 Tuesday
Some more of the men cleared out last night which is *"all serene"*. I am & have been scince Saturday employed taking the weight of rice & shall be till we are unloaded.

September 17 Wednesday
Taking the weight of the rice. One more man cleared out last night

September 18 Thursday
Taking the drafts of rice all day

September 19 Friday
Ditto

September 20 Saturday
Ditto

September 21 Sunday
This morning I drefsed up & went with one of the other boys in the captains *"sampan"* to church for the first time since I left home   I saw a lot of young Bostonians belonging to the bark "Sarah H. Snow." Text Romans 12th & 11th. In the aftn I went aboard the *"Snow"* & stayed there some time & from there I went to the *"Charmer"*   Saw the captain & applied for a berth to go home in her & he intimated that if our captain would let me go he would take me.

September 22 Monday
The old story again   Tallying rice

September 23 Tuesday
I have no time to write so I can only say that its *"all e same"* thing

September 24 Wednesday
The rice is almost out & we have got the masts scraped & varnished & shall paint the yards tomorrow

September 25 Thursday
There is some talk of our going to San Francisco from Shanghae but I guess it is all *"bosh"*. Busy at the rice all day

September 26 Friday

Nothing unusual happened today   the old routine of port life
Tallying rice all day

September 27 Saturday

The old man came down from Canton today & complimented the
mate on the fine appearance of the ship *"alow & aloft"* as we are
now beginning to *"look"* as they say like a *"tea ship"* & an *"India-
man"*

September 28 Sunday

No money was given today although we had liberty if we could
get ashore. I stayed aboard all day & did *"I dont know what."* The
mate went up to Canton to night.

September 29 Monday

We got all the cargo out today

September 30 Tuesday

Got some Kentledge in today & sent out some flour & Planks

October 1 Wednesday

The captain having got back from Canton again has concluded to
take a full cargo of sugar, fire crackers, furniture, &c to Shanghae
so we are good for another fortnight or 3 weeks here. The
Charmer is going day after tomorrow & I have sent a note to the
captain to try once more to get a place on board of her

October 2 Thursday

Captain Lucas sent me word that I could come & go home with him
& I am going

October 3 Friday

Preparing to go on board the Charmer

CHAPTER VII

FROM THE *SURPRISE* TO THE *CHARMER*

AND so Abbey left the *Surprise*. The passage he had made in her was good but not remarkable. Her time from New York to the equator in the Atlantic was 25 days; and from the equator to the Cape of Good Hope, 28 days. Thus she was 53 days from New York to the Cape. The record is 42, held by the *Sea Witch*. Her open-sea voyage (to Achin Head) was of 83 days duration. The record (to Java Head) is 70 days, 10 hours, made by the *Sea Witch* on the same voyage on which she set the New York–Good Hope record. The other legs of the *Surprise's* voyage to Hong Kong were as follows. She was 6 days from Achin Head to Penang, making 89 from New York. The run from Penang to Singapore took 4 days, and the run from Singapore to Hong Kong, 12 days. Thus the total sailing time from New York to Hong Kong was 105 days, the record being 81. This latter was set up by the *Oriental*, sailing direct of course and by a shorter route.

But if Abbey had returned to New York in the *Surprise* he *would* have experienced some fast travelling. He probably would have felt compensated for a later arrival home. The *Surprise* left Shanghai on January 2, 1857. She reached Anjer January 14, covering 2,663 miles in 12 days. The record is now 10, held by the *Sword Fish*. Two days later the *Surprise* took her departure from Java Head en route to New York. In February she encountered a hurricane in which she lost sails and had a boat and some bulwarks wrecked. As a result she took 31 days from Java Head to the Cape of Good Hope. She sailed home from there in 37 days, however—only 2 more than the record held by the *N. B. Palmer*. Accordingly she reached New York March 25 in 82 days from Shanghai. This smashed the record as it then stood. The present record is only 1 day faster—made by the *Sword Fish*. On this 81-day passage, the *Sword Fish* set the above mentioned 10-day record from Shanghai to Anjer. The two days spent by the *Surprise* around Anjer and Java Head spoiled her chance for an all-time mark.

The *Surprise* had a complete overhaul; among other items, the copper sheathing of her hull was badly torn. About this time many of the early clippers were so racked by years of hard service that their sails and spars were reduced to lessen the strain on the hulls. Not so with the *Surprise*, however. After her overhaul she sailed to Shanghai again and encountered a typhoon before reaching port. On her return passage she turned in another noteworthy performance. She made Anjer from Woosung (near Shanghai) in 13 days, and reached the Cape in 33 more. While rounding the Cape she encountered 15 days of heavy head gales. Nevertheless she crossed the Atlantic equator 72 days out and reached New York in 92 days, 22 hours. This can not rival the absolute speed of her preceding voyage but it was the finest run of the year, even so.

The *Surprise* continued in the trade between New York and the Far East for the rest of her career, making seven more round trips up to 1867 and several more after that. In 1860 Captain Ranlett turned her over to his son who kept her till the end. After he finally retired from the sea Ranlett, senior, died at the age of 101. The *Surprise* made one voyage to Penang after the one on which Abbey was in her. Strangely enough the time of the passage was 90 days—within a day of the earlier voyage. Taking her first fourteen passages from the Far East to the North Atlantic, she averaged just 80 days from Anjer to port, the individual times ranging from 70 to 93. This carried her down through 1866.

The *Surprise* was considerably rebuilt during an overhaul in New York in 1867. As to her rig, her skysails were eliminated and she was fitted with double topsails. Her speed and reputation continued high. She set out from New York on her last voyage in 1875. She was 29 days to the equator and reached the East Indies at Timor in 92 days. She picked up her Yokohama pilot on the 131st day but a head gale kept her out of the harbor. Next day, while seeking greater shelter, she went on the rocks and turned almost half way over. All hands got ashore safely, though only with a great deal of trouble. Four days later the ship was observed floating offshore nearly upside down. Thanks to the able assistance of a Japanese man-of-war, a good deal of her gear and cargo was salvaged, including 10,000 cases of kerosene. A reward of $1,000 was bestowed upon the Japanese ship's company. The *Surprise* herself was a total loss. It turned out that the "pilot" was a drunken beach comber. Thus after more than 25 years of smart service, the *Surprise* met an end like unto that of many other fine ships of her day.

When Abbey left the *Surprise* there appeared a little sidelight typical of the days when the world was expanding. The reader may remember the young passenger, Harry Price, who was wont to bring his guitar up on deck after supper on pleasant evenings at sea. His music would provide the accompaniment for the members of the crew who felt the desire to raise their voices in song until stilled by the striking of 8 bells. Young Price quite likely was leaving home for the first time, to be gone for a long, long time on his journey to far off China to try his luck in the wide world. Before he parted with Abbey he wrote this somewhat wistful note on the back flyleaf of the diary.

Dear Abby

When you arrive in New York please go to Wilmington Del and see my family   They will be glad to see you, knowing that you are a friend of mine. When you get out of the cars at Wilmington anyone will direct you to my fathers house. Be shure to see my mother and Mrs J A Griffin. If you cannot do so   write to both and say you left me well, but wishing to get home very much

By doing so you will oblidge your affectionate friend

Harry Price

Mrs Joseph T Price
Wilmington
Delaware
And
Mrs John A Griffin
Wilmington
Delaware

There was no last-minute hitch about Abbey being released from the *Surprise* and accepted aboard the *Charmer*. He was lucky, for he sailed for New York from Whampoa less than a month after he had arrived there. The *Charmer* was not the exceptional ship that the *Surprise* was; but she reached New York almost two months ahead of her and that was what counted with Abbey at this stage of his journeyings. The *Surprise* went from Whampoa to Shanghai and did not sail for home until nearly three months after the *Charmer* left Whampoa.

The *Charmer* was a fine new ship, on her second voyage only, and was no mean vessel, even if not one of the most prominent clippers. She had been launched less than two years before from the yard of George W. Jackman at Newburyport, Mass., her first owners being Bush and Wildes of Boston. She was a medium clipper, 181' 1" in length at the water line and 203' over all. Her beam was 37' and the depth of her hold 23' 3". Her tonnage was 1,055 by the old method of measurement and 1,024 by the new. She was a sister ship of the *Daring* and the *War Hawk*. Her figurehead consisted of a large snake with its tongue drooping out. After noting the expression on the face of the snake, one newspaper reporter opined that it must have just had a drink of water from Cochituate Lake.

The *Charmer's* career began auspiciously, as she sailed from Boston to San Francisco in 114 days, arriving there considerably less than six months after she was launched. Hers was a very creditable performance and under the circumstances was a fast one. Rounding the Horn she was delayed for 18 days by bad head gales which carried away her jibboom. Then she was forced by unfavorable winds to consume 7 days covering the last 500 miles into San Francisco. When she came home she was one of the first ships to profit by the building up of an eastbound trade from California. This was in the year 1855. She carried to New York 1,400 tons of wheat at $28 a ton.

Her next passage to San Francisco was slow, about 140 days. Coming down the Atlantic she allowed herself to get to leeward of Cape St. Roque and had a mighty wearisome time getting around it. She spent almost a month beating to the eastward through the light breezes and calms of the equator. She crossed the line from north to south no fewer than four times before finally getting clear, and by that time she was nearly fifty days out of New York. This is a perfect demonstration of the absolute necessity of getting well to the eastward up in the latitudes where the westerly winds prevail. In this particular case, however, it should be mentioned that other ships were caught in the same manner in this same period. The *Sancho Panza* was caught even worse than the *Charmer* and her passage was 7 days slower. Her captain was inspired to exclaim: "The devil take *Sancho Panza;* she is as bad as her namesake!" On this trip the *Charmer* was not yet done with light winds. They held her up for 7 days off the Horn and she was 11 days covering the last 800 miles into San Francisco.

She crossed to Hong Kong in 53 days and Abbey joined her at Whampoa. Captain Isaac S. Lucas was in command of the

Charmer. He had had her from the start, prior to which he had been master of the smaller *Hussar* for the first two years of her life. On the first page of the next chapter we shall find the names of nearly everyone aboard Abbey's new ship.

CHAPTER VIII

"ON BOARD THE CHARMER"

October 4 Saturday

Went on board & found one of my old shipmates on her. On the whole she has a very fine crew & no Chinamen

Officers of Ship Charmer

Captain

———— Lucas

Chief Mate

———— Crowel

2ᵈ Mate

———— Stone

3ᵈ Mate

Francis Conway

Passengers

Mrs Capt Lucas and sister

Mrs ———— Nye

& little Daughter

& Chinese servant

Crew

(Prussian)	"*Dutch*"
Charley	Peter Lost Overboard
Stephen (Yankee)	Jack (Irish)
Mitler (Swede)	Will Scott (Yankee)
Ned (Yankee)	Joe (Irish)
Joseph Hewlett (Yankee)	W Brien (Irish)
Big Bill (Yankee)	I. Williams (Irish)

Charles A Abbey ("*Bould American*")
Taylor ditto
Robinson (Prussian)
Charley 2ᵈ (Dane)
N. Washburn (Yankee)

OCTOBER 5 Sunday

Today a few of the Surprises hands came on board & gave me some letters to take home. In the evening "*Scott*" the boy who ran away from the Surprise came & told me he was going to "stow away" which he did

OCTOBER 6 Monday

Hove up the anchor & dropped down about a mile where we anchored for the night

OCTOBER 7 Tuesday

Hove up & dropped down a little further there being no wind

OCTOBER 8 Wednesday

Heaving up & letting go the anchor all the while. I had to lay up today having caught the Chills & fever. From now till some week or so all must be a blank As I remember nothing

OCTOBER 21 Tuesday

I turned to today though I can eat nothing at all but rice which through the kindnefs of the cook I used to get once in a while

OCTOBER 22 Wednesday

Usual sea duty, putting on Chaffing gear &c

OCTOBER 23 Thursday

Nothing particular transpired   very light winds & baffling

OCTOBER 24 Friday

Blank   Blank   Blank

OCTOBER 25 Saturday

I had no forenoon watch below today as I had to clean out the 2ᵈ mates room

October 26 Sunday

Set Studding sails today to keep ahead of a 6 topsail yard ship (the "*Aurora*" of Boston) that was trying to overhaul us. We spoke her in the course of the aft^n & found her to be 12 days from Manilla for New York.* Passed the "*Camels Hump*" a small Island which derives its name from its resemblance to that thing

October 27 Monday

Very squally weather   so much so that we are under skysails with reefs in the topsails, so as to be ready for "*Squalls*".† We crofsed the line last night which makes three times I have crossed it

October 28 Tuesday

Land in sight all around (Islands of course) the largest is "*St Johns*" near the mouth of the Straits of "*Gaspar*". Wind ahead as is usually the case in these parts. Double reefed the topsails in a heavy squall

October 29 Wednesday

Gaspar Island on the weather beam & we beating dead to windard trying to get through the abominable "*Straits of Gaspar*" the "*bugbear*" of these parts. Tacked ship every hour through the night

October 30 Thursday

Nothing but tack ship all day long & no prospects of any thing better for a while to come

October 31 Friday

Tacking ship night & day

* The *Aurora* was an extreme clipper ship with upper and lower topsails on all three masts. She had been launched at Chelsea, Mass., less than three years before and now hailed from Salem. She was very speedy but never had the good fortune to encounter favorable winds for a sufficient length of time to enable her to turn in any exceptional performances. Her best recorded run was one of 17 days from the equator to San Francisco and she had a number of very slow passages. The *Aurora* was a bad luck ship all around. She carried the American flag for less than ten years but, in that period, had a mutiny, broke her rudder-head, ran aground, was in collision, and was fined for the illegal transportation of coolies. After 1863 she flew the British flag and on one voyage had to put back for repairs. Some time after 1869 her captain and officers were convicted of loading her with bogus cotton and then burning her.

† This arrangement made it possible to carry practically full sail in the prevailing wind; then, in the event of a squall, everything but the topsails could be "let go," and the ship would be under reefed topsails immediately.

November 1 Saturday
We are through at last and nearing Angeir point

November 2 Sunday
At daylight this morning we had Sumatra on the weather beam & Angeir on the bow. Had 2 boats alongside with yams, potatoes, pineapples, pumpkins, corn, monkeys, birds, &c but no fruit that we could get as the captain bought it all   We went through* in six tacks on a dead beat which was doing well

November 3 Monday
Now we are clear of Angeir & the China Sea & have our head toward the Cape   I begin to feel as if we were getting towards home once more. Was taken down with the "*Shakes & fever*" again last night

November 4 Tuesday
All the studding sails set on the port tack & going about 10 knots. Sick yet.

November 5 Wednesday
Getting along finely though troubled with light squalls very frequently

November 6 Thursday
Still going along at a splendid rate. Nothing particular happened today excepting that I "*turned to*" again in the aft^n
Captain Lucas said to me well "Old Surpriseman" what are you turned to for   I told him that I had turned to work again "Yes" said he & if you "*turn in*" again Ill haul you out with a tackle.

November 7 Friday
The breeze still holds & we continue on our course at the rate of 12 knots an hour which is all we can knock out of the Charmer any how we can fix it

November 8 Saturday
Cracking breeze yet. This evening about 6 bells (we had all been

* The Straits of Sunda.

[94]

noting that the fore top mast & lower studding sails were to much for the boom which had no brace or topping lift & I had moved my seat to a spar under the weather fore rigging just in time as it happened) when the topmast stunsail tack parted & away went the boom & down came the sails & all giving us a job to *"clear the wreck."* We got the lee boom over to windward & set the sail again, in the next watch

NOVEMBER 9 Sunday

We had fresh pork for breakfast this morning by way of variety. This morning about 3 bells the mate came forward & ordered us to set the fore top mast stun sail again we got it up to the yard arm & when we had got the tack half way out the downhaul got foul & we were some time clearing it when we were hoisting it up again by some mismanagement the mate let the sheet go & it like to have taken the fingers off both his hands. He sung out, "make fast" & come up here & catch hold of this sheet. The sheet was slatting about like everything making it dangerous to go near it but we got hold of it & got a turn around the fore stay & passed the end aft to a man named Peter ———— (who had been in the ship ever since she left N. Y. & in fact he was the best man in the ship. I heard him ask the mate *"may I take a turn around the anchor shank sir"* but the mate said, "No hold on to it") we then 5 of us got hold beforehand & when ready took the turn off from the stay to let it go aft to its place The minute we did so it jerked right out of our hands & the next I saw was poor Peter flung over the rail head first. Man Overboard we all sung out at once & ran aft the man at the wheel stood ready with the grating (on which the helmsman stands) & as he passed the stern he hove it to him, but he had his head down in the water & was paddling dog fashion to all appearances stunned. I saw him for the last time about ½ a mile astern as his red shirt came up on the top of a wave. Just then the Captain came up from the cabin & asked in his usual tone *"who's overboard"* *"Peter sir"* was the answer he didnt say anything then till the man was out of sight when he observed *"Well he's gone, the best man in the ship"*. And still not a single effort was made to save him. Poor fellow, he was a good shipmate & sailor. He has a wife & child in Sweden whom he was making every preparation to return to.*

* Few tears have been shed by any who have heard that Captain Lucas met his own fate by falling overboard and drowning in midocean.

November 10 Monday

Nothing unusual happened today the wind is still good & we are cracking on towards the Cape at a rate which I should like to have continued till we reach N. Y.

November 11 Tuesday

I had the forenoon watch on deck today & instead of giving me & the other boy in the port watch our aft^n below the mate came forward & rousted us out & made us clean one of the Guns & intimated that we were getting to lazy & that we could not have any more aft^n watches below & a good many other things equally calculated to raise our spirits & get us to work better. Wind still good
Course of a necessity S. Westerly & thereabouts

November 12 Wednesday

Nothing unusual happened today except that the same operation was performed upon the two other boys that was on us yesterday
This morning the wind commenced a *"kickup"* & all the studding sails had to come in & skysails also. But our watch stuck them out again during the forenoon

November 13 Thursday

I had a forenoon watch on deck today & was not as I expected called up on my aft^n watch below. The wind is failing rather

November 14 Friday

Nothing in particular happened today. We had two sails in sight on the weather quarter but in the evening they were out of sight

November 15 Saturday

Nothing in particular happened to day but we are not going so fast & the wind is failing. We have got around on the starboard tack

November 16 Sunday

This is a beautiful day (or would be on shore) but here it is a *"dead calm"* the sea being as smooth as glafs. I should like dearly to be at home & able to go to church, but I cant. I went on deck in the aftn with a book in my hand & after reading awhile the day was so fine & everything so pleasant that I began to feel quite good & feel my spirits raised, when everything would be knocked in the head by the expectation of hearing *"Square the Main Yard"* or something to that effect & then the coldnefs of the officers & the harsh orders to do this & do that & no such thing as a smile & nothing but kicks & cuffs I defy any one to feel in good spirits who knows he can do better things.

Long. about 64° east
Lat.   "   22° south
in the neighborhood of the *"Mauritius"*

November 17 Monday

Dead calm almost all the while & very hot. Nothing in particular happened

November 18 Tuesday

Calm almost all day, but toward evening it breezed up & we *"Laid course"* pretty much all night, though it fell calm toward morning

November 19 Wednesday

We have got a breeze which by the way it comes in, "says, *"Im going to last"* & I guess it will for it is getting stronger all the while & to night we had to take in the top gallant sails

November 20 Thursday

Our fine breeze of yesterday has failed & here we lay "every thing flapping & slatting" enough to jerk the sticks out of her

November 21 Friday

Breezes constantly springing up & failing as fast so that it is "brace up" & "square away" & "shift over the stunsails" all the while & many are the imprecations which come from the men

November 22 Saturday

Pretty much all the same thing as it was yesterday   Nothing further to note

November 23 Sunday

Woke up this morning at 7 bells & found the men over the bows catching *"Bonita"* of which altogather we caught 8 & had fresh chowder & fried fish & duff & molasses   in fact quite a treat

November 24 Monday

Every thing as usual   light & baffling airs all day

November 25 Tuesday

No variation from yesterday & day before. Fine day as usual

November 26 Wednesday

We had quite a little breeze during the day but it died away in the evening & the wind hauled around during the night & then we had to i^st square the yards & then brace up on the other tack & then as in every night for a week we have to shift the stunsails from leward to windward & shift the gear too
Lat 28° 12′   Long. 45° −′

November 27 Thursday

About the same wind. Nothing in particular happened except a slight variation in the "*duff*" which was baked in a large pan & called in that state "*Dandy Funck*"   I liked it as well if not better than the boiled

November 28 Friday

Last night when our watch took the deck at 8 oclock we were under skysails & top gallant *stun sails* & when the other watch came on deck at 12, we reefed the topsails & it has set in for a blow. During the morning watch we had the topsails close reefed & I had just commenced to sweep down when (we were hove to) "*whew*" "*pish*", "*puff*" & we were "*all aback*" & going astern at a terrible rate   then out rushed the old man & I ran forward & rousted out the starboard watch & at 8 oclock (to tell the long & short) we were under a close reefed main topsail fore topmast & main staysail with a very heavy sea on

November 29 Saturday

Wind somewhat abated & under a little more sail

November 30 Sunday

This is a beautiful day & the wind having abated we made all sail & studding sails also

December 1 Monday

The winds are so variable now shifting here & there that it is allmost impossible to note the changes. Let it answer to say that in the evenings if it looks likely to blow perhaps we will reef the topsails & as likely as not shake the reefs out before morning & again perhaps set studdingsails

December 2 Tuesday

The wind has come out dead ahead & we are beating to windward on a race with a "*John Bull*" whom we are fast beating. But like all the rest of these breezes it wont last long

December 3 Wednesday

We have left "*Johnny*" out of sight to leeward during the night. The wind has hauled slightly so that we can lay nearer to our course & make more than by beating. There is a terrific sea on & there is evident signs of there having been a heavy blow about these parts

December 4 Thursday

We caught a beautiful breeze this evening & have been tearing away like mad a while but, alas, like all the rest of the breezes about hear it died away in the first watch & left us laying still as a log again

December 5 Friday

No wind at all to day. At dusk we spied a ship ahead
Now here it is the 5th of Dec & as hot as fire which seems strange to me who was born & brought up where it is always cold at this time of the year

December 6 Saturday

About the same as usual, the wind continued good though for a while & we are chasing a big ship which is ahead & passing a "*Johnny Crapeau*". The big ship went out of sight in the evening & "*Johnny*" crept off to leeward not being able to lay so high in the wind as we do

December 7 Sunday

The wind has held good all night & we passed the Cape of Aghulas last evening at 9½ o'clock with stunsails set

December 8 Monday

A tearing breeze which is sending us along at an awful rate bids fair to send us into the trades soon. We passed the English ship "Countefs of Seville" a Dutch brig & a French ship during the day. The "Countefs" gave us a tough match for we are not much account at sailing

December 9 Tuesday
Wind increased during the day & we took in the top gallantsails, but during the night we got the top gallant stunsails set
I was employed cleaning out the cooks coal locker & we got it filled up in the evening

December 10 Wednesday
Got under royal stunsails & caught the trades, which took us along at the rate of about 8 knots. Commenced to day to refit, rescrape, rewash, & "re" everything aboard the ship, & of course had "all hands" for the first time. Scraped the mizzen lower mast & topmast heads

December 11 Thursday
All hands again as it will be till we get into cold weather   Wind increasing as we get further north. Two of the men one of whom is "Long Jack" of the "Surprise" are laid up with (the captain says) either the "China Itch" or "Scurvy" he dont know which. I as well as all the rest feel scratchy but dont scratch for fear of getting it too
Lat 30° S   Course N W by N ½ north

December 12 Friday
All hands scraping masts again. Quite a fine day, & we continuing on our course at the rate of about 8 knots on an average.
This evening the mate told one of the boys & myself to take a pull of the main royal staysail halyards   I started aft with him but the "Old Man" & his "dog" were in the way. (Now he has set the dog on me so often that he wont let me alone any how but trys to bite me at any opportunity) the dog came at me & nabbed my knee tearing my trowsers (all the time the old man stood by with folded arms giving his silent approbation to the dog)   as soon as he bit at me I drew back & gave him a kick which sent him about a fathom & also sent my shoe after him   while putting on my shoe the Old Man drew back & gave me a heavy kick, saying, Let the

dog alone & he wont trouble you. I could not say anything though or I should probably have got ropesended in the bargain

December 13 Saturday

The same old story again but for a wonder we are done the masts & I dont know what will come next During the night we came up to & pafsed the bark Druid from Singapore for Barcelona 103 days out. We came up to & passed her as though she was at anchor having hardly time to speak each other
Lat 25°

December 14 Sunday

This is a very fine day & of course we had nothing to do. I had the forenoon watch below & employed my time in reading

December 15 Monday

Today we had a general clearing up about the decks took the "*Stream*" & "*Kedge*" anchors & their chains aft & put them below, serving the "*Guns*" the same trick. We had rice for dinner today & their being some left I took the pan & started for the galley with it. "*Now what are you going to with that*" said "*Big Bill*" one of the men. "Why take it back," says I, "Well now dont you do any such thing" says he, you take it & put it in the Pig Pen. So I went to put it in & the mate happened to see & stop me. He didnt tell me not to, but I had "*savee*" enough to take it too the Galley I was lying under the forecastle shortly after when the captain came forward & asked me if I done it & why I says "the men told me too." "You "dam'd" Son of a Bi—tch" says he & caught hold of my collar & jerked me, but he did not strike me

December 16 Tuesday

Scraped the jibboom & stump topgallant masts. Some of the crew at work on the rigging

December 17 Wednesday

Commenced this morning to scrub the Paintwork. It being my forenoon watch below at 8 bells I walked forward with the rest. The captain stopped me & told me to come on deck after breakfast. I did so & he told me that I couldnt have the forenoon watch but to go to scrubbing with the other watch & perhaps I should not get any more between here & New York. All this is because I was sick & uselefs for 2 or 3 weeks in the China Sea

DECEMBER 18 Thursday

Cleared out the forward lockers & scrubbed them.
The captain let his dog bite me again tonight, while he sat & watched us. If I strike the dog he will hit me & say *"Let the dog alone & he wont trouble you"* which he knows is a lie for he has set the dog on me so many times that he wont let me alone at all now

DECEMBER 19 Friday

Scrub, Scrub, Rub, Rub, dig, dig & get blowed out all the while you are doing your best. Of all men I ever saw on sea or shore this same *"Captain Lucas"* is the most Noisy Dirty Bawdy Obscene wretch I ever came acrofs   no one who has not sailed with him can imagine how far he carries it. He never opens his mouth but to Yell as loud as possible & all his language is filthy

DECEMBER 20 Saturday

Had a general cleaning today preparatory to painting

DECEMBER 21 Sunday

"Laid on our oars"

DECEMBER 22 Monday

Commenced painting & had all hands *"all day"*. Finished the bulwarks & cabin

DECEMBER 23 Tuesday

All hands all day, & in the forenoon touched off a little remaining on the bulwarks & painted the decks amidships (lead color) in the aft^n

DECEMBER 24 Wednesday

Our watch got its forenoon watch today & in the aft^n all hands were over the side scrubbing ship   We got a *"gleorious"* dinner today which must answer for our Christmas. This is Christmas eve and when I think where I was last Christmas & the chance I had then to improve my condition much better than by going to sea I cant help saying to myself, You stubborn fool. Never mind

I'll never spend another 24th or 25th of Dec. at sea if I can possibly help it

December 25 Thursday

Our ears were saluted this morning by the captains voice Yelling, "A Merry Christmas & plenty of work," & indeed there was plenty of work. All hands all day painting the outside of the ship
What are my friends doing today   I wonder if any of them are thinking about Carelefs Charlie & where he is. They suppose him to be in China I guess, & not so near as he really is. They are all wishing each other Merry Christmas, & I hope they are having one, but there is none for me & all the consolation I have is in thinking & saying to myself (when a new act of tyranny is enacted over me or I get a fresh bite from the dog) never mind "Abbott" (as they call me) 4 or 5 weeks more & you will in all probability be where you can "*dog*" those who now "*Dog*" you

December 26 Friday

Commenced holystoning this morning I had the forenoon watch below & before I went below at 8 o clock the captain told me to come out after breakfast but I didnt do it, & when I came out in the aftn he made me take a large grindstone (unshipped on purpose) which I could scarcely move & holystone with it. The men were all enraged at such cruelty This stone weighed at least 20 lbs while the common ones weighed from 3 to 5 I used it as I best could & took it easy but was determined not to use it again

December 27 Saturday

Went aft this morning to relieve the "*Stones*" & I went up to Scott to take his, the mate said "Take your own stone the grindstone" "I cant run that today" said I but still I got it & started slowly Mrs Lucas was watching me & persuaded the captain to let me take a small one, which I did & kept it all day, & thank heaven finished the decks

December 28 Sunday

Had nothing to do of course Kept a good lookout for the island of "Fernando Noronha" (which we "*didnt*" see) & crofsed the line during the night making the 4th time for me & the Last also for some time at least

December 29 Monday

Got watch & watch again & now the *"old man"* says, all he wants of us is to keep the ship clean & as she is till N. Y.

December 30 Tuesday

Forenoon watch below. Made a *"Blackball"* cap & commenced a general overhauling of my chest preparatory to coming on the coast

December 31 Wednesday

We got a squall from the N.E. last night & in a very few minutes our studding sails royals & skysails mizzen topgallant sail & topgallant & royal staysails were "all in a heap" alow & aloft. Boy *"Charley"* boy *"Hewlett"* & myself were up in the main top or *"up at the main"* &. In the 1st place we went up there at 15 minutes past 6 & took in 4 stun sails 2 staysails a royal & skysail & were down on deck at 7 oclock, (which I think is doing very well) & the minute I got down on deck the mate (a mean bugger) says *"Neow yeou boys have spent the whole watch up there"*. There were two men in the foretop & they couldnt beat us. New Years eve tonight I watched the old year out & the New Year in on my lookout & the minute it struck 8 bells there commenced the awfulest ding dong & racket from all quarters that had been aboard the ship in a good while. For instance the captain on the poop yelling Happy New Year the Carpenter & Sailmaker in their room hammering upon a Chinese gong one *"good" hand"* at the big bell ringing away like every thing & *"all hands & the cook"* making as much noise as possible with the wind blowing the ship rolling & pitching & every prospect of reefing speedily this was the way we watched the old year out & the New Year in.

January 1 Thursday

This is New Years day & here I am in a gale at sea. Never will I spend another one so. This evening the 1st mate Mr Crowel struck me a blow on the side of my head when no one was near, for nothing at all The biggest set of fools that ever lived are the officers aboard here. They appear to have no judgment at all. If there comes up a squall they will let it strike her all full & wait till it is spent & then it is clew up & haul down everything & furl all then get down on deck & lay up the ropes & often before you get cleared up they commence to loose sail again & dont stop till every stitch is on her again only to be taken in again in a like manner

January 2 Friday

The gale still continues with sometimes a short lull when the ("*4 fools*") crowd on sail   to take it in, often before it is set

January 3 Saturday

Got under topgallant studding sails with a roaring breeze & a clear sky & moonlight night

January 4 Sunday

Tearing along at a furious rate. Quite a fine day

January 5 Monday

Still going at the same rate   We have averaged 9 knots scince we passed the cape, a period of 4 weeks*

January 6 Tuesday

Today while setting the main royal studdingsail I went aft to help haul the tack out. The captain was sitting where I had to pass & his dog with him. The dog came at me & bit my leg & I kicked him off. The captain made no attempt to keep him away although one word from him would have done it. When I came down again I saw the dog waiting for me at the corner of the cabin & as there was not room for me to pafs between the rail & him I of course gave the dog a kick when he sprang at me   Then for the first time I saw the captain held him by the tail. Said he to me "*What do you kick that dog for,*" & at the same time shoved him at me saying "*Seek him*"   the dog bit me again on the calf of my left leg & I kicked him twice & sent him flying against the booby hatch. This so enraged the captain that he jumped up & ran at to kick me   he tried twice & the second time touched my arm with his foot. All the while the dog was trying to bite me too. He called me aft to show him the bites afterwards & as soon as I had done so he wanted to "Lie" me out of it by saying that they were not dog bites & the blood running from them all the while

* Quite remarkable if true. If it be correct, the ship's track must have been a good deal more of a zigzag than is indicated by the diary.

All the port watch saw the fracas & any of them will give their testimony in my favor when we arrive in N. Y. if I choose to call upon them
Lat 12° N
Long between 35° & 40° West*

JANUARY 7 Wednesday

The breeze threatened to die away altogather once today but it freshened up & is now as good as ever. Tonight it being my first lookout for the bell I went aft & sat down on a spar. I struck 1 2 & 3 bells & was sitting waiting for 4 when I got into a train of thoughts & fell asleep   the next minute the 3ᵈ mate pulled my arm & told me to strike 4 bells & then to come & walk the decks for the next 2 hours. I wouldnt do it, my lookout being out but stayed forward   he soon called me & told me to keep the weather gangway lookout. (on a fine moonlight night)   I told him I wouldnt do it. *"You wont do it"* says he, *"No I wont"* says I. A fracas then ensued in which he got worsted. He then asked me again if I would do it. *"No sir I wont"* he then walked aft & told the mate. He wouldnt make me & *"Conway"* couldnt so he con-cluded to let me alone
Scraped the main topgallant mast & blacked the lower rigging

JANUARY 8 Thursday

Was employed holystoning the mates room in the forenoon & in the 1ˢᵗ dog watch scraped the main royal stun sail boom & swept down
Lat 16° N
Long 53° W   Course N.W.

JANUARY 9 Friday

At daylight this morning espied a bark steering the same course as we. But as soon as she saw us she appeared anxious to speak for she set lee stunsails & ran off West (bearing down on our star-board quarter) but finding we were rapidly leaving her she came up to her course again & before 8 bells she was out of sight astern. We five boys cleaned the armory today
Lat 17° 42′
Long 54° 59′   Course N. W. by W.

* Probably a slip for "between 45° & 50°."

January 10 Saturday

Laid up last night with a tremendous boil on my knee. It swelled so much as to make me unfit to walk & so I went & turned in went to sleep & had a regular *"blowout"* all night. Saw a vessel by moonlight but it was so cloudy that we couldnt make her out perfectly
Lat. pretty near 20° N
Long 56° 30′ W

January 11 Sunday

Still laid up. The Captain came forward & looked at my leg today & told me to put a hot poultice on it every 3 hrs night & day till he told me to stop. Tonight & last night also it has looked like a change of wind to Leward but it has turned out to be nothing. Sent down the royal stunsails booms & all the blocks & gear attached to them *"and I am "*GLAD*" of it"*

January 12 Monday

Under double reefed topsails all day. Sent down the 3 skysail & fore & mizzen royal yards Saw a brig or other 2 masted craft
Course N N W
Lat 23° N
Long 61° W

January 13 Tuesday

Got under topgallant sails again Saw a vessel toward evening standing acrofs our bows
Lat 24° 40′ N

January 14 Wednesday

Reefed topsails & a dirty sea on. The sky looks lowering all around. Scraped a topgallant stunsail boom & set up the starboard main topmast rigging
Lat 26° —′
Long ——————

January 15 Thursday

Close reefed the topsails & have all the prospects of getting a North wester. Rained quite hard in the evening
Lat 28° N
Long ——— Course N by West

January 16 Friday

Boo ! Boo ! Boo ! Whew aint it a blowing "*Jehosaphat Bumstead*" & cold," it would freeze the tail off from a brafs monkey. It rained till 4 bells in the middle watch last night, with but little or no wind. When it cleared up the wind came out Southwest & it grew quite chilly   We got on the port tack & waited to see how it would come out   if it holds Southwest well & good, but if it gets a point beyond that it is sure to go to Northwest "always" & then lookout. Well before 8 bells we took in the foretopsail & then went below. When we came on deck again in the morning we found the ship hove to under a close reefed main topsail, main spencer, fore & main staysails. Before long it commenced to blow harder & at last all the sail we could show was a close reefed main topsail. And want it a blowing "*good gracious*" I never had an Idea it could blow so. Well here we are & here we must sweat till we get a fair wind

Pretty near the Gulf Stream

January 17 Saturday

The wind has hauled & we are now laying about W. N. W.   toward night we took in the fore topsail. In the i[st] watch the mizzen topsail & in the middle watch the foresail & it now blows harder than ever & is getting colder & colder all the while. Its no use trying to describe it, so I will only add (by way of variety) that I got washed from under the weather bulwarks, much to the amusement of all hands   But such jokes are but too frequent & are always taken in good part

January 18 Sunday

The wind has abated & we have set the topgallant sails over the topsails & are racing with a bark to windward of us. At dark she was about 3 miles ahead & to leward of us

commencement of the gale

6 o clock in the evening furled the topgallant sails   8 o clock double reefed the topsails. 12 o clock under the close reefed main topsail & reefed foresail.

January 19 Monday

Furled the foresail at 9 oclock & hauled down the topmast staysails. It now blows very hard with considerable sea. We stopped under this sail all day until 6 oclock when we hauled down the main staysail brailed up the main spencer & goosewinged the maintopsail. This was at 8 oclock the watch then went below. It now blew fearfully. I laid down under the weather bulwark so as to be able to hear the bell. I hadn't been there 5 minutes before I heard a crash & looking aft saw the mizzen staysail split from clew to earing We hauled this down. I then laid down again wondering what would go next. After another 5 minutes spell another crash met my ears & there was the main topsail (the only sail left) split from head to foot. We now called all hands & hauled up the lee clew of the sail & then the Old Man roared out *"Lay aloft all hands & furl that main topsail"*. I was the second one up & found it almost impossible to get on the yard however out I laid on the lee yard arm. A young sailor named Jack Dunn was my companion at the lee Earing. The split was about ½ way out on the lee yard arm & when we went out there (us two) there was a short lull which gave us the chance to get there, but before there were any more out, there came a squall which beggars description, & the sail Flapped & jerked so furiously that it was impossible for any more to lay out where we were. The men who were up were all in the bunt of the yard & momentarily expected the topmast would go & if it had Jack & I must go with it & no help for us. I being on the in side made a rush to get down & got in just the nicest pickle I ever was, & came near going overboard any how as it was I was wrapped up in the sail over a minute but I finally got in as did Jack also we then *"laid down"* it being impossible to furl the sail while it was blowing so. There being nothing to be done our watch went below. When I came on deck again I found the Main Topsail *"Tied up"* Like a bundle of rags the other watch having watched a lull to do it in

JANUARY 20 Tuesday
Got the fore staysail aft & bent it at the mizzen

JANUARY 21 Wednesday
The wind having somewhat abated we sent down the main topsail & bent a new one. Got under 3 topsails reefed foresail & main sail

JANUARY 22 Thursday
The wind keeps up to a gale all the while with short lulls

January 23 Friday

Blowing still & oh so cold

January 24 Saturday

Sent down the fore & mizzen topgallant yards & furled the fore-sail mainsail & fore & mizzen topsails. It has set in to snow & at 12 oclock it was an inch deep all over & every rope like an iron bar

January 25 Sunday

Hove to under a close reefed main topsail. It blows & snows & freezes like everything. At ½ past 7 oclock myself & boy Charley got a couple of heavers & commenced an attack at the braces, to knock the ice off of them so as to be able to wear ship. We did this at ½ past 2 oclock that night & had to take the main brace to the capstan

January 26 Monday

Got under 3 topsails again in the forenoon & furled the fore & mizzen in the aft^n

January 27 Tuesday

Close reefed main topsail all day but not hove to. At 3 oclock passed the whole side of a ships cabin & several peices of painted boards

January 28 Wednesday

Shook the reefs out of all the topsails & made for home as fast as possible

January 29 Thursday

Hove to all night being afraid to venture nearer in

January 30 Friday

Arrived at the Highlands this morning, got a steamer at ½ past 12 & arrived at our wharf (pier 9) at 7 oclock in the evening made the ship fast & went ashore, Where I mean to stay a little while

CHAPTER IX

THE UNLUCKY *TELEGRAPH*

THERE was nothing startling about the *Charmer's* passage. She was 116 days to New York all the way from Whampoa, though only 113 after clearing the Canton River. Her time from Anjer home was 89 days. This was a fairly good performance, spoiled principally by the bad weather of the last three weeks. Next to the Cape Horn run from New York to San Francisco, this course from China to the North Atlantic was the most famous and sporty of all the clipper ship race courses. It might be of interest, therefore, to consider some of the fast sailing accomplished on it. Below is a table comparing the *Charmer's* passage with that of the *Sea Witch* when she established the record from Whampoa to New York. Included also are the fastest times made over some of the sections.

	Charmer	Sea Witch	Section Record	Made by
Whampoa to Anjer	27	10	7:12	*Witch of the Wave*
Anjer to Cape of Good Hope	34	26	25	*Sea Witch* & others
Cape to Equator	22	19 ⎫	35	*N. B. Palmer*
Equator to New York	33	22 ⎭		
Anjer to New York	89	67	62	*Sea Witch*
Whampoa to New York	116	77		

It will be noted that the only first-class piece of sailing that the *Charmer* did on this passage was from the Cape to the equator— 22 days. Her Anjer–New York run was fair; but the Whampoa –New York time was spoiled at the very outset by the long time required to drop down the river from Whampoa, and then to get down the China Sea to Anjer. Although the name of the *Sea Witch* appears three times in the above table, no two of these performances were made on the same passage. Her first three passages home from China were so astounding that this opportunity for mentioning them will not be overlooked. On the first she established the present record of 62 days from Anjer to New

York (pilot). On her second voyage she sailed from Whampoa to New York in 77 days, a record still unbeaten. And on her third successive return from the Far East she set up the Hong Kong–Sandy Hook all-time "fastest" of 76 days. It is extremely doubtful if any successive performances of another sailing vessel can approach this collection.

A long life was still ahead of the *Charmer*, a life in which she carried out her duties consistently well and showed moderately good speed while so doing. Many were the trade routes that saw her—America, England, China, India, the Philippines. When homeward bound from Manila in 1860 she grounded on a reef off Banka Island. However, by throwing overboard some of the hemp in her cargo, she got off safely and finished her voyage in 128 days including all delays. The following year Captain Freeman relieved Captain Lucas temporarily and took the *Charmer* from New York to Key West and back. The return passage was made in 8 days. This is by no means slow; nor was her time of 5 days from Hong Kong to Manila in 1862.

On January 17, 1863, she sailed from Liverpool for Boston and, strangely enough, returned to port two days later. She was sold under the British flag and operated by W. H. Daunt of Liverpool. Captain Lucas severed his connections with the *Charmer* for good and Captain Cole took command. In 1870 we find the *Charmer* under Captain Harrington, the owners being C. Morrison & Co. of Liverpool. In 1875 her home port is Glasgow, J. D. Clinch & Co. the owners, Captain Hogg presiding over her. And the *Charmer* passes on.

It was beginning to look as if Abbey were going to follow his early oath never to look upon the sea again if he once got back home and ashore. A year passed by. And then, after a year and a half on dry land, he shipped in the clipper *Henry Brigham* as ordinary seaman—a step above "boy." She was bound from New York for San Francisco, around that man-killer, Cape Horn. The *Brigham* had not always borne that name. She was christened the *Telegraph* and *she was a bad-luck ship*. A fast extreme clipper, she was launched late in May, 1851, from the yard of J. O. Curtis & Co. of Boston. Her keel was 173′ in length and her deck 178. Her beam was 36′ and the depth of her hold 21½. By old measurement her tonnage was 1,078. It is fitting to note here

THE SHIP *CHARMER* OFF FASTNET LIGHT, IRELAND
From a painting by an English Artist.

THE CLIPPER *GAME COCK* ENTERING SAN FRANCISCO
From a painting by Charles R. Patterson. Courtesy of N.Y., N.H. & H. R.R. Co.

that the actual *weight* of the cargo, in tons, that the *Telegraph* could carry happened to be just about equal to the registered "tonnage" figure. Most ships could carry a weight well in excess of their register. The *Telegraph* was built exceedingly sharp, however. She was laid out by the famous designer, Samuel H. Pook, who had planned the *Surprise* a year earlier, it will be remembered. He included in his design of the *Telegraph*, some of the best points of his *Surprise* and *Game Cock*.

Her first voyage was a round-the-world loop from Boston to New York to San Francisco to Whampoa to London to New York and back to Boston. Then followed a fast and stirring race from the East Coast to San Francisco. The *Telegraph* sailed the same day as the *Game Cock* and a day ahead of the *Meteor*. Both the *Telegraph* and *Game Cock* were delayed badly at the Horn—14 days. When 105 days out, the *Telegraph* was within 600 miles of San Francisco but there encountered more bad luck with the wind. This was on March 1, 1853. Here is an account of the stirring finish as gleaned from the *Telegraph's* log:

Mar. 4—Clipper in Co. on Larboard beam.
Mar. 5—The Two clippers in Co. out of sight astern.
Mar. 7—A clipper ahead—coming up with her.
Mar. 8—Come up with the clipper Game Cock, spoke her 112 days from Boston.
Mar. 9—Tacked ship Game Cock in Co. strong breezes.
Mar. 10—Fresh breezes and passing squalls Layed to under double reefed topsails till four A M Made sail and took pilot at 6 A M. Ship Game Cock in Co. Arrived at San Francisco.

The *Meteor* was the other clipper mentioned, and she too entered the Golden Gate almost together with the *Telegraph;* a grand sight. Thus the *Meteor* won the race with a passage of 113 days as against 114 for the other two.

Soon the bad luck of the *Telegraph* was to begin. She sailed from San Francisco to Valparaiso and started home from there. Not much distance had been covered before she struck some large object floating almost wholly submerged. Such a bad leak resulted that she put back to Valparaiso where she was repaired by divers. The next time that she got away she made a 58-day run to Boston, which is the record; this in spite of the fact that a whirlwind carried away several of her sails on one occasion. It must be admitted, however, that a much better performance was made through these waters by the *Wild Pigeon* which once sailed in 58 days from Callao to New York—a good deal longer distance. This passage of the *Telegraph* that has just been mentioned is a typical example of her propensity for combining disaster with speedy sailing.

On her way back to San Francisco her experiences were surprisingly similar. She consumed 8 days getting through the Straits of Le Maire. Rounding the Horn she lost her bowsprit and attached sails, and sprung most of the yards on the mainmast. So she put into Valparaiso. Sailing from there, the *Telegraph* was at sea only 34 days before she was off Point Reyes, Cal.—northwest of San Francisco and only about 30 miles from port. This time has never been beaten. At this point, however, she encountered baffling winds, and required several days to get in. The *Reindeer* holds the Valparaiso–San Francisco record of 36 days. In spite of all delays, and even including the stop at Valparaiso, the *Telegraph* reached San Francisco in 135 days from Boston. And many clipper ships have taken a great deal longer than that.

After circling the globe again, via Manila, she started for San Francisco once more from Boston. On the third day out she was in collision and lost her main topgallant mast and much other gear. In spite of this mishap she was only 88 days to the equator in the Pacific, and reached San Francisco in 109 days. Good time. On her return she had some *good* luck. She is said to have been the first ship to obtain a cargo *from* San Francisco *to* the East Coast. California had begun to raise grain and produce, besides yielding gold, and also was shipping home again some of the oversupply of goods sent out earlier.

The *Telegraph* next got mixed up in the Crimean War. Archangel had been blockaded but the blockade was raised for a time. Along with eighty other ships, the *Telegraph* got in with a cargo; and she got out again too before being shut in. In 1856 she was sold at Boston for $34,000. She set sail for Australia but began to leak so badly that she put in to Savannah for repairs. When ready to sail again she caught fire and had to be sunk to save her. Some of the crew were suspected of setting the blaze. She was sold where she lay for $6,200 and was raised and repaired. Here she becomes the *Henry Brigham*. The change in name did not change her luck, however. Before she even got to sea again she dragged her anchors and went ashore at the mouth of the Savannah River. After she got off, one quarter of her was sold at auction for $5,150 to satisfy a $5,000 mortgage.

At last both the *Henry Brigham* and Abbey were ready to sail the sea once more. Abbey kept his diary for this voyage in a new ledger, not so picturesque a tome as the first one. The pages are faded blue and lined, and there are no days and dates printed on them this time. So, all that appears in the next chapter was set down by Abbey's own hand—apart from the first little paragraph which was written by his father. With the exception of a very few days, the diary is written in ink from August 24, 1858, onward. The text is inscribed to the right of a marginal line.

When Abbey joins his ship he finds that the *Brigham* has a skysail on the mainmast only, and is now fitted with double topsails throughout. The Captain is Stephen Dow who had recently had the *Skylark*. Mr. Brown is the First Mate and Mr. Jackson the Second. The Third Mate is Maurice McEntee, hailing from Abbey's home town, Rondout, N. Y. On one of the preliminary pages of the following chapter is the watch list; and in the starboard watch appears the name of Ed. Hjortsberg, ordinary seaman, from Brooklyn, N. Y. He is already one of Abbey's chums ashore. Our diarist is now 17 years of age.

CHAPTER X

AROUND THE HORN TO FRISCO

C. A. Abbey

N. York   July 26

1858

To be written in each day and kept carefully for perusal at home. Dont forget. Put down every thing of note with the lat & lon. of each day so that I can trace you afterwards on the map.

H G A

"Aye Aye Sir"

Journal of a voyage to San Francisco in the Clipper Ship *"Henry Brigham"* (alias Telegraph), thence to Honolula in the barque *"Francis Palmer,"* & back again, Thence towards New York in the Ship *"Intrepid"*

kept by your obdt. servant

Chas. A. Abbey

———— ‖ ————

Left New York July 26th 1858

1858

Aug 8 Signalized Ship Parana for Buenos Ayres
Sept 2d Spoke Schooner Blackfish from Rio 7 days
Sept 28th Passed Cape Horn under topgallantsails
Dec 6th Arrived at San Francisco

1859

Jan 7th Left San Francisco
Jan 23d Arrved at Honolula
Feb 17th Left Honolula
Mch 4th Arrived at San Francisco
Mch 25th Left San Francisco for N. Y.

Arrived at New York June 20th 1859

Port Watch			*Starboard Watch*	
Amer	*Martin Stitney*	North Adams	John Dow	Providence
	Bill Stewart	(Belfast)	George Price	(England)
	Amos Connick	(Halifax)	George ——	(England Falmouth)
(boy)	Wm Black	(Glasgow)	Harry Dexter	(Nova Scotia)
(ordinary	C. A. Abbey (Rondout) seaman)		Jim Doyle	(Ireland)
	Peter Noland	Liverpool		(Brooklyn)
	Edward	(Antwerp)	Ed Hjortsberg (ordinary seaman)	
Christian (Hans (My dance) Nelson (")			Wm H. Allee (boy)	New York
	John Smith	(")	Ned —— been at R. (cant say)	
	Chas Lent	(Liverpool)	Johnson Alex	(Down East somewhere)
			Alex. H. Baine	(Edinburgh)

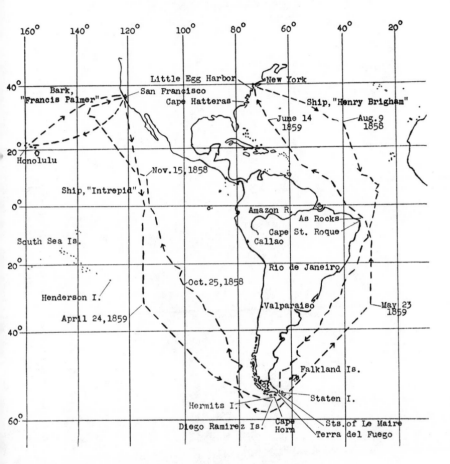

TRACK OF ABBEY'S VOYAGE TO CALIFORNIA AND BACK

"This is supposed to be the Henry Brigham as she often appeared after a blow   3 royals & flying jib"

From a pen-and-ink sketch by Charles A. Abbey

Monday July 26th 1858

9 oclock A. M. Got clear of pier 14 & hauled into the stream where steam tug *"Ceres"* took hold of us & towed us to the lower bay. We then anchored the wind not being very favourable & took leave of our friends of whom there were not a few on board

Tuesday 27th

Up anchor at 4½ A.M. & took our departure from Sandy Hook. 9 A.M. discharged the pilot & 1 stow away & Packed on the royals & topmast stun sails. 12 M. Clear horizon. About 3 oclock began to feel a little sea sick.

Wednesday 28th

Not very sick but sufficiently so to keep in my bunk whenever I liked. The officers are very kind & considerate, ask after a person as if he *"were"* somebody & not a dog.

Thursday 29th

Rather thick headed yet but managed to keep the deck my watches.

Friday 30th

Feel very well but have no appetite as yet though when I do get it it will be a voracious one I think. There is a contrast between this ship & the *"Surprise"* nothing to eat there, plenty here I have not seen a piece of salt junk yet. Saw a man of war but did not speak her

Saturday 31st

Fine weather &c   not much to do

Sunday August 1st 1858

This day began with fair winds & clear sky. It being Sunday of course we did nothing but loaf around & read. All drawing sail set SE by E½E   Lat 34°. 29′ Long 54°. 54′

Monday Augsᵀ 2ᵈ 1858

Fair wind & pleasant weather. Nothing remarkable transpired. Crew employed at ship duty
SE by E½E S. E.

[119]

Tuesday Aug 3d 1858

1 oclock A.M. took in the royals & foretopmast stun sail it being to breezy to hang onto them
S. E.

Wednesday Aug. 4th 1858

Weather as usual fine. Crew employed at ship duty. All drawing sail set. The Captain amused himself by shooting porpoises. Had a general dance & carousal forward in the last dog watch
Full & by about S. E. 6 to 10 knots

Thursday Aug 5th 1858

Had a squall this day in the 1st watch which brought in our mizzen topgallnt sail, fine weather as usual vessel going along easily. Crew variously employed
Full & by about S. E. 4 to 8 knots

Friday Aug 6th 1858

Fine day & pleasant weather Set the main sky sail for the 1st time not much wind quite calm in the last watch Saw a ship but did not make her out distinctly although we hope to sometime today as she is on the same tack as us & about 10 miles to windward. Crew variously employed
Full & by S E by S. 6 average Lat 30. 44 Long 44. 30

Saturday Aug 7th 1858

Dead calm all day long with some slight exceptions. Vessel of yesterday hangs around still
Any & Every Course

Sunday Aug 8th 1858

Spoke our neighbor who proved to be the ship *"Parana"* from New York for "Beunos Ayres". The first part of the day was fine with little or no wind, the latter portion finer with a good breeze. Crew employed in setting up the Main top mast stays & Back stay also the top gallant & royal. Course South or thereabouts
Lat 29° —' N Long 41.° 40' W

Aug 9th

Fine day & pleasant weather. Saw 3 sails, one an English another

[120]

a Dutch barque. The Englishman will no doubt report us. In a sudden squall clewed up the main skysail & 3 royals. I was on the fore royal yard ½ an hour & lamed my arm all because I had no one to help me & couldn't get the buntlines let go on deck. Course S by E with the NE trades which we got last night
Lat 27. 34n. Long 40. —w

Aug 10th

Fine day & pleasant weather. Nothing particular happened. We are now going along at a spanking rate. The mate *"read the riot act"* to the starboard watch, or rather, lectured them extemporaneously for not jumping at once when a word is passed forward. He said, "I never work a man up but if I have anything to settle with him I do it man fashion" further, "because we have treated you well thus far" (& this is indeed the case) "You must not think we dont know how to treat you otherwise". In all that he said he was right for if ever a good ship with good officers & good food & good treatment sailed the ocean this is the one. I cant find cause for complaint at all. Every one is called by his right name & all are treated like men & gentlemen at that
S. by E. course   Lat 21° 50 Long 31° 34' *

Aug 11th *Wednesday*

Fine day & pleasant weather, with the exception of occasional squalls. Crew employed at ship duty. Nothing further to note of consequence
Course S. by E   Lat 19° 07'.   Long
3d mate Laid up stiff with something akin to rheumatism. This has been the case for 3 days

Aug 12

Fine day &c as usual. Been trying to rain but couldnt do it so gave up in disgust   Crew employed at various odd jobs. Saw a *John Bull* Bark this morning   She came quite close to us but we were both going so fast that we only dipped our colors & kept on our courses. Course S by E ½ E
Lat 16° 30'   Long 35°. 40'

* Something wrong here. The longitude would properly be nearer to 40°. Even so, the run of the preceding 24 hours was an exceptionally good one—over 350 miles, apparently.

Aug 13

Of course it is a fine day. How could it be otherwise. The N. E. trades hold on good though they vary in strength Sometimes we go 10 knots then again 3 or 4 & *"vice versa"* As I have before observed this is the best ship that sails the *briny deep.*
Course S by E ½ E   Lat 14°. 42′   Long 35°. —

Aug 14th

Fine day & pleasant weather as usual   Nothing further to note
Course S by E ½ E   Lat 12° — Long 34° —

Aug 15

No variation from the above with the exception of some slight squalls and calms. We are losing the trades. Tacked ship & got the wind from the S. E. Clewed up the topgallant sails & laid course. At midnight Rained very hard
Same course   Lat 11° —   Long 31° —′

Aug 16

Fine day & light breeze   Nothing further

Aug 17

Heavy squalls & any quantity of rain

Aug 18

Horse Lat. weather   —Squalls & rain*

Aug 19   Thursday

Fine day & a spanking breeze but we can not lay course by it.
1 oclock tacked ship   Saw a barque   Course E by S. & W. S. W
Lat 8° —   Long 30° —   Got on the other tack & laid course

Aug 20th

Horse Latitude weather. Head wind. Everybody dissatisfied with the weather. Whales   blackfish   grampuses   &c quite plenty. Saw a barque   In fact we are seeing sails quite frequently   Course ——
Dont know where we are, having no observation today, it has been raining all the while

* The "horse latitudes" are really between the trade winds and the westerly winds of the higher latitudes. (See Aug. 7.) This calm belt near the equator, between the northeast and southeast trades, is called "the doldrums."

Aug 21st

Wind hauled today & we now lay near our course. Crew variously employed. Rained the most of the day

Aug 22d

This is Sunday & I have a little time (as well as all the rest on board) to think. If I was in New York I should go to H. W. Beechers & then down to S. Brooklyn or up town N. Y. & see some of my friends. The last time I was in this part of the world there was nothing I would not have foregone to have done so, but now It is different I am in a good ship have good treatment & plenty to eat & would not return If I could. I allow I should like to see my friends but I would not leave the ship & return now upon any consideration. Wind hauled during the night & we tacked ship. Course W. S. W. Lat at noon 5° 28′ Long 26°.

Aug 23d

Monday. commenced with fine breeze though a head one Ship going along at a spanking rate, that is as fast as she can 10 knots
Course S W by W. Lat 4° 11′ Long 28° —

Aug 24th Tuesday

This day commenced with fine breeze from the Southward. Towards 12 oclock the wind commenced hauling & at 2, 3 & 4, oclock at night we laid S. which is our course. Crew employed at various odd jobs though the best part of them were at work making sennet of which we need a large quantity. About 2 oclock in the aftn I saw two Monstrous Sharks under the lee bow. Flying fish abound in Myriads
Course S. W. by S. Lat 2° 31′ N Long 27° 30′ W.

Augst 25

This day began as the major part of the days have since we left Port fine & continued so throughout Not a cloud to be seen. Crossed the line at 1 oclock & 15 minutes in Long 29° or 30 West. Just as we calculated that we were about on it exactly, The mate raised a racket from the poop deck, & looked about as blank as possible. We couldn't think what was the matter but he soon let us know that a large Sperm whale had come up right under our starboard quarter barely shaving the stern with his tail. This was indeed a narrow escape for if he had happened to have been a moment earlier he would have hurt himself on our keel if he broke nothing even & then look out for squalls. There are accounts of 2 ships being lost in a similar manner & we might just as well make the 3ᵈ as not. It being a bright moonlight night we could not trick any of the green hands.*

Crossed the line at 1¼ oclock in the aftⁿ. Long 29°. 30'.

Course S. W. by S.   Lat at Noon 9' North   Long 29° or 30° W

Aug 26

Thursday today & as a natural consequence, "*Duff*" for dinner. Fine South East trades   ship going at the rate of 8 miles per hour. Watch employed in seizing off & putting caps on the fore rigging

S.S.W. Course   Lat 2° 23 S.   Long 30° 10' E

Aug 27

Fine day & pleasant weather   ship going 7 or 8 knots   Crew variously employed   Course S S W.   Lat 5°. 19' S.   L 31°. 18'.

Saturday Aug 28th

Opened with a fine breeze & beautiful weather   A real old trade wind sea characterizes this part of the ocean which is hard to discribe otherwise than by "A roll" "A pitch" & "A jerk" which at once sets everything taught & then slackens all again threatening all the while to pitch everything overboard   I will here give a slight description of the ship H. Brigham. She is a full Clipper of about 800 to 1000 tons burthen   very sharp & very stiff ("I.E.") doesent lay over to every breeze   She carries nothing higher than a main sky sail   & Is not at all lofty but very square in her rig, (it being about as much as one wants to do to hand the aforesaid sky sail when it blows any ways fresh). The ships company consists of the Captain   3 mates   carpenter   cook steward   16 men & one boy before the mast & 1 boy & 2 ordinary seamen in the house on deck aft, besides one dutchman who works his passage to San Francisco and acts a cabin boy, making in all 28 persons   The captain & mate think we will make the passage in about 120 days but the 2ᵈ mate gives her only 100 as she has performed the operation once in 108   for my own part I think if

* Ordinarily, when the equator is crossed, those who have never crossed before are hazed in some way by those who have.

we get there short of 115 days we will do exceedingly well as we are altogather too deep & any attempt to carry sail on her in a good breeze only forces her to bury herself thus impeding her progress considerably. What we will do in heavy weather Heavens only knows, but my private opinion is that we will stand watch about ½ way up the lower rigging for even in this pleasant weather she frequently lets go everything forward & *"drops herself overboard"* to use a sea phrase. *"Aweel" Aweel"* we shall see what we shall see, "There she goes again, "Bill shut"—*too* late, the house is full of water as she has just shipped a sea right abreast the house door" S.S.W. Course
Lat 7° 44′ Long 32° 12′

Aug 29

Sunday fine day & a ruined sea pie for dinner
Lat 10°. 55′ Long 33° something S S W Course

Monday Aug 30

Begins with N. E. instead of S. E. trades,* ship forging along slowly. Such weather in these latitudes is altogather unaccount-able, but it is so neverthelefs. The 3ᵈ mate (Maurice Mᶜ Entee) whose illness I have before mentioned is much worse the pain hav-ing settled in his left arm, which is as hard as a bone, almost, he cant imagine any more than the rest of us what it is. Paining like Rheumatism it has no other semblance of that disease. He is very despondant & talks of leaving in *"Frisco"* & going home, but I guess he'll weather it. We *"Trade'ed wind for a calm this evening"* which continues till the present.
Course S.S.W. Lat. 13°. 44′ Long 33° —

Aug 31

Wonderful to relate here we are totally becalmed within the limits of the S.E. trades a thing the captain never experienced or heard of before neverthelefs it is so. Crew employed in shortening the upper fore topsail. Saw a large whale make a most beautiful dive about ½ past eleven oclock in the fore noon. The Captain caught 2 Dolphins & I had a chance to observe their changing colors as they were dying which were indeed beautiful How long this "Paddys Hurricane" will last there is no telling but I hope to see

* N. E. winds perhaps, but not properly N. E. *trades* in this part of the world.

the end of it before long. 36 Days out & all hands well with one exception (3ᵈ mate)

All sorts of courses. Lat. about the same as yesterday   Long ditto

Sᴇᴘᴛ 1ˢᵗ

Becalmed as yet & no prospect of a breeze. Crew variously employed   Lat 14°. 39′   Long 34° 15′

Sᴇᴘᴛ 2ᵈ

Breezed up slightly in the forenoon. At 10½ o clock spoke the schooner Blackfish from Rio for Philadelphia 7 days out. Promised to Report us. Saw a brig. At 8 oclock in the evening there was quite a breeze & at one oclock just after I turned in we shipped a sea which swept us clean as a whistle fore & aft

Course S.S.W.   Lat 15° 20′   Long 34°. 44′   37 days out

Friday   Sᴇᴘᴛ 3ᵈ 1858

Ship kicking around like fun under 3 topgallant sails   I felt quite bad all day from some unknown cause   One of the Dolphins who were around the ship the other day hung around our bows & could not be persuaded to *come in out of the wet*. The Captain came forward in the dog watch carrying a light grainse of his own which drove up to the hilt in him. It is needless to say that he left incontinetly.

Course S by W.   Lat about 17°   Long 35.   40

Sᴇᴘᴛ 4

Still bowling along 9 or 10 knots with the topgllnt sails on her. Sky very lowering, frequent squalls   Crew variously employed

Course S.S.W.   Lat 21° something   Long 36° 38′

5ᵗʰ

Sunday & a fine day   ship still under topgallant sails though with a smoother sea   nothing to do as a matter of course. Kept breezing up all day & when I turned in at 4 o clock at night she had all she could stagger under. Course S.S.W.   Lat 23° 30′   Long 38. 39

6ᵗʰ

This morning when our watch came on deck we reefed the main topsail & main sail & furled the fore & mizzen upper topsails. This

is indeed as all expected a very wet boat for It is a sure ducking to venture forward of the fore rigging as she is continually scooping it up forward & the water is knee deep in the scuppers all the while
Lat 26. 05   Long 40°. —'

7th

The gale having finally lulled we are under royals & topmast stunsails once more with a light breeze. The weather has grown quite cold within the last few days & woolen trowsers & blue shirts are in demand. The Captain caught a Cape Pidgeon at noon. Our wake is flocked with them & Gulls.
Lat 27°. 30'   Long 41°. 00'.

Wednesday SEPT 8th 1858

Noticed that the sun was eclipsed yesterday by the moon. Fine day & pleasant weather   breeze continues to freshen & to haul & at 6 oclock we have square yards. At the time of writing the Captain is over the bows making furious attempts to harpoon a porpoise of which there is a school under the forefoot
Lat 29°. 17'. Long. 41°. 44'. Course S.S.W. by ¼ west

9th

Duff day & as a matter of course a fine one   Saw our first Albatross which measured about 12 ft. from tip to tip; he was last seen sitting on the water about a mile to leeward & when compared with the Cape Pidgeons which hovered above him looked monstrous   in fact I began to think that the story of Sinbad the Sailor might be true & one of these monstrous birds the Roc therein mentioned, but these are only my surmises. The Southern Cross & Magellan Clouds have been in view for 8 or 9 days. I stood the mates watch last night as he was laid up with a head ache & could not bear the force of the wind in his face. He laid down on the Carpenters bench & exclaimed when I came to him, *"My G-d Charley, I wish the "*OLD MAN*" (I.E. the Captain) would come out of the cabin & run his head against me"*. It seems that the Captain wished him to oversee the Caulking & Pitching of the top of the house, & when so engaged he got some of the smoke up one of his nostrils & gave him such an awful head ache that he fairly groaned with the pain. He is as good a man as ever lived & there is not one in the ship but that would do any thing for him. The 2^d

[127]

mate will leave in "*Frisco*" if indeed he is'nt kicked into the forecastle before we get there a thing by no means improbable
Lat 30° 49′ Long 43°. 42′ Course S.S.W.

Friday Sept 10th 1858

Commenced with fine breeze & pleasant weather 9 A.M. wind
began to haul, at 1 P. M. tacked ship & laid W. S. W. kept
breezing up & at 6 P. M. had the ship under fore & main topsails
(upper mizzen furled) & reefed spanker. A heavy head sea makes
her pitch terribly. Sometimes her bows will go up 30 feet & then
the stern follows suit I had the first lookout on the poop & could
scarcely keep my legs. The Old Man being rather Corpulent it is
laughable to see him Cutting Pirouettes & Pidgeons Wings over
which he has no control As the weather is quite cool he appears
on deck with a heavy watch coat & a red skull cap on, looking
more like some old Pirate than a Good Old man he is. Full & by
Lat 33°. 43′ Long 45°. 21′.

11th

While sheeting home the fore topgallant sail at ½ past 5 in the
morning the Lee sheet parted & the whip block came down &
struck the man behind me (Bill Stewart) & cracked his skull, it
then struck me & laid me out on "*the broad of my back*". Stewart
has had his head broke before by a fall in the Liverpool dock at
Liverpool & has a silver plate in his skull the old crack is now
open which makes it doubly worse. As for myself the shell of the
block (with which I was struck) was smooth & therefore did not
hurt me *very* much, but I had one roll over from it, Crew employed capping the lower rigging & caulking the top of the house,
an improvement much needed as my bunk has been full of water
once or twice from the leaks
Lat 34°. 41′ Long 47°. 19′
Mem. M^c has just been in here with a whole lot of Ambrotypes of
Rondouters. How little they imagine where we are & what we are
doing. I wonder what they are doing & where they are. Joe Von
Becks wedding has been the topic under consideration all day.

Sunday Sept 12th 1858

Oh how we do go, "& roll!" every movable thing has fetched
away. We frequently take water over either rail. There is a sail
ahead & fast going out of sight so that it must be a Clipper for

we are going 12 knots per hour. Sea Pie for the second time today
& a good one it was too. The "*whack*" which I stowed away would
astonish all Land Lubbers & indeed it astonished me. In the night
the wind freshened & being dead aft we rolled terribly fetching
away all sorts of things & showing us where more lashings were
needed. The decks are a foot deep with water as she takes it in at
the gangways & Hawse bights continually.
Lat   Dead Reckoning 36°. odd   Long. ditto. 49°. 00′

13th

Fine day &c   Stiff breeze   weather kind of rugged   got the sun at
noon & found our Lat to be 39° 30′ we having made the most
glorious run in the last 24 hrs*
Lat 39°. 30′   Long 50° —

14th

Rugged heavy weather   blowing quite stiff
Lat 42° 16′   Long   cant° say′.
The gale increased with the day & at 12^m (night) we were under
close reefs. While on the fore yard tricing up the stun sail boom
I remarked the beauty of the ships model which in connection
with the silver like appearance of the waves (which when combing
threw a glare upon the ship equal to the light of a lantern) &
the darknefs which frequently prevailed   made a spectacle un-
equaled in savage grandeur   As I gazed at the well formed hull &
the tapering spars now shorn of almost all their canvass, &
watched the awful struggles between the "Brigham" & the waves,
I almost believed her alive so finely did she ride over some huge
sea whose only errand appeared to be our destruction, seemingly
defying their fury, & trying to get free & bound away from the
iron grasp with which we held her in check. Just as I concluded
my meditations & began to think I was pretty cold there came a
wave which sent our foreyard into the water & I had my fears
that all on it would go to & they surely would had we seen many
such

Wednesday Sept 15th 1858

Got under 3 top gallnt sails again but took them in at 1½ oclock
at night & continued to take in canvass (calling the watch at 6

---

* Something wrong here. No observations had been possible the preceding noon.
Moreover, even if the entire run of the previous 48 hours had been made in the
last 24, the day's run would not have been extraordinary.

bells) until we were close reefed again, it blowing harder than at any time since we sailed. Mem. I wont say that it was cold, but, the main top galln^t sail was frozen stiff for the first time. Whoop blow your fingers, lee rail under water part of the time during the night. The ship behaves gloriously & proves herself a splendid craft   Lat 44° 03′   Long 57° 44′. Cape Flyaway 5 points on the weather bow at daylight, first made by Martin Stitney of North Adams, Mass.* Wind having hauled   laid full & by   S by E & S by E ½ E. Sent down the royal yards

16th

Lat 46°, 03′.   Long 58°, 07′.   Full & by,   about south.
Still blowing but not so hard as last night. Amused myself during the day picking oakum & in the dog watch by fishing for Cape Pigeons of which I caught one & after letting him get good & sea sick sat him on the rail to see him fly off   an operation which he performed, only, after several ineffectual trys. It is noted that no sea bird can rise from a flat surface such as the decks of a vessel though they manage to from the water easily. The Cape Pigeon is about the size of a very large domestic one & is white on the breast & under parts of the wings & black & white on the back & tops of the wings   I might go on & enumerate the different kinds of birds in our wake but as it is getting late I must conclude by saying that the Pigeons   Mowhawks   Moly mokes   *"Stinkers"*   & Whale birds form the majority with an occasional *"Albatrofs"* soaring about within from 1 to 10 miles of the ship. Biting cold all day & worse at night but as I am by no means short of clothes it mattered not to me, & so I cut Pigeon Wings on the *poop* all my lookout, & had a long yarn with the mate to boot. We were the same as hove to as we dont wish to make any more southing without the accompanying westing, if it can be helped.

Friday Sept 17th 1858

Quite fine to begin with but confounded cold & raw to end with wind hauled during the aft^n & we laid course with a spanking gale & 3 top galln^t sails set   Quite squally during the night. took in the miz topgalln^t s'l & flying jib   At the oakum again
Lat. 46° 42′   Long 57° something′ (So Bill at my elbow says

---

* This is horseplay at the expense of Stitney. It means that he mistook a cloud for land. Incidentally, "5 points on the bow" should be designated as "3 points forward of the beam."

18th

Unpleasant as the generality of days about here are. Although the major part of the day found under 3 top gll^{nt} sails the night found taking them in. We tacked ship twice & managed to get up to our course after persevering in a very praiseworthy manner all day. Very cold & damp. I here take occasion to remark that I find India Rubber boots are a *"big thing"* (to use a shipmates expression of any thing good & of importance). Wind all around the compass Lat 47° 58′ Long 60°. 2′.

All that I now have to observe is, that there is nothing further to observe at present. So I will conclude for the day

19th

Sunday & a very fine one at that. Crew in a fine state of idleneſs & good humor for we have a fair wind & are bounding along towards the Straits of *"Le Maire"* which with the present breeze we may reach in two days more, but we build no castles & therefore will not be disappointed should we have a South Wester & be at bay 20 days or more Steering S by W. ½ W
Lat 50° —′ Long 62° —′

20th

One of my shipmates has watered the ink until it is too pale for use so I use a Lead Pencil today. Very fine day with a light fair breeze rather cool though. Employed ripping up a topgll^{nt} sl
Lat 50°. 40′ Long, 65° —′

21st

Wind increased during the night insomuch that we took in the topgll^{nt} sls upper Topsails furled the foresail & mainsail & hove her to. *"Land Ho"* Terradelfuego & Staten Land on the Lee bow wind keeps hauling & we must lay over tonight & make our run tomorrow if possible* Look on the map for our bearings &c

Wednesday Sept 22d 1858.

Oh dear me, well if I wont give it up here we are off Cape Horn in the Equanoctial gales season & the weather is comparatively fine, though we had hail & snow enough last night Of course I dont wish for worse weather, on the contrary am thankful for that which we have had (smallest favors gratefully received

* Through the Straits of Le Maire, between Terra del Fuego and Staten Land.

larger ones &c) but as for Cape Horn being terrible at this season its all folderol (so say the old *"Shells"* forward) I suppose if old Nep should get hold of this page I should be happy to cry for quarter in short order, but in my chest & locked up there is not much danger of such a casuality By the way He has not favored us with a call as yet but If hearing is correct the green ones may look out for themselves on the line in the Pacific. I have no apprehensions on my own a/c having crossed the imaginary band 5 times already.* The weather is quite squally at times but not all the while & they seldom amt to much, though the weather wise say that if we had been off Hermits Island (the pitch of the Cape)† on the night of the 21st we would have had many a frozen finger but being well under the lee of the land we escaped with a cap full of wind & a sprinkling of hail. It was bad enough any way but not a patch for a patch of what I saw off the coast in the Charmer. Wind all around the compass course to correspond, ship heading for the most part of the day between NE & SE I dont know as we are any where on the chart today for what with the NE current & the head wind we have made no southing Mc says that its going to snow again, he having just taken an observation through a square hole in the side of the house denominated for appearance's sake a window, good morning

Thursday Sept 23d 1858

Sometimes clear sometimes cloudy. Tacked ship at 7 bells in the morning watch ditto at 2 in the forenoon. Course from 9 AM to 12 M, E S E, 5 knots Several snow squalls during the day & also hail. Very uncomfortable indeed it is to turn in at 8 bells (12 oclock at night for instance) & get well tucked up & warm & then be woke by a pinch in the side & informed very graciously that it is 4 oclock & your company is desired on deck. You all the while imagine that you haven't been asleep at all at least not 5 minutes. But there is nothing for it but to turn out & warm yourself in a snow squall (mayhap) as there are no fires to go to. Capt Dow is a man of about 40 or 50 years of age (to judge from appearances) & is my very beau ideal of a Sea Captain. In warm weather he may be seen lounging about under the quarter awning open shirt collar, loose baggy trowsers broad brimed sombrero

* During the hazing of those first crossing the equator, a sailor impersonating Neptune acts as master of ceremonies.

† Not so far south as Horn I. which is at the extremity.

on his head, & his only companion an immense Grass cloth hdkf. which he constantly uses, & as he moves about like a Polar bear on the line, every once in a while saying *"Whew aint it hot"* he would provoke a smile from any one. But now in cold & freezing latitudes he is apparreled in, first, a pair of very heavy cloth pants, an immense though fine fitting pilot cloth overcoat, reaching down to the calfs of his legs, a large pair of high topped sea boots, (french by the way) a round red cap which he obtained up the Persian gulf, & all the beard & mustaches he has been able to raise since he left New York, & as he moves about the poop with his spy glass under his arm ever & anon taking a view of the coast of Staten land & Terra del Fuego he is as I before observed my Beau Ideal of a Sea Captain

Friday SEPT 24th 1858

Continues fine sometimes cloudy, wind Light & baffling during the day, quite steady during the night, with one heavy snow squall which we appropriated for rain water (process a la squilgee) Last night while going along quite easily we caught our nose in a *"tide rip"* a circumstance which threw our head yards all aback but by cool management we coaxed her back though not untill many "a long pull a strong pull & a pull altogather" had been had at the weather braces. During a heavy snow squall this morning the first mate, Chas. A. Abbey & *"severial"* other well intentioned *"Sailieurs"* amused themselves by snow balling, washing the face of, & otherwise maltreating an exceedingly lubberly, fat, Dutchman (who never knew what good living was until he came on board here) & therefore fills himself at every opportunity (capacity about a ton & ½) & is the butt of the ships company. He being a lazy impudent Dutch hog & having succeeded in crowding himself into the pantry as a help to the steward, he soon waxed fat & saucy. I have the exclusive privilege of wakeing him up at 5 oclock every morning & here is my modus operandi. 1st get good hold of the cover he may have over him. 2^d make sure of one leg. 3^d jerk the cover slap off & immediately sieze the other leg & land him out on deck. If he is not thoroughly awake by this time a few kicks & yells properly administered finish the businefs. This is the ships part of the operation & if he growls at that, why then I proceed to wallop him on my own a/c when he immediately collapses

Lat 55°. 42′ Long 60° — Course S. E. or full & by

[133]

Saw a bark with loss of fore top gall^nt & main top masts,   Showed
Hamburg colors

Saturday Sept 25th 1858

Had the forenoon watch below & amused myself by beating
McEntee 3 straight games of *Euchre*. Tacked ship 6 bells in the
mn'g watch & laid W by N ½ N. Saw our friend again he having
dropped astern during the night & consequently, as we had
tacked,   we rose him in the same place as yesterday. He immediately tacked & is now dropping astern as fast as the law
allows him to. The day is damp &c   Wm H. Allee, Edward T.
Hjortsberg, & Chas A. Abbey were among the jolly sons of Nep,
who got routed out from their splendid banqueting halls to put
the ship about, (or as the Dutch cabin boy expressed it   to "*ship
the bow*") at 2 bells in the 1st dog watch   Beautiful night (I. E.
for Cape Horn) & a fair wind to match. The Chief Mate & myself
indulged in a yarn 4 hours long in the mid watch. Subject   Life
on the North Western frontier of America   The aforesaid individual having spent 3 years previous to this voyage on the said
frontier   I gained a great deal of intelligence from him as regards
the habits & customs of the Hunters & Lumbermen of that section, & also enjoyed a good many hearty laughs at his quaint &
funny anecdotes (of which he has an inexhaustible fund,) especially one of a fourth of July that got out there by accident & in
which he took a very prominent part. Mr Brown is a perfect brick.
If you knew what an amount of meaning was contained in that
simple word (brick) you wouldnt wonder that I put it in for
short   I did know our lat & Long but they have slipped my
memory & as it is time to turn in I wont go to the mate for them,
neither will I work the time today for I am already able to do the
days work   & therefore If I do miss today I shant forget by
tomorrow.

Sunday Sept 26 1858

Lat 56 32 S.   Long 62. 10 W
Uncomfortable as usual, quite cloudy,   wind hauled so that we
laid up to our course (W. by S.)   Clewed up the miz top gall^nt
sail about noon it being quite breezy & the ship staggering considerable. Set it again about 1 oclock. Clewed up the fore & miz
at 6 not being able to carry them any longer. Ship spitting fu-

[134]

riously at any one who dared to venture forward of the main rigging   I am the only one left out of the 28 that has not been wet

27th

Blowy snowy day   Lat 57°. 54′   Long 65°. 31′

28th

Tuesday   Just like all the rest. Wind hauled & we laid S by E some of the time so we put about & laid W. N. W. Lat. 58° 10 Long 66°. 55′
rounded Cape   Noon   65 days out.

29th

Wednesday   Medium fine day with frequent snow squalls   not so cold as usual   wind hauled around & died away during the night, then sprang up again in the morning though not very fresh
Lat 58° 07,′   Long 69°, 30′

30th

Breeze increased till at last we were going 10½ knots a gait which we held all day & the most of the night. Frequent snow squalls *"midout de vind."* The old man felt so good to see her going that he asked the 1st & 3d mates down in his room & gave them each a *"dthrop av suthin"* & told them that if the wind stood thus   24 hours we might laugh at Cape Horn until we came again. Long at noon 71° 25′, Lat 57°. 35′   Long at 12 o clock at night 76° 12′ Hi, Johnny aint it cold

Oct 1st

Breeze continued until 5 oclock this morning when the last puff died away with a receding snow squall & at the time of writing we have a new edition over the quarter   & the starboard watch (with the exception of boy Ned who is laid up with a cold & now sits forninst me shaving himself with some water I got for him from the cook) are squaring the main yard. Lat 57°. 02′   Long 77°. 16′

Saturday Oct. 2d 1858

Lat 55°. 02′   Long 80°. 47′
Sent up the royal yards & bent the cross jack,   during the forenoon & at the time of writing the starboard watch are getting the topgallant stun sail booms aloft preparatory to setting the sails.

Squared the yards at 12 oclock & kept her W by N. which with
2¼ points variation of compass makes a N W ¾ W course for
us. We are having the greatest imaginable luck having had fine
weather ever since leaving port & not having had a topsail clewed
up once, Cape Horn & all the rest put together. If we run our long
up down here where the degrees are short it is one half the aforesaid long saved*

Sunday OCT 3ᵈ 1858   Lat   no obs, Long ditto

Last night in the 1ˢᵗ watch the wind began to veer & veer until at
last it had *veered* so much that we were sharp up on the starboard
tack heading W. N. W.   At 4 bells the sails all flew aback & the
ship broke off 3 points *"ker whack"* but immediately began coming up again   the wind freshening every moment   5 bells   took
in the royals & I went up with Stewart at the fore   every thing
was hung on to then till about 1 bell in the next watch (starboard)
when in came the topgallⁿᵗ sls. When we came on deck again at 4
oclock the starboard watch were standing by the topsail halyards
& one of them by the forecastle door ready to call us before our
time if necessary   At 2 bells our side hauled the mainsail up snug
3   reefed the spanker & furled the upper miz topsail   3½   let go
the fore & main topsail halyards, & furled the fore topsail,   4
furled the main sail & main topsail & set the main spencer. Then
being nearly done got our coffee & proceeded to drink it   6 bells
furled the spanker & called the watch to reef & furl the foresail
8½ oclock (time of writing) ship hove to under 3 club topsails
foretopmast stay sail & main spencer & shipping any quantity of
water. Remainder of the day hove to under a close reefed main
topsail, wind blowing harder than at any time yet

Monday OCT 4ᵗʰ 1858   No Observation of any kind

Still blowing but not so hard. First part of the day under 3 close
reefs, Later 3 whole topsails   fore sail   main sail & sometimes 3
top gallⁿᵗ sails, very squally. Oh Christmas wouldnt we Catch it
if we were off the Horn now   But we aint there so whats the use
of talking so   Ship heading after wearing N. & N by W.

* Of course there is no point to this at all. A ship will try to sail as straight as
possible to its destination (unless better winds may be expected from doing
otherwise). If the *Brigham* here was purposely heading off to the left of San
Francisco, she was undoubtedly taking advantage of an easterly wind to get clear
of the coast in a region where westerly winds prevail.

Tuesday. Hazy windy rainy day, got no observation & as a matter of course have only a remote idea as to our whereabouts. Under the main topgll^{nt} sail the better part of the day & night

Wednesday. Blowing great guns ship hove to under a close reefed main topsail. When our side came on deck we loosed the fore topsail & sported gaily for ½ an hour when we came to the conclusion that we might better keep it than give it to Old Nep (a thing which we surely would have done had it been set during the squall which passed as we were on the yard furling it) so we quietly rolled it up & said nothing about setting it again. Nothing to do Nothing to say & as a natural consequence nothing to note, especially as it is cold & disagreeable in the house, the floor being wet & water running over it at every roll. Sunday the 3^d as I have previously omitted saying we were put upon an allowance of 3 qts & 1 pt of water per day but that is an old story & as a consequence of "*non importe*". Got the sun by flashes Lat by obs at noon 51° 27′ South Long, on the mates log book I suppose though I am not certain as to it. The 2^d Greaser has been laid up for 2 days & Mr Mc Entee has had to stand his watch notwithstanding his lame arm which continues about the same though rather better than formerly

Thursday Wind moderated considerable, got under three topsails fore sail & main sail Nothing further to note
Lat 51°. 24′ Long 81° 20′

Friday Oct. 8th 1858 Lat 48.12 Long 78.13
Ship still under 3 topsails fore & main sail weather quite squally at times, when she has all she can do to stagger along with her lee rail out of water. Barometer on the rise, which explains the press of sail, carried by the old mans orders. It is quite evident to all beholders that the Brigham is too deep, as she frequently settles her haunches into it with a smash that threatens destruction to herself & crew. Notwithstanding all this she has behaved gallantly during the recent gales which we have had & may be classed A No 1 as a seaboat & a strong one too for she does not leak worth mentioning whereas many a newer ship would have had her crew

at the pumps the most of the time under the same circumstances (for instance the Charmer My last ship)

9th Lat 48.40. Long

Saturday. Began with stiff squally breezes from the W. N. W. & thereabouts. Took in the Upper topsails fore & main sail about 3 o'clock at night, & had a regular snorter of a gale wore ship during the day sometime but at what hour I forget How long this head wind will last "*God only knows*"

10th

Sunday being a better day we consequently had better weather than during the week previous Got the main topgall^{nt} sail on her for the first time in a good while. Even Mr Brown the 1st mate does not recollect the lat & long for this day. He is standing by me now examining our library, which is in an awful condition, the librarian having been too busy on deck to give it the attention it demands. Dinner. Bill of fare Roast Pig (almost raw) & Soft Tack (bread) burnt & heavy Sailors life very gay. Got a fair wind at last

11th

Monday fair wind all gone to smash same old gale as formerly. Well blow away as long as you like & split yourself "*Sorra a one o'me cares*" if you blow a month. Lat 46°. 31′ Long 83°31′ Tacked ship at 8 bells in the evening

Tuesday OCT. 12th 1858 Lat   Long

Began with stiff breeze & squally, 5 o'clock in the morning took in the topgall^{nt} sails. During the forenoon watch sent down the main topgall^{nt} halyards & rigged them to set up in the top with two double blocks a new plan of the "*old mans.*" At 12 o'clock tacked ship Subscriber let go the cross jack sheet by the run which caused the Capt to request him never to do the like again, but as bad luck would have the same thing happened accidentally at the main whereupon the aforesaid Capt proceeded to give me a catalogue of the sheets to *let fly*, & the sheets to *ease away*, very much to the edification of the men & exceedingly more so to my chagrin But mark the sequel. While everything was shaking & aback I espied a gasket with a round turn on the Cross Jack brace & immediately rushed to clear it as it might easily have carried away the yard. just as I arrived on the yard (unperceived by the old man) he yelled "*Main topsail haul*" & away went the lee braces around swung the yards (& as the Cross Jack yard infallibly goes foul) back they swang again then around then back &c & so on, all of which sudden movements & the jerks attendant thereon placed the undersigned in a werry unenviable posetion, which the Capt just then perceived for the first time, & immediately roared out *Hang on like grim death there Charley* (but he might have saved himself the trouble for I couldnt have hung on better had I been lashed) & then Haul Away those Cross Jack Braces, quick, your play now, but by the time the yard was steady I was on deck. It is needless to say that my promptitude in saving the yard lost me no caste in the *Old Mans* favor. Set the topgall^{nt} sails in the aft^n & took the miz in towards night. I have been patiently waiting for a fine streak of weather in order that I may praise the Pacific Ocean but alas I can wait no longer & all I can say about it will be much to its detriment. Here are we 10 or 15 days around the Horn & in what ought to be fine weather whereas we have had nothing but gales & head winds, rains & hails & snows all of which lead me to think that the far famed "*Pacific*" Ocean is no "*Pacificer*" than any other however I may alter my mind some of these days if I do you will see it noted as a matter of course

C A Abbey

‖

Wednesday O$_{CT}$ 13th 1858 Lat 43°. 31′ Long 83°. 31′
Hazy foggy rainy weather ship under 3 top gall^{nt} sails. Crew employed during the morning watch by washing down an operation which has not been performed in some time in consequence of bad weather. 8 bells in the morning when I went below the starboard watch were at work at some Punch Mats & other little odds & ends about decks. Third greaser made himself very obnoxious this morning by putting on Airs & I proceeded to give him a piece of my mind at which he immediately became mum.* Forenoon very damp & uncomfortable. Aftn bright & clear wind hauled & we now lay course (N W by W) 1 or 2 points free. At 7 bells in the evening espied a Comet about 30 deg. above the horizon the tail of which appeared to be about 10 ft long & curved slightly. If

* A little joshing of the Third Mate who was a chum of Abbey's.

comets travel head first (and I think they should) this one was steering E. S. E.   his tail pointing W. N. W. The head was very bright & the tail quite distinct even unto the end where it broke suddenly off.* This makes 3 I have seen during my lifetime. Our Course is N W by W. 2 points variation   N W by N good & the comet bore West I should judge although I did not look at the compass   When I held the reel a few minutes ago she (the ship) was going 11½ knots good & true. Very heavy ground swell on. Every day I see some strange bird or a new species of Albatross there are 3 different kinds about now   the white   the black & white   & the Iron Rust with white beak   these latter are commonly referred to as old *"Barnacle Backs"*   there is one huge fellow astern at present that must measure 20 feet from tip to tip & the average is 10 to 12 ft. They are proof to all temptation in the way of bait & hooks & only approach the ship (that is   near by) at night fall, & then they come down with a swoop as though about to light but suddenly swerving from their course look at us with their heads aside & their very eyes say as plain as print, "Too old a bird to be caught with chaff"

Thursday OcT 14th 1858   Lat 40°. 47′   Long 84°. 38′

Began with fine breeze though squally occasionally & cloudy also. Had the royals set about an hour but could not carry them. Rate of speed sometimes 12 occasionally 13 & all the while 10. Rove the topmast stunsail gear at 4 oclock A. M. Set the starboard fore topmast stunsail at 8 bells   weather very fine the finest day in fact since we left 50° on the other side,   ship going 9 knots on the average with the wind 6 or 8 points free on the port tack. We must have made a glorious run last night for we averaged 11 knots   Weather during the afternoon fine though varied by occasional squalls now & then. A beautiful night & so warm that one could sit down or stand still on deck with comfort. Under fore & main royal at 12 O. clock M. Continued my letter home today

---

* This was no less than The Great Comet of 1858, perhaps the most brilliant and spectacular comet of a century or more. It was first discovered by Donati in Florence on June 2, 1858, and is sometimes called Donati's Comet. It became visible to the naked eye early in September and was nearest the earth on October 10. Its passage across the heavens was marked by a great number of rapid and radical changes in its tail, providing a notable show to all beholders. On October 3 the tail extended across the sky for a distance of 36°. Estimates vary as to the period required for it to make a complete circuit of its orbit. The average of these estimates, however, is close to 2,000 years. It is quite likely that the brilliant comet recorded by Chinese astronomers in 146 B.C. was this same celestial body.

Friday Oct 15th
Lat 38°. 21′ Long 87°. 30′   Course NW by W ½ W

Beautiful day. The temperature of the atmosphere has moderated greatly within the last two days. Got the two main topmast stunsail booms out of their snug berth on the port side of the deck & sent them aloft. The friends & acquaintances who escorted us to the Hook when we made our *"debut"* at sea would scarcely recognize the dirty, becoalcasked, bewatercasked, beboomed, besparesparred, belumbered decks they then saw, in the clear open ball room to be seen here now, for they are almost cleared up Weather continued fine throughout the day The *"greaser"* being detested by all hands trys to make himself as disagreeable as possible & so squared the yards today when the wind was abeam. Which was no sooner done than the Capt took matters in hand & braced up again, blowing the aforesaid *"Greaser"* at the same time, & applying all the epithets in the English language, denoting uselessness, carelessness, meanness, &c. Then the Greaser to be revenged began hazing his watch & even went so far as to accuse one man of informing the Capt that he had squared the yards, & thereby drawing his wrath down upon him. Oh pshaw I cant bear to go into particulars, let it suffice to say that the Greaser & his watch had a blow out which came near being a fight

Saturday Oct 16th 1858   Lat 36°. 21′   Long 90° —

Breeze quite stiff during the morning but commenced to abate & haul in the forenoon. Watch employed setting main topmast stunsail & topgalln^t do, overhauling the contents of the house on deck, the larzerette, &c, & bending an old main topsail & jib it being no longer necessary to carry the storm sails in use off the Horn. 12 o'clock M. dead calm. Quite warm out. Sea as smooth as a mil-pond, scarcely any movement at all to the vessel. This state of things continued until 4 bells in the 1st watch when there sprang up a light catspaw & we immediately ran away with Port braces only to run back with them in the course of a few minutes. Matters continued much in this shape until I turned in   W.N.W.

Sunday Oct. 17th 1858   Lat   Long

No wind & as a natural consequence a dead calm frequent drizzly rain squalls, from which we caught all the water we possibly could. Saw a sail in the aftn & made several attempts to strike some porpoises but only succeeded in bending our irons & killing one fish which we did not get. Hum back whale playing about the keel. Put a bullet in his hide, when he left   W N W

Monday   Oct 18th 1858   Lat.   Long

Amused myself (very "*poorly*" amused was I, though) by sitting & swinging under the Cross Jack Yard & varnishing the miz topsail sheets. 12 o'clock M. rose a sail which proved to be a sloop of war before the wind on the port tack but not being near enough could not signalize or read her colors. In all probability she was of the stars & stripe species. The weather is so fine that the Cape Pigeons (who are undoubtedly disgusted with our choice of climate) are leaving us, & returning to the Horn & cold weather The little scoundrels are never happier than when in a blow or amid the snow & hail. Notwithstanding the heat a few greedy fellows & one solitary old Albatross remain with us still. I suppose I ought to go to the Old Man about my Navigation but I dont feel very well this aft^n owing to the smell of the varnish which I have been using & an empty stomach (today is "*banyan*" day) so I will mend my trowsers (which I ripped by franticly endeavouring to step farther than I could) & turn in, giving as an excuse for so doing "my 8 hours out tonight & I wont get but 4 hours sleep till tomorrow night   W N W

Tuesday   Oct 19th 1858   Lat 35°. 05′.   Long 93°. 13′.

Commenced with baffling squalls of wind & rain. Improved our opportunities for catching water. 8 oclock dead calm. 8½ Capt had an Albatross on board which measured 9 ft 10 in from tip to tip   9 oclock caught another not quite so large (I appropriated this one & have his beak one wing & one leg all of which I shall endeavour to take home.) and still another smaller one at 10   I forgot to mention that I caught a Pigeon at 7 oclock & after keeping him all day & finding him a real good tempered little fellow putting up with all the inconveniences appertaining to one of his class from life on Ship Board, (& there was considerable for one who   like him   has always been used to living in a parlor 10,000 miles in diameter) I let him fly once more for I could not kill him under those circumstances. Boy Bill will no doubt be enraged, for he wanted to kill him & keep his beak & wings, but he'll have to travel farther on the water than he imagines before he will find him. School of porpoises ran across the bow but of course we did not succeed in striking any for we never do   no matter how good an opportunity offers. Light breeze from just the quarter we wish to go towards. Ship heading West. Employed in clearing out the topgallant forecastle preparatory to hauling up chain for the anchors. I tell you, I begin to think, "30 days or so more & then", well never mind whats the use. I want my supper, I wonder if it aint most 2 bells, I think Ill play the "banjo" until I hear it strike, so "*Adios*" Supper over the 3ᵈ mate & the boys held their Pow Pow in the boys Reception room. The "*comet*" is still in sight & going East I think, Bill says West, you decide for us, When first seen about 15 deg. above the horizon the tail pointing East by N or so. Now it is about 35 deg up, tail same way, and very near Venus which star it was beneath previously. We go North, & it is on our left hand & rising over us gradually   W.

Wednesday Ocт 20ᵗʰ 1858   *At Noon*   Lat 34°. 38′ Long 94°. 05
Began fine, but during the morning watch fell calm & began to rain in squalls. Forenoon watch, we tacked ship several times. Weather very fine the hottest day yet. I had a lofty job today & scraped the fore topmast. Crew variously employed. Wind continued light & good for nothing (ahead to boot,) until, well all day you may say.

Thursday Ocт 21ˢᵗ 1858 Lat 31°. 59′ Long 95° or so
Wind ahead until 3 oclock A.M. (I commence my days at Midnight) when it shifted 8 points in a less number of minutes & like to have taken the topgallⁿᵗ masts out of her. Clewed up the royals & found the ship on her course the wind freshning every minute. 8 bells (8 o'clock morning) ship under 3 royals foretopmast stunsail & Lower stunsail going 12 knots with the wind over the quarter "Rip," "*Scat*, "you *Witch*" "go it" "*get mad "old girl*" & such like expressions fall continually upon my ears. This will get us to the trade lats if it holds a couple of days & then, hurrah for "*Frisco*" & the news from home. Breeze gradually, very gradually, failing. 12 Oclock, M. very little wind. Quite a warm night

Friday Ocт 22ᵈ 1858 Lat 29°. 53′ Long 95.° 50 about
Beautiful day with light breeze. Engaged with Ed. turning in the fore royal backstays & setting them up One of the men in the starboard watch (Henry) refused to obey the 2ᵈ mates orders

whereupon he called the mate & they investigated the matter. No blows were struck as the man alleged that the 2^{d} officers order was contradictary to the 1st officers order which he previously had. A kind of an overhauling is going on preparatory to going into port, but so kindly & easily is it carried on & intermingled with the other work that it is scarcely perceptable. Indeed we have the ship scrubbed scraped & painted in a measure & I hardly notice where we have varied from our usual work. It all lays in the smartness of our Mate.

Saturday Oct 23^{d} 1858   Lat 28° 50'   Long 96° 02'
Cloudy day. Sometimes no wind, "sometimes some". Watch employed in setting up the jib guys   main topgallant & royal backstays. Aft^{n} clear, wind hauled & the ship fell off to W. & W. by N. We have very fine times in the port watch while the starboard (owing to a bad officer) have just the contrary. The Capt is *"down on"* them, while he thinks if any one is in the other watch he is all right   Every night the 3 boys (self included) & the 3^{d} mate hold a sort of a *"Conversazione"* in our *"library"* & canvass all sorts of subjects under the sun & much fun & many hearty laughs we have at the various jokes & anecdotes thereat related From talking we go singing & any other thing that pleases us & when in the heigth of the pile perhaps the bell strikes 8 & instanter every one leaves, some to take their lookout, some to relieve the watch on deck, & some 1 or 2 lucky ones to *turn in.* Any night at sea a stranger would be surprised at the change in the aspect of affairs between 5 minutes of 8 & 5 minutes after. At the former he might hear, laughing, joking, singing, playing, dancing, almost any thing, but the moment 8 oclock comes every one stops & 5 moments after nothing would be heard but the tread of the officer on the poop & the man at the lookout. There are a great many who write of the monotony of sea life, & the horrors of being confined as though in a jail   As for monotony I never found any as there is always enough to do, & to keep your thoughts on something else. And I never felt confined unless I knew there was some land within 100 miles of me, then indeed I have often thought "we have hardly room enough just now". The *"idea"* of confinement when there is nothing to obstruct your progress for months at a time   "Pshaw" get out with such nonsense Ye *"Old fogys"* & *Longshoremen*

Sunday Oct 24th 1858   Lat 28°. 29′   Long 97°. 24′

A splendid day & as a matter of course an idle one   Engaged
myself in conversation all the forenoon. Mr McEntee giving us
an a/c of his naval & mail experiences, which were very interesting
& amusing. The mate gave *boy Bill* (sen.) a tow line upon condition that it should not be seen by *Stephen* (Capt Dow)   He
wouldnt give me one,   so I have but one alternative I.E. steal one.
The wind hauls once in a while & we are gradually edging up to
our course (NW.)   Laying W.N.W. at present. The Comet keeps
rising   I have previously spoken of it as being near Venus but
upon further consideration I have come to the conclusion that it
is *not Venus* but Jupiter, which star it is now above. Came up
during the night to our course N W by N. 11 o clock took in the
main skysail   wind puffy & not to be relied upon

Monday Oct 25th 1858 Lat 26° 15′ Long 100°. 19

Took the royals at 1 A M & staggered along under 3 to 'gan'
sails up to the time of writing 8 A.M. There the mate has just left
the door where he gave some orders to some of the starboard
watch, to one he gave the *fish hook* with orders to scrape it, to
another the *cat hook* & another he told to *freeze on* to *that Devils
Claw*. These articles are all used in anchoring & heaving up, & stop-
pering the cable & though the names may seem *queerious* to you
they are all very appropriate, & had you heard the mate as he rattled them off a moment ago it would have caused you as it did me to
smile. The starboard watch are rattling down the topmast rigging.
I received intelligence through Ned that the mate had said that he
& I knew enough & he meant to put us together in the starboard
watch out of Frisco & take Bill with him & let him learn something. *"Bully for him do it again"*. Weather remained fine
throughout

Tuesday Oct 26th 1858 Lat 24°. 07′   Long 101°. 23′

Commenced tarring down. Subscriber performed prodigys in his
bowline & for a wonder did not get overboard. The wind remains
steady & we lay within one point of our course N.W. The next I
have to observe is that there is nothing further to observe.

Wednesday   Oct 27th 1858 Lat 22. 19   Long 101° —

Wind remained the same until 8 oclock this morning when it

hauled sufficient for us to lay course. A trade wind sea is for the first time perceptible & we will probably get the trades by evening. 6 oclock the day is most spent and we have not yet got the trades, although we have a N.E. breeze which answers very well.

Thursday OCT 28th 1858 Lat 20.° 45′ Long 103°. 19′
Fine day with the wind 3 points free & a fore topmast stunsail set. Very, very, strange, no trades. They generally prevail in 30° & sometimes in 35° & we are now in 20° & have not got them yet. Weather during the night cloudy & squally.

Friday OCT 29th 1858 Lat 19°. 45′ Long
First part cloudy & squally, took in the royals at 4 oclock A.M. Second part clear, & dead calm 3d part got a breeze & jogged along 6 or 7 knots up to the time of writing 8½ A.M. Day remained

Saturday OCT 30th 1858 Lat 17°. 45′. Long 105°. 37′
First part beautiful 2d ditto, so Pete says & he ought to know, for he has had nothing to do today but watch the weather & boy Bills girtline (he is tarring at the main rigging) But I must go to sewing or else bymebye I wont have a whole rag to my back.

Sunday OCT 31st 1858 Lat 16°. 09′ Long 106°. 11′
Wind dies away & comes again by spells Rained quite hard during the morning watch. 8 o clock nearly calm. A number of "*marlin-spikes*" flying about & uttering their shrill cries add to the oddity of the morning. The day remained very beautiful after a while a light breeze sprang up & we continued on our course Continued my letters but couldnt think of anything to write

Monday Nov 1st 1858 Lat 13. 59 Long. "didnt get it"
Began fine & continued so up to the time of indictment The Southern Crofs only makes his appearance at 3 or 4 o'clock in the morning while the Comet has gone after some cream in the Milky Way. His tail is "*slewing* around over him" & is now almost perpendicular. Tarred down the *mizzen* all the forenoon & wrote during the aftn 97 days out

Tuesday Nov 2ᵈ 1858   Lat 11°. 16′   Long, *"No Savee."*

First watch very fine breeze sprang up & we were going 10 knots at 8 bells (4 oclock A.M.)   died away in a measure & sprang up again in the 2ᵈ* & at 8 o'clock A.M.—10 knots again. Betting has commenced as to the number of days we will have –

Wednesday Nov. 3ᵈ 1858   Lat 8°. 13′   Long

Wind free & the ship rolling along 10 knots all the morning & forenoon watches. I was occupied all the forenoon in tarring down the main top mast stays. The Southern Crofs I searched in vain for last night. He has watched us a long time & now his vigil is over for a short while but I long for the moment we shall sight him again as we shall then be homeward bound

Thursday   Nov 4ᵗʰ 1858   Lat 5° — Long

Passed much the same as all the rest of the days have since we have had fine weather   I was painting yards & blocks up at the mizzen all the aftⁿ. Night fine   furled the main skysail at 2 oclock

Friday Nov 5ᵗʰ 1858   Lat 2° 59   Long 111°. 00

We commenced painting this morning on the poop   I completed my share by daubing the top of the monkey rail & the stanchions, while thus engaged I accidentally got my brush knocked out of my hand. Forthwith I told the mate that it was overboard (& consequently past praying for) & he remarked "you are very smart," then paused. I waited for another brush but he presently said "very well you need not wait, if you cant paint on deck without losing brushes you cant paint at all." Now listen reader. Since this ship left New York there have been 8 marline spikes lost & two prickers (all overboard) & by able seamen too. Only one of them ever got a reprimand for it. Since this ship left Sandy Hook I have been the chief dauber & in fact have done all the painting (until this morning) & during that time I never lost or dropped my brush nor spilt paint on deck (as one or two unlucky ones have lately)   I have handled marline spikes too & never dropped one of them either. But this morning in an unlucky moment I lost a brush & am Immediately spoken of as being careless &c. &c., dont care, &c. &c. It has never been so before & perhaps the mate is

* In this sentence the first and second watches apparently mean the 12 P.M. to 4 A.M. and the 4 to 8 A.M. watches—the first two watches of the calendar day.

[147]

crofs about something else that made him do so. I dont care if he is. I have had the name of doing well all the passage & I can do so still & better if encouraged too. Expect to cross the line tomorrow dont know how it will be though, as the sky is dark & lowering as I write (so is my sky for that matter) & we may at any moment have a change of weather. I have not mentioned that we have had the trades for some days of late   their prevailing so far north perhaps will be beneficial to us by carrying us through the *"dol-drums"* The tarring is all done. The mate & myself had quite an argument last night & regard to navigation & because I would not agree with him where I thought I was right & he said I was not, & couldnt tell me why & the reason, he referred the case to Capt Dow whose judgement I may hear tonight, perhaps.

At Noon
Saturday Nov 6ᵗʰ 1858   Lat 00°. 49′S Long 112°. 00′ W
Began with good breeze, though inclined to be squally. The water has changed from blue to green during the night, though we are near no land that I am aware of. Painting going on all day. The mate gave me a brush & set me at it again notwithstanding my losing that one Yesterday. Crossed the line at 8 oclock in the evening, with a *"wet sheet & a flowing sea"* making 6 times for me. No *Neptunal* demonstrations this time   Weather continued fine throughout.
Crossed the Line in the Pacific   Long 112°. 00W   103 days out

Sunday Nov 7ᵗʰ Lat 1°. 13′ N   Long 113°,   something
North Lat hereafter until homeward bound
A beautiful day with a finer breeze & everyone in good spirits. Oh — if we could only keep this wind for 14 days! we'd be laying in Frisco on the 15ᵗʰ. A school of *"Bonita"* (the first we have seen) are under the bows. The Carpenter managed to hook 2   one of which he got aboard   Some of the starboard watch have manu-factured 2 pairs of boxing gloves & the men have been practicing the *"manly art of self defense"* all the morning. Some of them are quite proficient in it. Altered our course from N.W. by N. to N. N.W. & set the main togallⁿᵗ stunsail at 1 o'clock P.M. Weather continued fine throughout.

Monday   Nov. 8ᵗʰ Lat 3°. 15′ N   Long 113. 13 W
Got our only rough spar off the deck & stowed it under the rail,

[148]

thereby clearing the decks of every obstacle. When we left N.Y. we could cross the decks at only 2 points (around the booby hatch & around the fore hatch) now you can walk any where you please, all the coal casks being smashed up for firewood & their contents burned   all the spars either sent aloft, stowed along the water-ways, or made into battens for the rigging, & the watercasks lashed on the main hatch. Struck two porpoises during the day but owing to the inefficiency of the harpoon it drew out both times. So we got neither of them

Course due North

Tuesday Nov. 9th Lat 5°. 48′ N Long   W

Fine day & beautiful breeze. Varnished the decks during the fore-noon. Having lots of dried apples the Capt. ordered the steward to give us applesauce once a week, so today we got our first in-stallment.

Wednesday Nov. 10th Lat 8.53 Long

Fine day as usual   Course altered to N.W. by N. wind right astern, stun'sails set on both sides. Everybody in a fever & talking about "*San Francisco.*" For my own part I cant see any land yet, & so I made no fuss at all. Fine day throughout.

Thursday Nov. 11th Lat 10°. 42′ Long —° —

A squall came up at 1 oclock A.M. which shifted the wind & we braced up 2 or 3 points. Hove the log & found her going 9 knots continued this rate until 5½ oclock A.M. when it came on to rain & fell dead calm. All hands catching water & scrubbing paint-work. 1 o'clock, cleared up & got a breeze on the quarter. Course N W by N 3 or 4 knots. Having lost several Porpoises lately by the poorness of the irons one of the men ("Geo" Price) produced a new edition from his chest which we have sharpened & got over the bows line & all attached & now let the fish come for if this iron once goes into one he must either come on board or else the iron must break for when it receives strain it toggles on the end & has to be cut out. Martin (our harpooner) is so vexed to think that he should lose 2 in one day that he says he wont miſs another one this passage but put the harpoon right through & through I watched the one he struck Monday, after he got loose from the iron, until he rolled belly up on top of water about 3 ships lengths off, & died. his track was one line of blood for the iron went

[149]

through him right behind the blowhole. The way his mates left him was a caution

Friday Nov 12th Lat 11° 05′ Long —

Calm & foggy, consequently damp, feel very stiff. Rained quite hard at times, during the morning. Almost calm at 8 oclock. The boys (myself excepted   it being my watch on deck) went swimming off the Dolphin Striker Last night   The "prince" (Bill) was swinging in the bight of a rope & going into the water once in a while (he's rather *skeery* in the water not being a *"tip top"* swimmer) & I proposed jestingly that he should drop astern & see what our stern mouldings were,   he not exactly believing in this sort of business, clapped his thumb on the end of his nose in a sort of *"No ye dont"* style peculiar to himself alone, when *"kerswash"* down went the Brighams bows & *"Dolphin Striker"* under water, a catastrophe entirely unexpected by him, & he being some 6 feet below either of them you can imagine where he went to. He came up when the ship did but alas his mirthful mood was gone, gone to give place to the most terrified expression I ever cast my eyes upon. It was done so quick & he was so completely astonished, that it was some 10 minutes before he dared venture near the water again. Went in myself this morning & had a fine swim. The Mate has had me *sailorizing* all the aftn while smarter *sailors* are scraping steps & belaying pins on deck. A Tremendous fleet of *"Portugee men o war"* passed us this aftn. I caught one & put him in a book entitled "Young Man from Home" but whether he'll keep or not I dont know. Oh! Scissors how hot it is. Later still:— . The Captain went past the house with a bucket in his hands   an occurrence so unusual that I looked out to see what was up, & saw him throwing it over the stern & out of the mizzen channels. What to make of it I did not know but being on the poop soon after I saw 3 beautiful "Portugee men o war" & one *"Button"* (thats all the name I ever heard for them) on a piece of pasteboard, so the mistery was cleared up.

Saturday Nov. 13th Lat 11. 26   Long ——

Dead calm, & Oh————h-how, hotttttt. Not a ripple is on the water & there is scarcely any perceptible swell. The pitch oozes from the seams in the vessels side & your feet scorch through the soles of your shoes as you traverse the decks. I was serving the main togallnt Royal & Skysail backstays on the sunny side of the

rigging &, well, I thought I was so burnt & tanned that to be more
so was utterly impossible   but oh, if ever any body was mistaken,
I was, for at 8 bells every body said, "well you are burnt, for a
certainty" & sure enough a looking glass proved the truth of their
observations. At 6 o'clock all hands prepared to go in swimming,
(notwithstanding the presence of 4 or 5 "*Pilot* fish" the sure
precursors of sharks) & overboard we went   10 of us   the 1st &
3d mates included,   we swam off some 100 yards from the ship &
oh, "how pretty she looked," so long low black & saucy rising &
falling with the swell as though she was alive & vexed that there
should be no wind to send her on her course   The Capt came up
on deck & watched us for some time as we dove for buttons, (you
can see one until it is some 100 or 150 feet beneath the surface)
the sharks did not make their appearance therefore we infer that
there are none around. I saw a very large sunfish today "which
boy Bill took for one of the shark species." Oh for a breeze now
we have been in the same spot for two days

Sunday Nov. 14th   Lat 12°. 12′   Long 115°. 20′

As a matter of course it is a "*beautiful*" day   So cool & such a
"refreshing breeze." The pitch oozes out of both seams & un-
seasoned wood   our "breeze" is a dead calm & the only objects
of interest are several pilot fish & one curious specimen of the
finny tribe which no one can name. Occupied myself with reading
lazing around under the awnings, writing a letter & lastly by
listening to "*Stephen*" who is coursing the quarter deck & "cursing" Lieut Maury for as he says sending him into such a calm
streak & then saying nothing about it in either his "*Reports*" or
"*Sailing Directions*". I dont care much how long we are in getting
in for we cant make a good that is extra passage, but for one
reason I should not care if we were a month more "*More days
More Money*" is a saying peculiar to sailors & I believe in it
sometimes.

Monday Nov. 15th   Lat 12°. 19′   Long 115°. 22′.

No perceptible deviation from yesterday. The Greaser had some
of his watch over the bows on a stage trying to clean off the moss
which has collected for about 1 foot above our copper & impedes
us greatly in our sailing, (in fact one of the men observed to me
when speaking of it "*bloody old Hooker*" stay out another month
without cleaning that stuff & she wont move at all" an observation

[151]

partially believed by me) but they did not succeed in doing much for the mate gave the order to haul the stages up observing that there was more fun than work going on & indeed those who were over there *were* having *"fine fun"* getting washed overboard from the stage every once in a while & once in a while getting a dab at the mofs with a scrub broom each one was provided with & could apply but one hand to at a time After being at it 2 hours they were ordered to *"Come in out o' that"* & no one could see that the moss was any the *"worse for wear"*. Thus the Greaser keeps his watch fooling around if he has not got orders from the Mate or that gentleman is not on deck.

Tuesday Nov. 16ᵗʰ Lat   Long

About 5 bells Bill came down from aloft (scraping) seasick Not long after Ned followed suit. The ship pitching in a short head sea, threw their breakfasts clear off their stomachs The *"Old Man"* was very mad about it but when after dinner he saw me come down & turn in his rage knew no bounds & he raved stamped & swore like a pirate. Hope it did *him* good but it didnt benefit me any When I went below I forgot to say any thing to the mate about it & in the dog watch he came to me & said "You wont make 4 times by that, "Ill pay for it this time" "Now you see" &c. Very good Mr. Brown thought I, if it comes to that after all the pains I've taken to please you, I guess Ill *"traverse you just a little"*. He made me walk all my lookout & I kept 3 hours in the bargain & would not let me lay down when I came off it.

Wednesday Nov. 17ᵗʰ Lat 14° —' Long 118° —

Brown sent me up at the main this morning to scrape Ned had the royal mast ½ done & I was working on that when I heard the mate sing out to me, "Thats a two handed job" (I chanced to be holding on with one hand & scraping with the other at the time a slight deviation from the usual plan of spitting on your *stomach & sticking yourself fast to the mast thereby*) "You can take your time Ill keep you up there all day" &c. "Ah, ha," says I if thats your play "Im there". I got the royal mast done by 3 bells then he yelled at me as before stated. After that for 3 hours till 1 bell I did not scrape a spot 6 inches square he came up to see it & what he thought I dont know, but as he didnt keep me up I infer that he thought it wouldnt do to try any such game on me. Ive been "Good Boy," all the way from N.Y. & if he commences *"hashness"* I wont be so any longer. The Capt told him he might discharge all of us boys in Frisco & we all have determined not to give him the chance but to apply for it at the first opportunity. Then if we are such a scandalous set we shall know it

Thursday Nov. 18th Lat 15°. 24′ Long 119° —
Fine day & pleasant weather. Good breeze from N & N by E. Ship going 7 or 8 knots (she ought to go 10). A sail to windward but what class she ranks as I cant say but she looks to me like a barque. It mought "be our friend the Rambler" which sailed the same day we did. Employed scraping but did not perform much in that line, being rather sick.

Friday Nov. 19th Lat Long
Got the anchors over the bows & stowed the cables & hawsers in the house. Ship going along 7 or 8 knots & heading from N.W. to W.N.W. full & by is the course If you can find it which I very much doubt. The Lat & Long for the last two days have not been correctly put down by me in consequence of us boys being in bad favor aft, at present, "Dont care a *Darn*" "May go to blazes for all me" "Hope they'll discharge us in Frisco" "Go in a *Fruiter* down among the islands" "Better wages" *"Bully times"* "Dont care a *Darn*"

Saturday Nov 20th Lat Long
Fine breeze but rather inclined towards the squally. Took the royals in at 6 bells. Cleaned the brasswork this morning. Boy Bill upset the oil on some new paint "Mate mad & loose" swore we shouldnt get our breakfasts until we had cleaned all the brass in the ship. Did it, & got done just, at 8 bells. Old Man came on the poop & saw the spilt oil—didnt say much (but to use the words of the old Dutch man) guess he thought *"G-d d- -n"* Scraped the fore down & oiled the fore & main masts Got imposed upon a little in that too

Sunday Nov 21st Lat 21°. 51′ Long 126° 20′
Began with a terrible *"stink"* on the quarter deck (I.E.) a row among the aristocracy Greaser had his men scrubbing paint work after the decks were washed down, the mate seeing it sent him word to "Stop," he engaged in conversation with the

Carpenter and did not seem to mind the order, upon which the Mate roared out "Put those Lye buckets away" Mr Jackson assented *of course* but gave the Mate such an insinuating smile, that it roused all the fight swear & tear in him & he sprang out on deck—from his room—and swore by all that was good & great he'd knock the "*Skillets of Burgoo*" out of the 2ᵈ Officer Mr J. being a very quiet cool sort of man, & morover knowing he had "No papers" to get in to a row with the mate, said *Nary* word   Mr B. then said that he could lick any 4 such men in the world but Jackson again said *Nary* word. 1ˢᵗ officer upon this got so "werry wroth" that he fairly jumped & jerked about like one distracted, & was just on the point of knocking Jackson down When Stephen stuck his head out of his state room window & says in *very* bland tones, Oh—dont—strike him Mr B. He only wants to make you pay for it. *He* then came on deck & walked up & down talking very cooly all the time, his remarks when he did make any suddenly were rather facetious. He says to Jackson You are the dam'dest trash for an officer that I ever saw, & Ive seen some pretty small ones. Then again he stopped sudden & observed   The ship looks pretty nice; what have *you* done towards it? & this strain he continued for some time provoking smiles at every turn, from all who listened to him   Course NbyW

Monday Nov. 22ᵈ   Lat 24° 03′   Long 128° or so
Under 3 topgallⁿᵗ sails all day. The mate had me on the quarter deck all of the first night watch, as he is angry with me for some cause or other & would not let me sleep the same as the rest do when they have no wheel or lookout   He has always said that "he never works men up" or hazes them around & upon being asked what he meant by keeping me up, said, it was his duty, if its your duty to keep him up it is the same with all the rest & so why dont you keep them up too, said his interrogator, to this he made no answer but he evidently thinks better of it, for he let me sleep this night, although I had his previous orders to keep in sight on the quarter deck until we get into port. On the lookout for "Hendersons Islands," all day but did not sight them.* Rousted up our mooring chains this morning & got all ready for the cables to follow. Blowing quite stiff at times. We

* And for good reason! for the *Brigham* was in 128° W and 24° *N* whereas Henderson I. is in 128° W and 24° *S*.

keep her full & by & head all over between W.N.W. & N. by W. our correct course is N ½ W.

Tuesday Nov. 23^d Lat 26°. 13′   Long dont know
Oh! *"sceezeours"* "aint she a schooting" 9 & 10 all the while & the lee cathead under water. Cleared the rubbish & other stuff out from under the topgall^{nt} forecastle, & made other preparations for going into port.

Wednesday Nov. 24th Lat 28.14   Long
Rather nasty squally weather. Mizzen top gall^{nt} sail & flying jib have been stowed for 36 hrs Oh if this wind would only break us off a little more or let us lay a little higher 3 or 4 days would put us along side of a dock in *"Frisco"* Every one anxious & expectant. Frazers River is all the talk & I dont think there will be any body to stay by the ship. Cant tell though

Thursday Nov. 25th Lat 29. 32   Long 133.
Thanksgiving day at home I suppose so we killed a pig & had a good dinner in honor of the occasion Tacked ship at 1 bell (12½ oclock M.) & laid E.N.E. which is within 2 points of our real course, N.E. on this tack. Very diligently employed doing nothing all the forenoon. I had no room to mention on my last page, that at 6 o'clock last evening we were struck by a heavy squall which hove her down allmost on her beam ends, far enough at all events to upset our tea pots, pans, &c, & deprive us of our supper. We let go topgall^{nt} halyards & furled them, together with the miz topsail. Reefed the Spanker & Mainsail at 8 o'clock also furled the Crossjack. In this manner we sweat it out until 8 oclock this morning when we again packed on the rags.

Friday Nov. 26th Lat 30.13   Long
Went up on the mizzen topgall^{nt} yard to measure the lift (length) * & the distance from the sling band to the lift bolt   a dutchman who was assisting me took the yard arm end of the measure & I of course trusted to him to hold the end square. We came down & the mate had a lift made. Just as I was going below I heard a rumpus aft & ran out to see the mate holding

* The length of the lift.

my "dutch friend" by the throat with his fist all ready to strike
him (what it was about I didn't know but listened to hear)
Stephen came up on a dog trot & said to Mr B. "if you lick
him, lick him good" Suddenly I thought may be that lift is
too long or too short, if so "Charley look out for you too will
be implicated" It hardly passed my mind when Stephen sung
out to me *"Here You I want"* & asked me if I couldnt measure
a lift without getting it too short told him as how I thought I
could He was mad & I didnt care so I said nothing further. He
went on with a sort of tirade, of which I remember nothing with
the exception that I thought at the end that if he didnt like me
he could lump me in a few days.

Saturday Nov. 27th Lat 31°.21' Long 137° —

Loosed the royals during the forenoon. Wind dying away
gradually & at time of writing almost calm. We are about to
have a change of wind no doubt it will be fair when it comes
but at present it is dead in our teeth Bent the cables & ducked
"Martin" overboard during the operation but he had a bowline
around him so he *"went not far"* Furled the royals at 6½
o'clock in the evening & sailed along under 3 topgall^{nt} sails the
rest of the day. Light squalls continually passing. I hear the
Lat. almost every day but sometimes get it wrong therefore my
readers must make allowances for the incorrectness of my
figures. Went about at 4 oclock & back again at 6

Sunday Nov 28th Lat   Long

Oh dear me ! are we never to have a fair wind, but always this
tantalizing N.E,er & there abouts. No matter, we sail right
along the adge of it & go in every nook & corner it displays, our
head varying from N to W by N. So it gains no more on us
than we can possibly help. Almost up to the Lat of San Francisco & 15 deg. to the westward of where we ought to be Confound Lieut. Maury & his sailing directions as far as they relate
to these Lat's. Weather the same as yesterday with frequent
passing squalls. Never mind. "More days more money". Tacked
ship at 4, o'clock & laid E.N.E.

Monday Nov 29th Lat 33°.13' Long 135°. 28'

Sometimes up to course sometimes 1 or 2 points off. Variously
employed weather fine with light squalls. Furled the royals at

7 o'clock & kept them stowed all night. Rained some during the small hours but cleared up after a while.

Tuesday Nov. 30th Lat   Long
Under 3 topgallnt. sails at daylight. Weather very fine though not clear.

Wednesday Dec. 1st Lat 34°. 00. Long 130°. 11′
Beautiful day. Ship bounding & rolling & pitching like mad, right straight at "Frisco" The mate told me that he hoped to get in by friday night I dont care if she gets there tonight. Hauled down the flying jib at 1, o'clock as it was not safe to hang on to it any longer at least while these squalls (we have one every 10 or 15 minutes. There thats the mate, "Clew up the mizzen topgallnt sail, haul in that lee brace Jim; stand by the fore & main to'gallnt halyards" Then comes a sea & wets my window to say nothing of its drenching the cook & washing the gally floor! Ah! he shuts the weather door to gaurd against a similar occurrence. I am wet myself as she shipped a sea on me when I went to the galley Boy Bill & the 2d mate both got wet up to their waists & Bill came fearfully near getting "left behind" but he hung on to the rail & saved his bacon ! Took in the fore & main togallnt sails during the aftn, & furled the mizzen topsail in the last dog watch. Wind moderate with a nasty heavy sea

Thursday Dec 2d Lat 34.37 Long 127.51
Loosed & furled the mizzen topsail & crofs Jack during the morning. 8 oclock, blowing quite stiff Ship under fore & main topsails mizzen reefed. A fair wind & no sail on her "Oh My dont you say so George." Kept taking in sail until 12 o clock when we found ourselves reduced to a close reefed main topsail main spencer & foretopmast staysail, & it, blowing great guns. Ship labored very heavily all the first watch there being a terrible sea on. Carried away the lashings about the main hatch & every thing fetched away, that is, 5 or 6 water casks & the carpenters bench together with lumber, ropes, tackles, rigging, &c, &c. There they were & nobody dare venture near for some time (as a broken leg & two or 3 smashed ribs are delicacies not much desired any where) at the same time a lot of the cargo down the booby hatch got adrift & on the whole we had quite a time.

Could not sleep any the first watch she rolled so. At times I almost thought the house must go, for I lay on the partition instead of my bed although I employed sundry overcoats Blankets &c to wedge me down. Tacked ship twice during the day

Friday Dec 3ᵈ Lat 34°. 33′ Long 127°. 00′

Gale abating gradually, got the 3 close reefs set at 1 oclock & foresail & mainsail & reefed upper topsails at 4. 12 o clock M. shook out all the reefs & were under whole topsails once more. Set topgallⁿᵗ sails in the aftⁿ & proceeded on our course. Went about at 4 oclock & back again at 8. 12 oclock (midnight,) under 3 topgallⁿᵗ sails & forging along as fast as the prevailing heavy sea would permit.

Saturday Dec 4ᵗʰ Lat   Long

Morning found the sea considerably lighter & the "H. Brigham of Savannah" going it to the tune of 7 knots. Our distance yesterday noon, from San Francisco, was 300 miles N.E. course. With a fair wind we can make it in 2 days. Oh dear, when under the line we talked of 105, 106, 8, & 10, days as our passage, now we are out 130, & have a fine prospect of seeing Christmas at sea to boot "What cant be cured must be endured" may be very fine to read, but to have to practice your endurance is quite another thing Breeze hauled sufficient for us to lay N.N.E. this aftⁿ & every one telling the other how soon they would eat ashore, &c, got all hands into fine spirits. Got a topmast stunsail up & bent it. (having unbent all our studding sails in anticipation of not using them again) Well we set it, & in about 5 minutes a squall of wind rain & "nasty weather" was seen bearing down in full style, previous to this the day had been uncommonly fine & this seemed to be a sort of punishment for daring to bend & set a studding sail after having them stowed for good once. It of course became essential to furl the royals, as the breeze became stronger & the squalls more frequent. Went to the mizzen topgallnt halyards at 4 bells & saw all clear for letting go at a moments notice. Stephen however seemed to have come to the conclusion that he had given the Brigham very little pain since leaving N.Y. & now that he had got a chance he would drive her under, & fast & furious did she pitch & roll. At intervals as a squall would pass, her motion would become varied & she would lay over with a surge that sent the foam seething from the waves under the lee. At such times the men gaze aloft then at the old man, at the same time nearing the sheets & clewlines to be in readinefs & when a puff heavier than usual passes sieze hold of some of the running gear to keep from going acrofs decks against their will at the same time giving vent to their suspicions as to the old mans sanity. At 5 bells I had become pretty well used to them & was promenading along the poop when I saw Stephen stop & look up under a cloud to windward & immediately he roared out Clew up the mizzen topgall^{nt} sail I let go the halyards & went up & furled the sail while going aloft the squall struck us & oh—how she jumped & kicked I heard a terrible racket on deck & in the air & caught a glance of the main topgall^{nt} yard sticking almost perpendicular. I had however enough to do to take care of my own yard which was in much the same situation besides too furl the sail. On returning to the deck I found every thing tranquil & the ship easy 8 bells soon struck & I turned in. I was awakened several times though by the motion & noise of the ropes & blocks as the wind whistled through them & was in momentary anticipation of being routed out to shorten sail. Not so however. When our side took the deck at midnight things looked very checquered & the squalls were still flying by as thick as peas. All went very well & we hung on all, until almost 4 bells when we were struck by a terrible gust. Away went every thing in the shape of halyards & every thing in the shape of a downhaul was extensively manned. It did not go as it came however but kept puffing away & trying to split our canvass for over 10 minutes the lee rail was under water all this while, & we were just the mussyest looking Clipper extant. Mr. Brown stuck it out some time but at last sang out call all hands & shorten sail this we did & were soon under 3 close reefs, for if ever a sailor will work it is when he has been routed out of his bunk in the middle of his short 4 hours below. Hove the log & found her going 5 or 6 knots notwithstanding our short sail

Sunday Dec 5th 50 miles from the Farralones at noon
The gale like all of these puffs about here abated with the night & 8 bells this morning found us once more under lofty rags. 10 oclock "Sail Ho" right ahead & bound to the westward. A

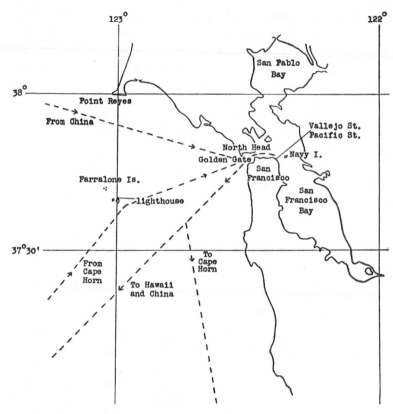

SAN FRANCISCO HARBOR AND VICINITY

Barkentine under short canvass as she proved. 12 oclock M.
coast of Cal. in full view & the Henry Brigham skimming the
water like a wild cat. Passed several pieces of cord wood during
the forenoon. Hove to off the "Farralones" all night. A welcome
sight was the revolving light on "Los Gros Farralone" to us
poor weatherstained fellows & our little barkie.

Monday Dec. 6th 1858 off the Heads—

With the earliest streaks of dawn all hands were roused &
preparatory measures taken for going into port. Some were
getting the anchors off clear, & others getting the cable out,
while a few prepared lines for mooring & towing. Never did
Stephen look so rosy & happy (at least within my recollection)
as when spy glass in hand he scanned the coast in search of a

pilot boat. 8½ o'clock A.M. took a pilot from the *"Fanny"* of San Francisco." Going in met the *"Challenge"* China bound." She left N.Y. 10 days a head of us & came out in 117. The "Golden Fleece" from Boston the same day we left N.Y. arrived out in 112 days, the quickest run of the year. I saw much to comment & enlarge upon in the land marks and other things upon the coast but I cannot do so at present being pressed for time. Had rather a narrow escape after taking a steamer by catching in a "tide rip" off Navy island but we got off with a whole skin. Ran up to Pacific street wharf where the pilot meant to anchor us, but owing to our cable fouling on the windlass & the anchor not holding we passed it & almost made a hole in the Clipper Ship "Silver Star." The pilot then left saying he would be off at 10½ P.M. when we would go alongside of the wharf, but 10½ P.M. found us aground & immovable. So of course we remained *"in statu quo"*. I got my letters before coming up to the town, & as a matter of course perused them eagerly but received no bad news. Passed a very uncomfortable night on my chest & awoke in the morning as stiff as a "Poker," but I am getting ahead of time so just be kind enough to turn over & you will see what happened on

Tuesday DEC 7th 1858   off the wharf
Found the Brigham deep in the mud this day so we got not to the wharf. Went ashore on 2 hrs liberty & examined the "Post Office" but could get nothing as it was closed.

Friday 17th   DEC 1858
Left the Henry Brigham

CHAPTER XI

GUANO AND COOLIES

NEAR the end of the last chapter, Abbey mentioned two very well known clippers, the *Golden Fleece* and the *Challenge*. As our chronicler stated, the *Golden Fleece* did arrive from Boston in 112 days; but he was not correct in saying that this was the fastest run of 1858. There were seven passages earlier in the year, each of which bettered *110* days.

This was the second *Golden Fleece*, the first one having been wrecked in the Golden Gate in 1854. Perhaps the most note-worthy performance of this second vessel came some years later when she took only 12½ days from the equator to within 200 miles of San Francisco. (The remaining distance required more than a week!)

In 1871 she suffered a very strange mishap. While enroute from Boston to Calcutta, laden with ice, the cargo caught fire!—that is, the sawdust, etc., in which the ice was packed. The fire could not be extinguished so the ship put in to Halifax. There a great quantity of water was poured into her; finally 20 feet of water had to be admitted by making holes in the bottom. Later, after the hold had been pumped clear, the fire broke out once more. A final and successful flooding followed, and eventually the *Golden Fleece* sailed the seas once more

When the *Henry Brigham* "met the *Challenge* China bound" Abbey saw a renowned ship. The *Challenge*, according to reliable records, came out in 114 days on the passage mentioned in the diary—3 days faster than stated. She was one of the most famous of all the clippers and was possibly the very sharpest. When launched in 1851 she was the largest merchantman ever constructed, her tonnage exceeding 2,000. She was 27 feet longer than the largest U. S. man of war, the ship of the line *Pennsylvania*. The *Challenge* was the first 3-deck clipper and the first American sailing vessel to be braced with iron. Her mainmast was 3 feet in diameter and its extremity rose 200 feet above the water. Her main yard was 2 feet in diameter and 90 feet long. With stunsails set, her lower sails spanned 160 feet; one complete suit of sails totalled 12,780 yards of canvas. It is interesting to note that her spar plan was reduced subsequently on three different occasions.

The *Challenge* was beset throughout her entire career by mutiny and pestilence, death and disaster. However, in the year 1852 alone she established probably a greater number of important records that stand to this day than any other ship has ever made in an equal period. First came a passage of 33 days from Hong Kong to San Francisco, an all-time record. She required but 18 days to San Francisco from a point opposite Japan, much faster than any other recorded passage. After a quick turn-around of 7 days she sailed again for Hong Kong. She was off Honolulu in 8 days, another record. The best time ever made from San Francisco to Hong Kong is 32 days and, on this trip, the *Challenge* took 43; but with only moderate winds, she was within 400 miles of Hong Kong on the 23rd day. In other words, she was in a position to break the 32-day record by 7 full days! At Hong Kong old Captain Land departed this life. The *Challenge*, however, carried on. Bound for England, she established the still unbeaten record of 65 days from Anjer to Deal, the standard part of that much travelled China–London race course.

After the safe and peaceful passage which the *Brigham* enjoyed with Abbey aboard, she sailed from San Francisco to the South Seas for guano, and reached New York after Abbey did. There Captain Dow was relieved by Captain Potter. Under the latter, she made a second voyage similar to the preceding one, i.e., New York–San Francisco–South Seas–New York—and without mishap. Then her old jinx overtook her again. We find her loading coal in Liverpool. From there she had a momentous passage of 141 days to San Francisco during which she opened seams in her hull, lost several sails, and had part of her bulwarks stove in. At one time she acquired a dangerous list and some of her cargo had to be thrown overboard in order to straighten her up.

When the *Brigham* reached San Francisco, she was seized by the U. S. authorities. The Civil War was in progress; her ownership was Southern and this fact had not been covered up successfully. Two months later, while anchored in San Francisco Bay, she was fouled by another vessel and incurred $1,000 damage. The Government sold her and she sailed again under

Captain Potter. In 1865 he required 168 days to make San Francisco from New York; this was a result of unfavorable winds all the way.

After this protracted voyage, the *Henry Brigham* was sold into the coolie trade under Peruvian owners and renamed the *Compania Maritima del Peru, No. 2.* (Incidentally, the *No. 1* was the clipper ship *Twilight.*) This debased occupation of carrying coolies was pursued until her final destruction. In 1866 she became the Italian *Galileo.* On her first passage under the flag of Italy she reached Hong Kong from San Francisco partially dismasted. The next year she had the same experience; in 1868 she burned at sea. Thus ended the turbulent career of the *Henry Brigham.*

Abbey's next venture was a round trip from San Francisco to Honolulu. Though only 17 years of age he was shipped as an A. B. (able seaman)—i.e., qualified to perform all the duties required of a sailor. His ship was the little clipper bark *Francis Palmer*, of 302 tons. She was launched in Robbinstown, Maine, in 1852, her builder being J. M. Balkesn. Her length was 125', her breadth 25', and the depth of her hold 11', 9"; all in all, a rather small craft. Her owners are recorded in 1869 as being Kesing and Brown of San Francisco.

CHAPTER XII

TO THE SANDWICH ISLES

DEC 31st 1858

Joined the Francis Palmer

Friday JAN 7th 1859

Made sail at the wharf and started for Honolulu. Had a fine breeze & consequently soon ran through Golden Gate. Took the wheel at the wharf at quarter past one & kept it until four. 6 o'clock P.M. passengers (of which there are 8 or 10) all begin to quake & feel thin in the shanks, & one by one suddenly remember something or other which it is necessary for them to look after below, & it occupied them some time for they dont make their appearance again for a couple of days "of course they aint sea sick". Breeze continued fine throughout the night

Saturday JAN 8th 1859

Morning, no land in sight, not even "le gros Farralone" had the forenoon watch below & slept it away. So far we have had what I think for a sea going ship is tip top living, but the men who have been in the ship say they never lived so poor before. The bark has two capt,s both of which are on board. Capt. Stott who owns her & has been running her, is now going down to the islands to stay, & he acts as *"The"* capt yet. Capt. Paty is to take her as soon as Capt S. leaves her, & then, (if the reports of the men who have been with him & thought enough of him to wait two months in order to go with him again come true) we shall have still finer times. I am shipped as able seaman here & have more sailorizing to do than ever I had before but *"You Bet"* nobody shall know but that I have been to sea for at least 10 years

Sunday JAN 9th 1859

Fine day & pleasant breeze. Nothing more to observe

Monday Jan 10th 1859

Ive ransacked the forecastle & sorra' bit o' ink can I find so here goes with a lead pencil. Breeze about the same hauls a little occasionally when we have to brace the yards. Passengers pretty much over their sea sickness, & all over the decks, asking no end of silly questions & getting no very satisfactory answers. One man in the forecastle has been on this coast a long time & knew R. H. Dana when he was in the brig Pilgrim out here, previous to his writing his "two years before the mast"*

Tuesday Jan 11th 1859

Much the same as yesterday. It is great fun to stand at the wheel & hear the passengers talk "large" about things they *"no savee"* I.E. aboard a ship. Course South South West, & changed during the night to S W by S. ½ S.

Wednesday Jan 12th 1859

Fine day & fair wind

Thursday Jan 13th 1859

Good breeze & fine weather

Friday Jan 14th 1859

Strong gales, reefed topsails at midnight & had a great time altogether

Saturday Jan 15th 1859

Blowing quite strong

Sunday Jan 16th 1859

Wind abated got under royals again

Monday Jan 17th 1859

Weather pretty warm. Fine day & fair wind. This vessel sails well going 10 & 12 knots under ordinary sail.

Tuesday Jan 18th 1859

A heavy squall passed over us but luckily we escaped the worst part & made sail as soon as possible quite rainy & squally

* More than twenty years after his voyage in the *Pilgrim,* Dana revisited San Francisco on a fine passenger steamer in August, 1859—this very same year.

Wednesday   Jan 19th 1859
Rained all the morning, consequently got very wet indeed.

Thursday Jan 20th 1859
Weather fine, rushing along for dear life   Watch variously employed

Friday Jan 21st 1859
Came on to blow during the night   consequently reefed topsails

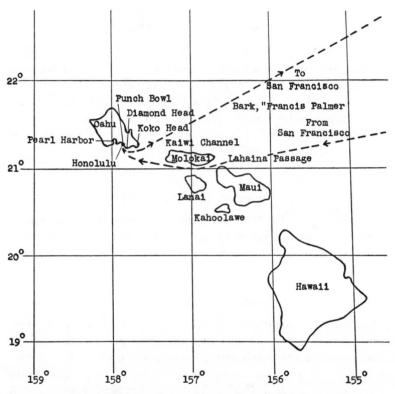

TRACK OF ABBEY'S VOYAGE TO HONOLULU IN THE *FRANCIS PALMER*

Saturday Jan 22d 1859
Made the island of Maui at 9 oclock & oh what a sea there was & always is along the north side of it. However we bruised along through it & at noon made Malakoi another of the group. The wind blew like sixty & so we concluded to keep away & run through

[169]

the Lahaina passage. Took the wheel at 6 oclock & from then until 8 had all I wanted to do to keep her straight. 8 oclock made every-thing snug but the main topsail & went below (our side)   after getting asleep I was suddenly awakened by being thrown nearly out of my bunk & before I had time to rub my eyes heard someone calling us out to reef. Went & came back in about an hour & did not get any more sleep that watch   12 oclock made Cocos head on Oahua & soon Diamond head. Ran into smooth water & lay off & on the remainder of the night.

Sunday Jan 23ᵈ 1859

Made sail at daylight & kept tacking until the Propeller "*Pele*" (which word signifies a volcano) came & hooked on & towed us in. There is quite a number of whalers yet here   the total for the season was 74 but the most of them are gone to the "Ochotsk" sea the Clipper Syren* is waiting for freight also, & yet another called the "*Gladiator*". I inquired for the "Gracia" in which vessel I have a relation but could not hear of her.

Monday   Jan 24ᵗʰ 1859

At 9 oclock I saw the Missionary brig "*Morning Star*" come in.† I have a 10ᶜᵗ share in her but I guess I wont make any advances on the strength of it. Warped in to the wharf & began to discharge

Tuesday   Jan 25ᵗʰ 1859.

Continued discharging & at night I took a stroll on shore to see what was to be seen. I found the town quite pleasant & regularly laid out. As I sauntered along I heard music ahead & *of course* determined to see what was up. It led me into a large room on the ground floor with a Darky fiddler at one end (tamborine & triangle also.) & a bar at the other   in the intervening space were about 20 men "tripping the "heavy Bombastic we" instead of the

* Built in 1851 and listed in Lloyd's as late as 1920—as the bark *Margarida* of Buenos Aires. Accordingly, and in spite of many mishaps, the *Syren* holds the longevity record among the old clippers.

† See footnote page 64. The Danish brig, *Morning Star,* there mentioned, had held American registry before she flew the Danish flag. Could this, by a strange coincidence, be the very same vessel?

CLIPPERS AT VALLEJO STREET WHARF, SAN FRANCISCO

When the Henry Brigham reached California in December, 1858, she berthed just two blocks away from here. From a Southern Pacific Co. photograph taken in the 'sixties.

THE SHIP *SYREN*

From a photograph taken at New Bedford, Mass.

In port at *Honolulu*"

"light fantastic", & what with being about half slung & in good
spirits they were having a merry time, one fellow became infatuated with the idea that he could dance (but he couldnt) &
consequently kept the floor all the time dancing on his own hook
one step to every tune & nothing else at all but it pleased him &
caused much merriment throughout the crowd which lined the
room I was requested to "*take a hand*" but declined displaying
my terpsicorean activity in the presence of so refined an assembly
as was there collected Not knowing any one or any thing about
the town I thought I might as well stay there as long as the
amusement lasted. Presently our "*Bob*" of the Palmer came in.
Now you must know "our Bob" is a good dancer & of course well
known in such a circle as he now entered, consequently he was soon
on the boards, & judging from the envious looks of the English
"Johnny haultaughters" from the "*Calipso*" (which vessel is in
port) I concluded he was the champion of the room Not caring
to be seen by Bob, for I never drink, & I surely should have had
to had I been discovered by him, I slipped slyly out & finding that
it was raining concluded to "Catchee one piecey Pie" & go aboard.
So I did. The Chain gang pass us every morning noon & night
on their way to labor

Wednesday Jan 26th 1859 ("*6 mo,s from home*")
Discharging freight all day. Amongst our freight is a lot of
"*Champagni Cider*" & the owner on its coming up on deck, asked
me for a pot & gimlet (both of which were provided for him) &
drew us about 2 qts of it. It is needless to state what became of it.
I saw a lot of runaway sailors taken aboard their vessels this aftn,
they were in irons

Thursday Jan 27th 1859
Finished discharging

Friday Jan 28th 1859
Working at the rigging & sails

Saturday Jan 29th 1859
I was engaged all day painting the main mast. There has been

[171]

some talk of sending us down to Owyhee on a pleasure excursion
to see the volcano which is now in eruption but we are not going.

Sunday Jan 30th 1859

Rigged up & went ashore. Did as I always do in a strange country
(I.E.) went straight ahead until forced to turn & finally found
myself up the valley abreast the *"Punch Bowl"* a large hill (formerly a volcano) so called from its resemblance to that article.
Concluded Id go back, went back, slipped into a Tarrow Patch &
got my shoes all muddy. Extremely disgusted. Saw the Presby-
terian Church coming   concluded to go in, did so, got a seat &
tried to behave myself,   how I succeeded I don't know, nor have
I any means of ascertaining, but I know that I all at once found
myself enclosed by Kanackas   Never having been used to sit in
the back seat with the niggers, I left, went aboard, and read the
day away.†

Monday Jan 31st 1859

Working at the rigging all day

Tuesday Feb 1st 1859

Working at the rigging

Wednesday Thursday & Friday 2d 3d 4th

all the same

Saturday Feb 5th 1859.

Fizzling around

Sunday Feb 6th 1859

Fine quiet day. Went aboard the Melita & had a *"lot"* of *"Lime-
ade"*

* This note and the "mourning band" were added after arrival at San
Francisco upon hearing of the death of a brother on this date. See March 4,
1859.

† The Hawaiian or "Sandwich" Islands composed, until 1893, a kingdom of
Polynesians (brown race).

In port at *Honolulu"*

Monday Feb 7th 1859

Had a general overhauling of all the Iron work on board. Pounded the rust off of it

Tuesday Feb 8th 1859

Painted her outside & overhauled the colours

Wednesday Feb 9th 1859

Birth day of King Kamehameha the ninth

Dressed the ship in flags & had a holiday. Aftn, I got a horse (for which I was obliged to disburse one dollar) & proceeded to follow the example of every one I could see & *"have a run"* Started at a break neck gallop for up the valley. Rode smack up into the fog which always pervades the mountains of *"Oahu"* & came back. Horse very much *jaded* but not I. Went aboard & waited for the great time to come. And finally with the shades of evening it did so Every one on the go some for the "Hula Hula" at "Japan Sea" some to the dance at the *"National"* & some to another at *"Liberty hall"* I first tackled the *"Hula Hula"* which consisted of 6 or 8 men with as many calabashes & 3 girls in ballet costume with the exception of their feet which were bare. They Hula'ed while the men kept time on their calabashes The dancing is indiscribable & the gestures peculiarly savage. Got enough of that & went to the National found almost every body there & a cotillion in full blast Company varied & drunk, so I cleared for Liberty Hall where I obtained admittance readily (not being drunk) I found all the respectability of the town collected & having a good time, sailed in & danced until tired then went on board the Francis Palmer & turned in

Thursday Feb 10th 1859

Seven oclock in the evening finds Honolulu quiet all our men with the exception of one in his bunk & myself on my chest writing this paragraph Been raining all day. Surveying Schooner *"Fennimore Cooper"* came in the other day & was the gaudiest drefsed vessel on the station yesterday, not excepting her Majestys Frigate "Calypso," so Hurrah for the "stars & stripes."

[173]

In port at *Honolulu*"

Rumor says we are to go on Saturday but if we are gone by next week thursday we will do well I think

Friday FEB 11th 1859

At work sawing up & taking in wood & scraping & painting

Saturday FEB 12th 1859

No deviation from yesterday. Went to the "Royal Hawaiian Theatre" in the evening to witness a promised immaculate personation of the *"dumb girl of Oran"* by Miss Rowena Granice Very lame indeed, although the performers did not feel ashamed for themselves, I *did* for them Melita left for Frisco

Sunday FEB 13th 1859

Very rainy day. Went aboard the Surveying Schooner "Fennimore Cooper" during the forenoon & staid aboard the rest of the day

Left Honolula on the morning of the 17th up to the night of the 18th Oahu was still in view. Got a breeze which increased to a gale & lasted 4 days ship heading N & by W. & making good time

Wednesday MCH 2d 1859

Among our passengers are Miss Rowena Granice who has been playing an engagement at the Royal Theatre & Mr Hamilton a *"Banjoist"*. One more, Mr Hawks a Lawyer of San Francisco (which place he represented in the Cal. State Senate in 55, & 56.) last from *"Tahiti"* to which place he went to complete his recovery from an attack of the consumption He is now on his way home to die, & it is very doubtful if he will live to get into port. He eats nothing, but drinks enormous quantities of Jamaica Rum, which is all that keeps him alive. His disease is brought on by dissipation. I sat with him two hours last night during which time he was quite rational, but he is generally delirious, & cursing & swearing in his whispering, husky voice. All hope he will live to get in but it is doubtful. Mch 30th 1859 He died 3 days after arriving

[174]

Have had heavy weather for the past 4 or 5 days but are now going it with a fair breeze right for the Farralones which we expect to make tomorrow night if the breeze holds, as our distance at noon today was 320 miles due E.

MARCH 4th 1859

Arrived at San Francisco.
Sad, sad news from home

MCH 5th 1859

Left the Francis Palmer

CHAPTER XIII

CAPTAIN GARDNER AND THE *COMET*

On the round voyage just completed, the *Palmer* was off Honolulu in 15 days from San Francisco. This is not far from average time for a small clipper. The record is held by the *Challenge* which made it on one occasion in 8 days. The record to Honolulu anchor is 8 days and 18 hours, held by the *Fair Wind;* here too the *Palmer's* time was almost exactly 7 days longer. The *Fair Wind* on her record passage sailed only 2,104 miles; this is just 20 miles more than the shortest possible route. The time of the *Francis Palmer* from Honolulu to San Francisco was the same as for the outward passage—15 days. Honolulu is far to the southward of the eastbound track of clippers sailing between China and San Francisco. Consequently no fast Honolulu–San Francisco runs are available for inspection. It may be said, however, that 15 days eastbound is a better performance than 15 days westbound.

After reaching San Francisco, Abbey was berthed on the steamer *Northern* for two weeks. He then joined the clipper ship *Intrepid*, a splendid new craft hailing from New York City. Her master was the noted Captain E. C. Gardner. Captain Gardner's career was so outstanding and his reputation so high that it will be found worth while to follow his movements through the clipper era. At the start we find him in 1845 in command of one of the first of the fast vessels, a 400-ton bark called the *Candace*. From 1850 to 1851 he had the brand new extreme clipper ship *Celestial*. He made one long voyage in her; and he did not tarry along the way. He was 105 days from New York to San Francisco and required only 38 to make his destination from 50° S. in the Pacific Ocean. That is fast sailing. The greatest performance of this round-the-world circuit was his run of 33 days from San Francisco to Hong Kong. This has been surpassed only by the 32-day passage of the *Southern Cross*. From Hong Kong the *Celestial* went to Shanghai and sailed thence to New York in 117 days.

Here Captain Gardner was given the *Comet*. These two names of master and ship are almost synonymous for high-grade clipper ship performance. The *Comet* was another extreme clipper, brand new when Gardner took her. She was built in New York by Wm. H. Webb, one of the most famous builders of clipper ships. Her tonnage was 1,836 by old measurement. She was 241' long, 41' 4" broad, and her hold was 22' 2" deep. Her performances demonstrate conclusively that she was indeed a flyer. On her first voyage she reached San Francisco in 103 days. She required only 32 of these days to sail from the equator in the Atlantic around the Horn to 50° S. in the Pacific—which is very fast travelling. From San Francisco she made Hong Kong in 37 days, another good run. She reached Anjer from Whampoa in 14 days against the monsoon. Her time from Anjer to New York was 83 days, the breezes being so light that Captain Gardner had his skysails set all but 12 days. On this passage (1852) he brought home the largest and most valuable cargo of teas and silks that had yet been imported from China.

The next voyage was a round trip to San Francisco and it was an eventful one. During a severe gale at the outset, the wind shifted suddenly and blew with terrific force from the new direction. The *Comet* lost her foretopmast and main royal mast, with topsails and other gear from both fore and mainmasts. One of Currier's lithographs depicts her in her extremity. Captain Gardner rerigged his ship and finally reached the equator in 33 days. From there the *Comet* was only 79 days to San Francisco—total, 112—a great piece of work. On the way home she had a thrilling race with the *Flying Dutchman*. Gardner sailed a day after his rival but passed her. Then the speedy *Dutchman* caught up and they were in close company all of one day. The *Comet* pulled ahead again but was passed later on. She reached New York first, however, by a small margin. Her time was 83 days, 18 hours. A few additional notes will show the exceptional quality of this race. The *Flying Dutchman* on this occasion established the San Francisco-equator record of 11½ days. The *Comet* required just 12. The *Dutchman* made the Horn in 37 days from San Francisco; the *Comet* took 38; the record is 35:07. The *Comet* averaged 185½ miles a day for the whole passage.

This was just a warm-up, however, for the next run over the same course. After a comparatively slow outward passage, Captain Gardner drove her home in the still unbeaten time of 76 days, 7 hours; on the way he set up the above mentioned record of 35:07 to Cape Horn. He consumed only 21 days and 19 hours from the equator to the Horn—extremely fast going. On the first page of the next chapter our diarist has mistakenly recorded the time of this passage as 73 days. At that, the *Comet* was within 220 miles of Sandy Hook in 73:18. The *Comet* seems to have been not only very fast herself, but also very lucky with her winds; for, few ships have turned in such a large number of exceptional performances. From New York Captain Gardner took her to Liverpool and sailed from there to Hong Kong in some indeterminate time approximating 84 days. Whatever the actual time was, it may have been the fastest ever; at any rate it was not far from it. On this occasion she attained the almost unbelievable average of 212 miles a day for the entire journey. No other ship has ever sailed at this rate of speed for such a length of time. On her way home she casually set the present record of 7 days from Hong Kong to Batavia. This latter city is on the island of Java close to Anjer, Sunda Strait, Java Head, etc. Thence the *Comet* went to Bremen in 91 days, and back to New York.

It would not be fair to the builders of the *Comet*, even to imply that Captain Gardner was in great part responsible for her remarkable speed. No ship will have such a career without an unusual master; but at the same time, neither can any captain obtain such results without an exceptional ship. The *Comet's* subsequent career establishes the speed of the ship itself. In 1855 Gardner was relieved as master of the *Comet* by Captain Arquit; as it happened, the latter had had the *Candace* too after Gardner had her. Under Arquit the *Comet* established the still unbeaten records of 14 days from the Atlantic equator to Sandy Hook, and 12 days from the Pacific equator to San Francisco. On the whole it is seen that the *Comet* came pretty close to being the fastest ship that ever sailed the seas.

She was sold in 1863 to British owners and was aptly renamed the *Fiery Star*. Her fate was a sad one; in 1865 she caught fire when 21 days out from Moreton Bay, Australia. Efforts to extinguish the blaze were fruitless and the boats were launched. These would hold only 80 persons and there were 98 aboard. The Captain, the passengers and some of the crew abandoned ship. The Mate and 17 others remained aboard. The boats endeavored to stay by the ship but had drifted out of sight by the following morning. Those remaining aboard continued for days to fight the fire, and were taken off by a passing vessel just before the old *Comet* went down. None of the boats was ever heard from again.

This brings us to the handsome clipper ship *Intrepid*, for she was the next command given to Captain Gardner by the owners. He held a part interest in her, besides. She was a medium clipper model and was built by Wm. H. Webb of New York who had also constructed Gardner's last two ships, the *Celestial* and *Comet*. Altogether, Webb built 138 vessels, totalling 177,872 tons. The *Intrepid* was one of only eight clippers completed in 1856 for the Cape Horn and China runs. Her tonnage was 1,173, length 179′ 9″, breadth 37′ 8″, depth 23′; a vessel of "style and distinction." Though he had sailed the *Comet* and others for many years, Captain Gardner claimed later that the *Intrepid* had never met her equal in sailing qualities. The following pages will convince the reader that there was some justification for this opinion.

Her maiden voyage, New York to San Francisco, was not auspicious. After its completion she was accused by a ship that had been in distress of not having given aid. Captain Gardner proved, however, that some other ship must have been the guilty one, since the *Intrepid* was a thousand miles away at the time. This first passage required 146 days. The time from Cape Horn to San Francisco was only 52 days, but 94 had been consumed in reaching the Horn. Next Captain Gardner took the *Intrepid* to Shanghai and from there made a round trip to India for rice. Soon after leaving Shanghai for New York he took 96 Chinese passengers off the wreck of the clipper ship *Waverly* and brought them in to Hong Kong. From there the *Intrepid* sailed to Sunda Strait in 20 days and to the Cape of Good Hope in 38 more. The total sailing time between Shanghai and New York was 110 days.

While Abbey was coming out in the *Henry Brigham* and then sailing to Honolulu in the *Francis Palmer*, Captain Gardner was bringing the *Intrepid* from New York to San Francisco. The time made by the *Intrepid* may have been 135 days—identically equal to that of the *Brigham*. So then, we find the *Intrepid* and Captain Gardner in San Francisco, and there Abbey ships under the famous master. The Chief, Second and Third Mates were Messrs. Hurd, Peterson and Croatman.

SAMUEL HALL
famous builder of clipper ships. The Surprise
was one of his products.

WILLIAM H. WEBB
who built the Comet *and* Intrepid *and 136
other vessels. Founder of the Webb Institute of Naval Architecture, The
Bronx, New York City.*

ROUNDING CAPE HORN

From a painting by W. N. Wilson reproduced in Cutler's Greyhounds *of the Sea.*

CHAPTER XIV

CAPE HORN AND TRAGEDY

MARCH 23ᵈ 1859

Went on board the Ship Intrepid Capt Gardner, bound for N.Y. Hauled out into the bay & anchored

Friday Mᴄʜ 25ᵗʰ 1859   Bay of San Francisco

Sailed from San Francisco   Homeward Bound
We had got ready to go & had the anchor apeak but the Captn not making his appearance we concluded not to leave him behind, so let everything sweat, and continue to do so as yet   The Intrepid is a fine ship of about 1200 tons register belonging to Buckland & Crane of N. Y. and commanded by Capt Gardner. She has just come out from home and is going back *"flying light"*   What sort of a passage we will make it is impossible to tell, but this Capt took the *"Comet"* home in 73 days, the quickest time ever made, so we talk of, & hope to, get home by the 4ᵗʰ of July. My old ship-mate Ned, shipped at the last moment, after trying ineffectually for a long time, of which I am glad. 3, o'clock P. M. Pilot & Capt having come on board we hove up the anchor & made sail   The wind being ahead we had to beat all the way through the *"Golden Gate"*. 12 oclock Midnight off North Head the pilot left us & we at once squared away for N. Y. It was our 8 hours out but the starboard watch of course had not had their watch below from 8 to 12 so it being now ours, we got to windward of them by going below besides having the forenoon watch below the next day

Saturday Mᴄʜ 26ᵗʰ 1859   off the coast of California

Nothing much to do. The old hands say that this Capt has no work done on Saturdays except slushing down* & cleaning out the forecastle.
8 months from home

Sunday Mᴄʜ 27ᵗʰ   Lat 32. 42   Course S S E

About as quiet a Sunday as ever I had at sea.

* *"Washing* down" (the decks) is undoubtedly meant here.

Monday Mch 28th 1859   Lat 28°. 14′.   Course S.S.E.
Contrary to all expectation we were not set at work

Tuesday March 29th 1859   Lat 24°. 26′   Course S.S.E.
Still nothing to do. The anchors are still on the rail, the fish
pendant aloft, and numerous other things are left undone which
in any ship on any voyage are done as soon as they get outside.
For instance the anchors are taken aboard and lashed on deck, the
fish pendant sent down below and the men kept busy all the time.
But we have nothing to do but trim sail & sit in the forecastle.
Night watches we turn out & dress ourselves & then turn in again,
if any thing is wanted the lookout calls us & we go & do it & then
come back & turn in. Some say that he means to put in somewhere
either to Callao or Valparaiso, but I dont hardly think that he
will for it would have been as easy to have shipped his men for
any place as N. Y. Yet the anchors &c look very suspicious. She
steers as wild as a kite & brings down more than a few curses on
herself

Wednesday Mch 30th 1859   Lat 20°. 06′.
Beautiful day as in fact all the days have been since leaving San
Francisco   Nothing to do but sit in the forecastle & once in a
while trim the yards   Course S.S.E.

Thursday Mch 31st 1859   Lat 16°. 56′
Fine day as usual & quite hot. Shin pants much in vogue. Commenced work at last by taking the anchors down on deck & stowing
them. Aftn began scrubbing & al *frescoing* the "*tween decks*"
with whitewash *beautiful!* white! Making 4 deg,s a day now by
means of a 4 knot current hereabouts*

Friday Apl 1st 1859   Lat 14°. 16 N.
Very much like all other fridays at sea   finished whitewashing the
tween decks

Saturday   Apl 2d 1859 Lat 10°. 48′ N.
Unlike some, Captn. Gardner takes every precaution to avoid
Scurvy among the men, consequently he gives them every Sat-
urday to clean out the forecastle & wash & mend their clothes. So

* The *Intrepid* averaged 10 knots for four days in succession, quite a good
performance. It is safe to say that no 4-knot current aided her for any such
length of time, if at all.

today we took every moveable out of our den & cleaned it thoroughly. During the melee I had the good luck to upset a *"whole pot of coffee"* in my bunk & my white blankets consequently present a *"Maroon"* appearance not at all to my liking. Well we cant complain. Seven days out last night at 12, & only 11° north* thats capital luck, every ship dont catch such a steady leading breeze as we have had Talking of fancy jobs, it aint every ship that allows one to spend every Sat forenoon aloft touching the sheaves of all the blocks with an oiled feather, this one does though Some have bets on the passage, & say we are going home inside of 100 days, others in 110 I say 115 to 120 which is I think the nearest to right. I should like to be home by the 4th of July but if the 20th sees me there I shall be satisfied. Every one is mending up their thick clothes to receive Cape Horn, once around & overboard they go, as thin duds will be the order of the day until we arrive. All hands having got the *"pricking"* mania I (perhaps foolishly) sat down & had a spread Eagle put into my arm, it is said by all to be very well done, but I cant see very well for myself. Course S.E. by S.

Sunday Apl 3d 1859 Lat 7°, 42′.

Beautiful day & a splendid breeze. Unlike any Captn I ever sailed with this one keeps continually bracing & squaring the yards when there is no change of wind at all. I almost begin to think that he means to *"fan"* her to N. Y.

Monday Apl 4th 1859 Lat 5°, some′

Our fine breeze which has not failed us for a moment since we left port, died away during the Morning & we are now laying almost becalmed & moved only by occasional "cats paws" Here I sit on the topgallant forecastle "having abandoned the forecastle itself as altogather to hot," & oh! how hot it is. I have just stopped sewing & Ned is sitting by me finishing up his. Oh what a stack he has got, he has let them go so long, shirts, pants, drawers, & jumpers, laying about him in heaps. We began to holystone this morning, but the Capt sent word for us to stop, as we made to much noise for his sick sister, who is aboard. We were all very glad of this & bless the lady for coming aboard, as holystoning is by no means an enviable job Oh how beautiful & still the sea is all

* The record from San Francisco to the equator is 11½ days.

around us   only moved by that long heavy ground swell always prevalent

Tuesday APL 5th 1859 Lat "all over"

No wind but any quantity of rain. Caught 3 or 4 casks full.

Wednesday APL 6th 1859 Lat, 4°, 12′

Head wind & quite enough of it too. This is a fancy ship,   for instance the Captn told a Dutchman (who cant talk English) that when he coiled up a rope he must have "each succeeding bight of a corresponding magnitude with its predecessor"   to all of which the dutchman replied "Yaw"

Thursday APL 7th 1859 Lat 3°, 26′ N

A very fine day   stopped raining early in the morning. Watch employed cleaning the between decks. A very light breeze enables us to make a little headway in a S. W. by S. course. Sighted the Southern Cross & had the North Star in sight at the same time, an unusual circumstance*

Friday AP– 8th 1859 Lat 2° 26′

Weather still fine   breeze rather stronger than yesterday. We generally on coming on deck at night lie down with our jackets for pillows & seldom stir *"tack or sheet"* until 8 bells sends us to our bunks,   thus not infrequently do we obtain 12 hours in. This is not the case on all ships.

Saturday APL 9th 1859 Lat

We are making preparations to shave "boy Joe" in accordance with the 2d mates orders, as we expect to cross the line today some time towards night. We have got the S. E. trades & are in a gay humor fore & aft   Towards evening the mate came forward & requested that we would do without that shaving   so boy Joe *of course* went clear. Crossed the line   Long 115°W.

Sunday APL 10th 1859 Lat 1°. 18′   Long 115° 10′

A beautiful day & a quiet one too.

Monday APL 11th 1859 Lat 2° 56′

At work in the *tween decks*. As the bell struck 4 (6 o'clock) it

* Not unusual. The feature here was the fact that the North Star was in sight from such a low latitude as 3°.

found the port watch playing *Euchre,*   there being nothing doing
we kept on although it was our watch on deck. All at once we
heard some one say "what are you doing with a light lit in that
port forecastle" "come out of that every one of you or Ill be in
there directly". So we came out & now have to stay on the poop
all our watch on deck

Tuesday APL 12th 1859 Lat 5°. 16′S. Long 116°. 10′ W
Cape Horn 56.27
Caught the S. E. trades and are now bounding along at the rate of
9 knots towards Cape Horn This day 3 years agone I commenced going to sea. I like it very well & but for some things I
should probably follow it up, I may still for all I can now fore-
see.

Wednesday APL 13th 1859 Lat 9°. 5′ S.
Nothing extraordinary happened, consequently I have nothing
extraordinary to note. I helped the carpenter readjust the force
pump & that is all I did do. How we do go though.

Thursday APL 14th 1859 Lat 12°. 27′ S
Down in the hold shifting dunnage all the forenoon. I feel quite
sleepy & dont know what to add more so Ill stop

Friday APL 15th 1859 Lat 16°. 18′ S
Only varied by a squall which carried away the fore royal sheet.

Saturday APL 16th 1859 Lat 19° 49′ S
Clear fine day. No part of the ocean is so pleasant as that where
the trades prevail one steady everlasting breeze always coming
from an inexhaustible source, and clouds of all shapes continually
rise, bank upon bank million upon million.

Sunday APL 17th 1859 Lat 22°. —′
The trades are somewhat abating & the wind is inclined to haul
although it has not done so yet. Trades all gone & any quantity
of head wind & rain are now our portion

Monday APL 18th 1859 Lat, dont° know′ S
Wind variable & baffling. At work in the between decks when not
hauling at the braces

[185]

Tuesday APL 19th 1859   Lat, cant° say'

Came in with strong gales & heavy rain. Took the top gallant sails during the forenoon, Upper topsails & jib in the aftn, Mizzen staysail & Mainsail towards night & finally the fore & mizzen topsail foresail, & foretopmast stay sail. Hove to all night, the wind blowing a hurricane & the rain falling in torrents.

Wednesday APL 20th 1859   Lat.no° idea'

Morning finds us in the same condition   The wind abating during the forenoon   made sail, only to take it in again as quick as the law allowed us. Night found us all tempest tossed, weatherbeaten, tired, & wet. I have not a dry suit to put on but turn in wet & turn out smoking. Oh its pleasant, and then to stand your regular two hours at the wheel with the sleet whipping your face, is pleasanter still

Thursday APL 21st 1859   Lat. somewhere about 30° S.

Wind abated during the night, & 6 oclock tonight found us once more under 3 royals   I should like to make some remarks concerning Capt Gardner but it is almost 8 bells, & my wheel, so I'll defer it until some future & more suitable occasion. Pitter, patter, I hear the rain on the decks so I must put on my oil skins & prepare for my two hours of *"grinding water,"* there goes the bell, Good night my friend

Friday APL 22d 1859   Lat about 29°, —', S.

Got tackles up & set up the fore & main rigging. Our watch had the forenoon on deck & as we kept all hands we were ALL DAY *on deck*. The old man is as grouty as possible. We finished the fore & main rigging.

Saturday APL 23d 1859   Lat 30° ——— S

Capt G. got out of bed wrong end first this morning & as he could find nothing else to snarl about, he set us to taughtening the rigging again, all of which we did.

Sunday APL 24th 1859 Lat 32° 20' S. Long 116° W.

Quite a fine day & fresh pork for dinner. There has been some complaint in regard to our bread & it was promised that we should have more of it, but it was not much larger than usual today notwithstanding.

Monday APL 25 1859 Lat, dont° know'

Very fine day with a fair wind & square yards. Capt G. in a fine humor. Towards night it began to breeze up & sprinkle & we took in the fore & mizzen royals & miz. topgallant sail. It rained very hard during the night

Tuesday APL 26th 1859   one month out and 34 on board

Morning found us under whole topsails & noon under 3 topgallant sails. It seemed inclined to rain & blow so we did nothing during the forenoon but the starboard watch went below to work after dinner.

Wednesday APL 27th 1859   Lat

Windy rainy squally weather. Nothing unusual to note. Several Cape Hens made their appearance

Thursday APL 28th   Lat

My 18th birthday. I got no presents & had no unusual fun, with the exception of some sugar which I hooked out of a barrel between decks. It was marked *"Crew"* so I had a right to it, although I suppose Capt G. would dispute it if he knew it. We caught 5 Albatrofs & one Moly Moke this morning, (as they & the Cape Pigeons have made their appearance in numbers), the largest of which measured 10 ft 6 in from tip to tip. Under close reefs all day

Friday APL 29th 1859   Lat

Oh, will we ever get out of the squally weather. Main topsail up & down 9 times per day, & a split 8 feet long in it at that.

Saturday APL 30th 1859   Lat.

Heavy windy weather. Got 3 whole topsails on her during the forenoon. Starboard watch are now engaged in bending a new main topsail, & a fine time they are having up there in the cold *"You bet"* Monotony varied by frequent hail squalls that cut through your skin

Sunday MAY 1st 1859   Lat 43°. 30'

Came in with strong gales from S.S.W. ship heading S.E. & going quite fast. Continual heavy squalls all day and night.

[187]

Clewed up the mizzen topsail and mainsail in the dog watch. Standing at the wheel the other night, with my head bent to windward to (in a measure) keep off the sleet I was somewhat surprised to hear a voice close by, which I instantly recognized as the mates, calling my name and asking if I had ever seen a *"corposant"* I replied in the affirmative whereupon he directed my attention to the trucks, above each of which was a ball of fire. As I looked they ascended a little then disappeared, to return again, and then disappear entirely. They are seldom seen except in a heavy shower, and when the atmosphere is overcharged with electricity as was then the case.

Monday MAY 2ᵈ 1859 Lat 47°. 22′ Long 96° —′ `

The heavy scotch mist that has prevailed for some days is growing heavier every hour. Set the main topgallant sail during the forenoon, & the fore & mizzen in the first watch Mr Hurd the chief mate is as fine a man as ever it has been my lot to meet. He always speaks kindly, never angrily, is a good sailor & an excellent officer, in fact what Capt G. would do without him I dont know for he sails the ship navigates her, & does everything that the Capt should, while he is below, instead of attending to his duties as he should. More of this anon

Tuesday MAY 3ᵈ 1859 Lat 49°. 18′

Dull heavy atmosphere & a very uncomfortable day. Watch variously employed. Wind continues from the west & southard. The mate said Sunday, that in 8 weeks we would be in N. Y. & that this wind would take us around the Horn Weather not so cold as it might be

Wednesday MAY 4ᵗʰ 1859 Lat 51°.06′ Long 90°

Clear fine day & *quite* cold. Ship heading E. S. E. with square yards & going at the rate of 7 or 8 knots. Watch employed, whitewashing in the lower hold. Dont feel like turning in, or like writing either, in fact, I dont know what to do, no sewing, to dark to read. Wish I had an oil Jacket, lost mine overboard the other day. Doubling the Horn without one, no joke. Guess I'll turn in. Adios.

Thursday MAY 5ᵗʰ 1859 Lat 52°—Long 86°

Squally day (so Bell says). Under fore & main topsail the last night, set the miz. during the forenoon. Some heavy hail squalls during the forenoon. Got under 3 topgallant sails during the night. Watch *employed* doing *nothing*.

Friday   May 6th 1859   Lat 54°=Long about 80°

Joe Purdy if you dont go and turn in I shant be able to write anything at all   You scoundrel I wont malign Joe Chaffers character for you   Capt Gardner has on two coats today, lemonading the quarter deck,   he thinks its very cold himself but dont think anything about a poor fellow at the wheel when he shivers & chatters his teeth as Joe Purdy does when he feels like it. The starboard watch have gone down in the hold to whitewash & some have mittens on. I guess they'll play Euchre instead of doing as Mr. Croatman thinks they do. Joe Purdy has been prompting me to all the above. Saw a sail for the first time   a clipper (Frisco bound) I suppose   Two days more of this breeze will take us into the Atlantic and clear of Cape Horn.

Saturday   May 7th 1859

Under 3 topsails all day & expecting to make the Horn every moment. Saw 2 sail & one light. To steer her now is almost impossible & every one comes from the wheel cross & mad. The mate told me that he guessed he'd have to make us an old wheel out of a flour barrel & let us practice in our watch below.

Sunday May 8th 1859   Off Cape Horn

Awoke this morning to find Hermits Island and Diego Ramirez off the weather beam distant six miles.* Upon sighting it we loosed the topgallant sails & got along as fast as we could. At 12 o'clock we were heading N. E. and the Cape to leward. At 6 we were heading N.N.W. with Cape Horn on the weather beam and a head gale beginning to blow. Such is the nature of this place; when almost in the other ocean a wind comes down from that side and beats you back again.

Monday May 9th 1859

Under the fore & main lower topsails and holding the helm down. Wind blowing great guns & it snowing very hard. Wore ship at 12

* Hermit I. is near Horn I. (Cape Horn), about 35 miles NE of the Diego Ramirez Is. The *Intrepid* probably sighted two of this latter group.

oclock & took the main braces to the capstan. Decks & rigging covered with ice. Almost impossible to stand up.

Tuesday MAY 10th 1859   Lat   dont know
Dark, cloudy, dreary, day, & very cold withal   Under very short sail & hove to. Wore ship twice. Unable to form any correct idea as to our whereabouts.

Wednesday MAY 11th 1859
Passed the Horn sometime during the night
Bitter, bitter, cold, & snowing very hard   The man at the wheel looks like a statue as he holds the helm down; his weather side covered with snow & ice; & the officer of the deck & man on the lookout move about like a pair of automatons; stamping their feet occasionally to keep the frost out. From calculation the Capt surmised that he was to the eastward of the horn & consequently he changed the course from E. to N.E. which with two points Easterly variation makes an E.N.E. course good; what confirms his opinion, was the fact that a little brig which we saw was standing to the westward on the wind, (S.S.W.) whereas had he been around the cape he would have made a fair wind of it & run her free. We rose her about 3 miles ahead & to leward & had a good view of her notwithstanding the snow was falling very, very, heavily. Oh what weather she was making of it   it seemed as if the water was continually pouring in at the bows & over the stern & sometimes she stood on her nose at an angle of 45 deg & vice, versa, (the other end). Our wake is full of Cape Pigeons,   they look like a cloud when they club together to settle down on some food. How handsome they are too, the prettiest sea bird that there is, & so lively   animated & quick. I wish I could get one home, but it is as impossible to carry them across the line as for a right whale to "the same"   The mate has a beautiful bird, that settled down on the rail exhausted. It is all white but the legs which are black & the beak which is black & yellow. He calls it a crow. Capt Gs sister & 3 children are aboard, (pafs.)   Mrs B. is very sick   in fact she came this way to try & recruit but for the last week we have expected to hear that she was dead,   the Capt & mate have their hands full as there is no woman on board to assist her, & consequently the carpenter has stood the mates watch,   thus we have a new officer

Thursday May 12th 1859 Lat 54°. 52′. Long 61°. 47′.

Having seen no land we are now sure of being to the eastward of
"Caphorn" & so stand N.N.E. (N E. good) Got the sun & found
our lat & long; as above. Constant squalls of snow hail &c pass
us, & pelt the poor fellow at the wheel unmercifully, & Oh! its
bitter cold. Toward evening it began to lull (please remember
that for the last 3 days it has been blowing as only Cape horn
can) & we got 3 topsails the foresail & mainsail on her but had to
stand by the halyards constantly. During the first watch set the
top gallant sails fore & aft, & during the mid watch the Main royal
which has not been aired for 20 days was sheeted home & hoisted
up. The weather suddenly became clear & mild at midnight & we
now consider our selves clear of the worst of the passage.
Course N.N.E.

Friday May 13th 1859 Lat 51°* —′ Long 58° —′

I have got out my writing materials, & dont know what to say. It
is always so, that is what makes my journal so uninteresting
Having been interrupted by a squall, I again resume my pen.
What to say I dont know so I'll stop.

Saturday May 14th 1859

Mrs Babcock our Capts sister, died at 12 o'clock at night just as
the bell struck 8. We have been expecting it for some time & consequently were not astonished

Sunday May 15th 1859

Carpenter at work preparing a coffin & the men employed tarring
canvass &c, as the capt intends to try & preserve her.

Monday May 23d 1859 Lat 33°. 58′ Long 31° 30′

60 days out and two months on board

Having had very unpleasant weather for the past week I have not
written up as usual. But to sum it all up we have been on our
course nearly all the time. Mrs B. was encased in blankets tarred
parcelling &c put in a coffin which was tarred & white leaded &
coppered outside then placed in another & buried in the ballast
in the lower hold. It has been reef & furl, loose & set all the while
but we are homeward bound so never mind

* It would seem that this should be approximately 54°.

[191]

Tuesday MAY 24th   Lat 27°. 54′ *
Fine night though marred by one squall which drove in our royals, & clewed down our fore & mizzen topgallant sails. I have nothing particular to note. The Capt. is in a good humor, & since his sister died "makes no bones" of carrying sail, a thing which he guarded against before, in order to keep the ship as steady as possible & consequently make it more comfortable for her. Commenced work again   Weather all at once quite warm. Wind N W to W, ship going at the rate of 8 & nearing home fast
Course N by E   ½ Point Westerly Variation

Wednesday   MAY 25th   1859   Lat 25°. —′. S.   Long
Nothing unusual occurred. Breeze fine   Weather delightful &c

Thursday   MAY 26th 1859
Caught the S. E. Trades & right hurriedly are they sending us along, although they are not so steady as is generally the case. Signalized an English Brig Belle of Dundas from London for Mahone Bay 47 days out   She was built of iron & evidently belonged to that class of vessels known as Aberdeen Clippers. As to her destination however we are in doubt   She showed 4283 which is Mahone Bay, while 4287 is Straits of Le Maire and if she were going to the before mentioned place she would scarcely be so far to the westward.†

Friday MAY 27th 1859   Lat 18°. 40′ S.
Beautiful day with strong trades. Work having again commenced we are all busy   some rattling down   some repairing the rigging some sailmaking & some tarring & refitting battens   to the latter gang I belonged & had the main under my supervision, as may be plainly perceived from the state of my hands which are of a dark maroon tint & feel like two pieces of sole leather but all traces of tar will be obliterated ere we arrive at our destination, which the captain says we will do in 25 days. Early this morning sighted a sail dead ahead   at first we gained on her then we did not & so it

---

* If this position and the preceding one are correct the *Intrepid* made at least 360 miles in 24 hours, an average of 15 knots—a splendid performance.

† "Mahone Bay" probably means "Mahonti" (Lourenco Marquez) on Delagoa Bay, in Portuguese East Africa. It is not at all unusual for sailing vessels bound around the Cape of Good Hope to be this far west in these latitudes. (See tracks of *Surprise* and *Intrepid* to the Far East, facing pages 29 and 205.) Also it would be unlikely for the "destination" of a ship to be the Straits of Le Maire.

continued all day long until at evening she was hull down off the weather beam we having changed our course from N by E to N ½ E.

Saturday MAY 28th 1859 Lat 14°. 12′ Long 30°. 30′ W.
Beautiful day again. Last night while carrying on the royals we were overtaken by a squall which threatened to take the sticks out of us, it was just 12 o'clock & the watch had just been called, but were not out of their bunks. The royals halyards were let go but the yards would not come down, & some *"Gilute"* let go the fore one's sheets before hauling down on the clewlines the consequence was that the buntlines slapped clean & clear over the top of the pole the weather sheet parted, (an occurrence which happened twice before today) & the yard became cockbilled (to use a sea faring term) & everything went wrong, one miserable soldier who belongs to the main royal shirked out of going aloft & as it happened I went in his place, to help Ned H. furl the sail. As a consequence I came down wet, mad, & furious, for there too everything went wrong the yard was not down & kept swinging up & down first jerking one lift & then the other, (please bear in mind that the mate observed today that "the lifts of the fore & main royal were both nearly gone") & the sail kept slapping one in the face so incessantly that you could do nothing but hold on in momentary expectation of going overboard

Sunday MAY 29th 1859 Lat 9°. 12′ *
Rainy squally windy &c. Nothing of note happened. Had fresh pork for dinner, & as there are several who have always played the grab game we all played it to day & stood outside waiting for a chance to dive As soon as I sighted the kid I made a rush & secured about 3 times my share in order to get even with the crowd. They understood it & no one asked me for any so Ned & I *"scoffed"* it between us

Monday MAY 30th 1859 Lat 6 21
Rainy squally day. Passed Cape St Roque with a land breeze which sent us along at a furious rate. The mate came to me on the lookout & told me to keep a bright lookout for land & Breakers, as we were in the vicinity of "Roccas" marked "dangerous" on the charts. We did not see them however but by the morning had the

* Another fine day's run—more than 300 sea miles.

trades again having cleared the land. It was not to be seen but judging from our olfactory's we could not have been more than 10 or 15 miles from it*

Tuesday MAY 31st 1859 Lat 3°. 20′

Fair day comparatively. Nothing of note occurred during the day. But in the night the 2d mate had some words with one of his men & struck him whereupon Bill, told him that if he did it again he'd "rip his guts out," the 2d officer called Capt Gardner & they put Bill in irons & stowed him down aft on the Port side.

Wednesday JUNE 1st 1859 Crossed the line

This morning Mr. Croatman found Bill had got over on the starboard side close to some liquor that was open, & in endeavoring to put him back Bill drew his knife on him, the consequence was Mr Bill had his irons taken off & his arms clasped around a stanchion & then the irons on again so that he cant get far just now. This ship keeps her name for luck good, for the S. E. Trades have hauled around to N. E. & here we are going it towards home & north of the line

Crossed the line in the Atlantic Long 38° or 40°

Thursday JUNE 2d 1859 Lat 1° 12′ N

The N E. breeze which we hoped was a trade wind has failed us & we are now becalmed in a measure & dependant upon the current from the river Amazon (which it is plain we are in both from the distance we go without any wind and from the color of the water) which runs here at the rate of 2 or 3 knots per hour†

Friday JUNE 3d 1859 Lat 2° 20′ N Long about 40°.

Beautiful day for those who are not in a hurry & can find a dry place to stay in. It has been nothing but squalls since last night & rainy ones at that. Every light suit I have is wet & I am soaked. I "turn in wet" & turn out smoking" & to tell the truth I feel pretty stiff.

Saturday JUNE 4th 1859 Lat 4°. 40′ N

Calm & placid as usual and no squalls either of wind or rain, had

* Often land can be smelled distinctly, many times this distance.

† This would be the Great Equatorial Current—flowing toward the Amazon mouth at this point, not away from it.

bath in the evening & then tried to catch some "Portugese men o' war" fleets of which we were sailing through all the time. They were the largest & most beautiful I ever saw some of them would spread a sail in the shape of Queen Vic's crown about 4 inches high by 6 or 7 broad* the color is a strange though most beautiful (especially when the sun is just below the horizon) mixture of purple, pink, sea blue, green, & white. I got a bucket & was about to catch one with it when the 2ᵈ officer told me not to put a wooden bucket over the side but to take the draw bucket. Consequence as might be supposed, draw bucket to small mouthed and so I got none

Sunday June 5ᵗʰ 1859 Lat 6°. 00′ N
A beautiful day and the real, veritable, N.E. trades to brighten it. Nothing but reading & tract distributing going on. A glorious sunset ended the day, all of which I viewed while eating my supper upon the topgallant forcastle.

Monday June 6ᵗʰ 1859 Lat 8°. 00′ N Long 45° W
Fine day and a good breeze. Men at work scraping & tarring down

Tuesday June 7ᵗʰ 1859 Lat 11° 30′ Long 50° 30′
Weather as usual, and wind also men at the same work

Wednesday June 8ᵗʰ 1859 Lat 14° —′ Long 56° —
No deviation

Thursday June 9ᵗʰ 1859 Lat 17°. 20′ N Long —
All e same

Friday June 10ᵗʰ 1859
A day corresponding with the 3 foregoing

Saturday June 11ᵗʰ 1859
Fine weather

Sunday June 12ᵗʰ 1859
No deviation

* Evidently argonauts (paper nautiluses) rather than Portuguese men-of-war.

Monday JUNE 13th 1859
All the same

Tuesday. JUNE 14th 1859 Long 69°. — W Lat 28°. 30′ N
A Fine day with the men at work painting scrubbing &c preparatory to entering port, a manouvre (which if this breeze continues)
we will perform within 4 days

Wednesday JUNE 15th 1859 Lat 30. 15 N Long — W
Beautiful day & a splendid breeze ship going it like mad.

Thursday JUNE 16th 1859 Lat 32°. 12′ Long —
Commenced holystoning & finished up the poop "Very vile"
vewy" extheedingly tho" Breeze holds as yet.

Friday JUNE 17th 1859 Lat 34°. 58′ Long 73°. 30′
Began by holystoning the topgallant forecastle. 9½ A.M. struck
an awful ragged chop, jig a jig, sea and at the same time struck
into a breeze which was somewhat fresh 12, M Mr Hurd called
me aft to draw some water, & he thereby ascertained that we were
in the gulf stream (Temp. of the water 83°. Farenheit) turned
in in the aftn & was rousted out at 3½ P.M. to help take in sail.
We got a smell of Cape Hatteras & a rough one too. Wind hauled
around to the westward & once we thought we should make a head
wind of it but we were only knocked off a point after all
Seeing vessels every day

Saturday JUNE 18th 1859 Lat 37. 42 N Long 74°. 33′ W
Six sail in sight at daylight. We are fast leaving them. Went to
the wheel at 6 oclock & found her full & by heading N by E.
I had not been there ½ an hour before I had brought her up to
N by W, her course. All of which Capt Gardner said I must do
If I wanted to go to church tomorrow afternoon Got the anchors
on the bows

Sunday JUNE 19th 1859 Lat 39°. 29′ Long 74°. 00′
A beautiful day but scarcely any wind. Pilot boat 16, that has
been hanging around us all night, succeeded this morning in putting a pilot on board of us, who brought papers of the 15th the
day before he left. We have any quantity of sails in sight & Little

Egg harbor beacon looms up on our port bow like the Bunker hill monument. At 12 today we were within 65 miles of Sandy Hook & are now praying for a breeze to carry us in. As soon as the pilot came on board he addressed the capt as follows. *"Well, Capt, where's your stun'sails, down below! you'd better get them up, Capt. Dont carry them sir, get along faster without. Impossible! what do you find for your men to do. Oh, we manage to keep, them busy &c. &c."* And indeed we do get along faster than anything we have seen as yet and are passing all the vessels in sight, although they all have stun'sails set.

Monday J UNE 20th New York Harbor

Home again once more. Oh it is a miserable day. Raining & chilly withal Made The Narrows at daylight got the health officer at 5 o'clock. Steamboat Jacob Bell, same time & to the Wall St ferry (Brooklyn) at 9 A.M. when we knocked off & went ashore, considering that we had fulfilled our agreement & brought the *boat* home & tied her up alongside of the *"Great Republic"*. I find that the Henry Brigham is not in.

Friday J UNE 24th 1859

Went to Rondout on the *Tom Powell* & found D. waiting for me with the carriage & about 10 fellows whom I had not forgotten *"You Bet"*

CHAPTER XV

A SHORT RUN ON SHORE

ON June 20 when the *Intrepid* docked, the diary mentions the *Great Republic* and the "steamboat" *Jacob Bell*. The latter was named after the famous shipbuilder, as was the clipper ship of the same name. This steamer is, with little doubt, the same one that saw such active gunboat service in the Civil War as the U. S. S. *Jacob Bell;* for, when war broke out, the Navy took over this latter vessel at New York as a "tug."

The *Great Republic* was, by a wide margin, the largest clipper ship ever built. The vessel mentioned here was the rebuilt edition of the "first *Great Republic*" which caught fire at the dock and had to be sunk before she ever hoisted a sail. Even this cut-down "second" ship registered 3,356 tons. She was 335 feet in length and drew 25 feet of water, which draft often necessitated the use of lighters in handling her cargo. In 1856–7, three years after the original launch, she made her first run from New York to San Francisco. And it was a remarkable one. Without delay she established a record that still stands—15 days, 18 hours from Sandy Hook to the equator. On the fifth day she made 413 miles. For a 19-hour period on that day she averaged 19 knots! On the last leg of the passage she was within 500 miles of San Francisco in 87 days and so had a fine chance at the record of 89 days. She required 5 days more, however, to reach port. Even so, her run from the equator was made in 19 days, a feat which she performed three times altogether.

The *Intrepid* had just completed a splendid passage, having sailed from San Francisco to New York, anchor to dock, in 86 days, 18 hours. Although this is not a record, it is 62 hours better than the fastest run ever made in the other direction—or 68 hours faster, allowing for the 3 hours difference in time each way. And this performance was made, it will be remembered, without any crowding of sail during the first 50 days—i.e., until the death of Captain Gardner's sister.

This was such a fine passage, made by such a fine ship, that it might be of interest to analyze it and compare it with the best ones of all. Ordinarily it was not quite such a feat to get around the Horn from west to east as it was from east to west. This was not Abbey's experience; but westerly winds are to be expected there more often that easterlies. Accordingly, for times, the San Francisco–New York passages are divided up a little differently from the westbound ones. In order to tabulate the exact number of hours for the different sections of the *Intrepid's* run, it is necessary to make a few slight assumptions as to the exact hours at which she passed certain points. Therefore, from the text of the diary, it has been assumed that the *Intrepid* crossed the Pacific equator at 6 P. M., April 9, 1859; passed Cape Horn at 12 P. M., May 10; crossed the Atlantic equator at 9 A. M., June 1; and took her New York pilot at 9 A. M., June 19. In each case the hour is believed to be very close; the dates are exact.

First of all, then, we shall compare each section of the *Intrepid's* passage with the fastest time recorded for that section.

	Intrepid	Record	Made By
San Francisco to Pacific Equator	15:03	11½	*Flying Dutchman*
San Francisco to Cape Horn	46:09	35:07	*Comet* (Capt. Gardner)
Cape Horn to New York	40:09		
Cape Horn to New Point, Va.		37	*Flying Mist*
Atlantic Equator to New York	19		
Atlantic Equator to Sandy Hook		14	*Comet*

This form of tabulation naturally has an appearance unfavorable to the single ship. Let us make a more fair comparison by setting the *Intrepid's* whole passage against the fastest whole passage (*Comet*), each one divided up into sections. This tabulation constitutes a real saga of Captain Gardner for he was in command on both occasions! This passage of the *Comet* included the San Francisco–Cape Horn record listed just above.

	Intrepid	*Comet*
San Francisco anchor to Pacific Equator	15:03	13½
San Francisco pilot to Pacific Equator	14:18	
Pacific Equator to Cape Horn	31:06	21:19
Cape Horn to Atlantic Equator	21:09	26
Equator to New York	19:00 (dock)	15 (anchor)
San Francisco anchor to New York pilot	85:18	
San Francisco pilot to New York pilot	85:09	76:00
San Francisco anchor to New York	86:18 (dock)	76:07 (anchor)
San Francisco pilot to New York dock	86:09	

This is mighty fast sailing. It will be noted that it was between the Pacific Equator and Cape Horn that the *Intrepid* fell behind. It is reasonable to assume that the sickness of Captain Gardner's sister held the *Intrepid* back in this stormy section more than in any other.

Abbey was still far from through with the speedy *Intrepid* and her famous master. Only a month after reaching New York we find all three of them together again. The *Intrepid* is anchored in New York harbor off Bedloe's Island on which the Statue of Liberty stands. This time she is bound for Shanghai, the most distant of the important Chinese harbors. Practically every member of the crew has shipped again. One of the mates and several of the men had been with Captain Gardner for years, and his Chinese steward had sailed with him since boyhood. Abbey starts this voyage with a new ledger, a third one. His diary is inscribed in ink, inside of a left-hand marginal line, and the handwriting is still better than before, as he advances toward manhood. As we start this next part of the diary we find the *Intrepid* awaiting the "steamtug *Underwriter*." This is with little doubt the same vessel that later became the U. S. S. *Underwriter*, the little steamer with such an eventful Civil War record; for she was taken over by the Navy in New York in 1861. Strange to say, she engaged in many operations with the *Ceres*, the tug which took Abbey's ship down New York harbor on the voyage before this one. In 1864 the *Underwriter* was captured temporarily and burned by a body of Confederates in small boats—one of the most thrilling of the minor naval exploits of the Civil War.

CHAPTER XVI

"JOURNAL OF A VOYAGE IN THE SHIP INTREPID"

Tuesday July 26th 1859   New York Harbor

Having hauled into the stream yesterday & anchored, we expect the steamer hourly. 10½ A.M. Steamtug Underwriter came alongside with the captain, pilot, & my father, brother, Ned H. Hen S. & Geo B. on board. As I passed the Capts things on board he requested me to be careful of his wife whom I held in a piece of paper in my hand. The wind being ahead the tug could not come alongside but had to go ahead of us, consequently I was obliged to bid my friends good bye, which I did with a very bad grace, for never did I leave home so reluctantly before. I have been but a month ashore, but in that short time I have enjoyed myself so well that I was inclined to stay ashore. But as the song runs "when duty calls we must away." They went off in a small boat & kept waving their hats to me & I returning the compliment as long as I could distinguish. The last glimpse I had of them the boat it was going in at the Hamilton ferry. At that sight my spirits fell, as I thought how long it would be, & what changes might take place ere I saw them again. Oh! I cant write much   It is now Wednesday night & to sum it all up we discharged the pilot & steamer at 3 P.M. & clapped on every stitch we could carry. At sunset we lost sight of the Nevesink Highlands, but I kept looking in their direction long after they had disappeared & thought & thought & ——— but no matter what I thought, I may recur to it some time or other. I am in the starboard watch & have (my usual good luck) the best bunk in the forecastle. I wonder what my friends are doing, now, tonight   I hope they are thinking of me. Bell has just come in & wants to know if I have his name in here yet.

Wednesday July 27th 1859

Begins with fine breezes from the northward & continues fine throughout. Got the anchors in & stowed them. I stood my wheel & put on two battens today & that is all I have done or been asked

to do. But it is most 2 bells & I must not keep this light burning
any longer so good night & pleasant dreams

Yours &c C.A.A.

Thursday JULY 28th 1859

A beautiful day & a light breeze, every thing goes smooth & easy.
It is the same old Intrepid yet. Somehow or another, as I stood
at the wheel my thoughts would revert homeward & I wished myself at New York again & again until I found myself 2 points off
my course & going farther rapidly. I soon brought her back however & was more watchful after. Mr Peterson (2^d Officer) sat
down on the break of the cabin at one bell & stuck his left leg out
at me, a proceeding which I was at a loss to understand until he
told me to pull it, *"he is rather Rheumatic."* Being A. B. now I
dont have to run at the cry of "Lay aft here one of you boys."
Mr P seems bent on giving me all the chance in the world to improve & has me knotting splicing serving & seizing, all the while,
at which I am very well pleased for this is my last voyage "before
the mast" if I cant help it. We saw no vessels today. I have not
troubled myself about the Lat. & Long. as yet for I know we
are but 2 or 3 days distant from N. Y.

Friday JULY 29th 1859   Somewhere due East of N. Y.

Almost a week out & we have made little or no southing. It is the
same old Intrepid yet, I find. Everything is quiet, & every one
satisfied, work goes on but with such smoothnefs that you are
not aware of its progrefs until it is completed   Mr Peterson the
2^d officer in whose watch I am, is every whit as good as Mr Hurd
the 1st mate used to be & is still. We have had head winds for two
days, but the weather has been pleasant all the time & we have not
lowered a royal since we set them off the *"Hook"* Capt G. is himself again & airs himself at certain times on the poop. We have
one pafs, his nephew. A New cook has made *some* alteration in our
food, not in regard to quantity or quality, but *style.* We have two
green hands, *boys,* who have not yet got over sporting 2 or 3 suits
of clothes per day, so they are regularly conned, quizzed, &
"codded" as they come on deck at 8 bells. The week notwithstanding it is the first has passed quickly, as, I hope will the rest.
I am looked up to as a sort of an oracle in any question about the
ship having been in her before. Our watch are all good natured
kind & obliging fellows, mostly foreigners who have not been in

many American ships long. We have some from every place almost one from a slaver, & another from the Rifle Brigade of India, he regaled us all with an a/c of his adventures, a few nights since, & was very interesting withal.

Saturday Aᴜɢ 6ᵗʰ 1859   Lat about 32 ᴺ

We have just finished washing down & altho' my watch on deck I have nothing to do as this day of the week is a holiday here I have been disabled for 3 or 4 days which accounts for my not writing before. Wednesday while setting up the head gear, I put a strap & tackle upon the weather Martingale back rope to take the strain of the lanyard while we unrove it. Having done so, I proceeded to put another upon the lee one. I was standing down under the bow (almost down to the water) upon the bowsprit shroud, with one hand I held myself & the end of the strap to the backrope while with the other I passed the turns, at this moment the weather lanyard parted & of course the lee backrope gave a quick short jerk, which quick short jerk taking effect upon the subscriber threw his shoulder out of joint in considerable lefs time than it has taken him to relate the occurrence So I have been carrying my arm in a sling for a short time. There goes 7 bells & that rascally port watch will make so much noise that I cant continue at present.

Sunday Aᴜɢ 7ᵗʰ 1859

3 oclock P. M. All is quiet it is my watch below, & my watchmates are all in their bunks & asleep with the exception of Alex who is swallowing the remains of his dinner. The day is beautiful with scarce any wind at all. Saw a sail this morning full rigged ship on the wind *homeward* bound. I know not what to add and as I look around I can see nothing but *Ned* Capt G's nephew a passenger with us climbing around the mizzen channels, & Capt G. standing in front of the cabin attitude a'la Napoleon I occupy the most of my spare time, reading and so do the rest. A Frenchman in our watch assists me greatly in some of Chas Levers works by interpreting for me all that I cant understand. A thunder shower passed over us last night between 2 & 4 o'clock accompanied by 4 of the most vivid flashes of lightning I ever saw.—and I've seen some terrific ones—they began by an awful blinding flash which hissed & crackled & trembled & quivered for an instant that seemed (as I stood at the wheel) an hour in each instance. The first came

so unexpectedly that Mr Peterson fell back upon a ventilator by my side & had not the wheel box supported me I should have fallen too as it was it startled the breath out of my body, & I listened to hear the crashing of spars as they fell, for I thought most assuredly that it had struck our vessel but we escaped without injury (If I except a severe drenching which I received) either from wind, water, or what was worse fire in the shape of Lightning. My arm still perseveres in feeling lame & wont consent to be raised above a level with my shoulder. I wonder where we are on the map of the world it is a question which has scarcely presented itself since leaving. Lets see Long must be about 50° W. It is 3½ P. M. about 2 o'clock in N. Y. & R. Pa is either at home or in B. taking dinner. Uncle G. Aunt S. & Dave are reading in the old hall, Willie is 'I *dont know where*,' and I am in the starboard forcastle of the Intrepid sitting near the door inditing this epistle. Oh how I should like to be in either of the first two places for 5 or 6 hours at the least, just to see & talk with the folks & take tea, but, Alas, I must travel to China & back full 40,000 miles,—and how much farther God & the owners know,—before I can see one relation. Oh I wish Ned H. had come this time, I have no one to talk to & that is the worst for me. There are boys on board to be sure but they are such as I cannot sympathize with or talk to as I would like to, and save Bell, I have no one who I am willing to call *"friend"* in the whole ship. He is a real good kind wholesouled fellow, (not as people on shore believe, as sailors go) but a good hearted generous friendly young man who can talk & reason on *most* common subjects as well as any one & Is always ready to assist me or back me in any thing I propose if it meets his approbation independant

Friday Aug 12th 1859 Lat Long

The wind which has been ahead for some days has veered a little & we are now almost able to lay course. We met a ship Sunday night & passed so close that we could hear the officer of the deck sing out "C-o-m-e, bring that light aft here, one of *you*" & judging from his tone he was not in the best of humors We have seen several sails lately, the last a little brig, which we met last night. Bell caught a small Dolphin a few days ago & while carrying him in his flesh tore out & he got away again. We were more successful with Bonita & had a supper of them the other night. My chum (Bell) has been *"barberizing"* some lately, on all who have been

[206]

green enough to let him practice, he has left his mark. Thus one has a crofs on the back of his head, anothers looks as if some amateur farmer had been mowing on it & so on, every one marked My arm troubles me some yet, & when it pains I wish I was home where it could be taken care of. Oh these old sailors, I wish they would *turn in*, but no; there they sit, sewing, & talking about Australia (they have been in the mines) & burning Chinese gambling houses, & driving the Celestials out of the diggings. The breeze is freshening & there goes 4 bells so Au Revoir.

Cha's A Abbey

Tuesday Aug 16th 1859   Lat 18°. —   Long 40°. —

Going our course at the rate of 8½ knots   the wind has lulled & we are of course not thumping into it quite as much as we have been for the last week or so. I know not what to say, every day brings the same things again, working about decks, serving, tarring, &c, &c. We have easy enough times though & if there was food to match would be quite contented. I heard something about the Lat. & Long. yesterday which are something like the above. I have been aloft since 6 o'clock, up in the miz. topgallant rigging. Oh, dear. I aint very well & dont feel comfortable. Lets see, beans for dinner=nothing for dinner   my next wheel, oh, well not so bad after all   I've got but 2 hours to work to' day & then I'll have a supper that I can eat & relish too. No, by thunder, its too bad, today is pork day (I dont like pork) & I can get no beef, so I must hold on,   lets see   tomorrow is Wednesday, Rice, it would be good but that blasted steward is so afraid of his molasses that it is never sweet enough   So to morrow "brings no comfort". Well Thursday, Ah! ha! *"Duff & Applesauce"* & a plenty of it too, & well there need be, for, from then until Sunday we get comparatively nothing & from Sunday until Thursday ditto again. Oh well   I have stood it 3 years & I am now on my last quarter, I hope. So that after this voyage I shall go where I have good food and sleeping apartments at the least. Oh, twould make an Epicures mouth water to see the cabin dinner sometimes. I've a notion to waylay the steward & steal it. Oh, no, though, never do, one week in irons, & a very unenviable time of it for the rest of the voyage, never do; would it   C A A

Friday Aug 19th 1859   Lat about 11° or 12° N.

Well here I sit again pen in hand, & thoughts everywhere but

[207]

where I want them to be. We have lost the trades & for the past 24 hours we have experienced genuine *"doldrum"* weather, though just now we have a fine breeze from the S. W. but it is not likely to last long. I hear from the mate that we are not going through Angier but around the *south* of Java *via* Straits of Balba,* then outside of Borneo, the Phillipines, Loo Choos, &c up through the Pacific Ocean, instead of the China Sea By doing so we lengthen the passage some thousands of miles† but expect to make up for it by having fair winds. It will take us about 140 or 50 days, but we might be more the other way, as we have the N. E. Monsoons strong against us not to speak of short tacks, & a head current.‡ Oh how hot it is you may see the bottom of the page is wet from the perspiration which is constantly rolling off me. We jog along much as usual, being occupied mostly in making mats & cotton swabs the mats to keep the tea chops (or boats) from rubbing the paint off our sides, the swabs to rub the coal dust off the inside after unloading. Oh I cant write with this *"hubbub"* all around me

Friday Aug 26th 1859   Lat 3°. 00′ N

One week to journalize. Now let's see what has happened. We have had a head wind for the most of the time & plenty of it, (that is for our purposes) so we thump along first on one tack then on the other making something all the time. Signalized a Portuguese ship standing E.N.E. on Tuesday last. He ran up his Ensign & "Whats your Longitude per Chronometer" in answer to our Ensign. We answered 31° 20′ he then ran up "Wish you a pleasant voyage." fearing that he would get out of sight before he knew who we were the mate ran up our numbers, to which he answered "Wish you a pleasant voyage" again, & more he seemed disinclined to show although there were 6 or 7 passengers officers &c on his poop. Consequently we by unanimous consent denominated him a *"Muggins"* & as we couldnt well help it let him go. The capt is in a bad humor & the officers not daring to take any responsibility on themselves dont know what to do with us, so we have been scraping

* Bali? The straits of Bali are at the eastern end of Java. This would be no suitable point, however, at which to pass through the chain of islands composed of Sumatra, Java, etc. As a matter of fact the *Intrepid* went through the Ombay Pass, 600 miles farther east.

† Roughly 1,500 miles longer.

‡ The current would be with them, not against them.

old iron & blocks for a week or more, to while away the time. The weather is pleas   . I broke my pen & could not proceed last Friday

Sunday Aug 28th 1859 Sighted the rock of St Pauls 55′. 5″ north of the line and 29° 13′ West of Greenwich

Wednesday Aug 31st 1859

Last Saturday forenoon we raised a brig standing N & E, he was hardly out of sight when we sighted a large ship on the weather beam. From appearances he could not lay so near the wind as we & consequently was coming to leward gradually, & at the same time ranging ahead some   Towards dusk raised a schooner stng NE by E, he ran up under our lee & showed a board with 26°. 15′ on it to which Capt G. answered "Aye, Aye," & hailed "Where are you bound" Ans. "London" & then he asked "What ship is that," Ans. "Intrepid." "Where bound" Ans *"Shanghae"* Our speed was so great that by this time we were out of hail. And he kept away course having luffed to speak us. He showed Danish colors but as they have no fore & aft'ers he must belong to St Thomas besides he was American built Sunday morning discovered our large antagonist on the weather Quarter & farther to leward. As soon as the sun rose he began to overtake us, as our sails were dry & the wind had not so much effect on them as in the damp night air. He proved to be an American Frigate but where he was bound or where he was from his name or any thing more he would not or could not (perhaps the latter) answer. So "as we could not well help it" we let him go, and he went, away off to leward & finally clewed up his royals, though why I cant conceive for we experienced no change of wind, although we were to windward. The mate from observations through the glass thought he was getting his anchors on his bows, if that is so he must intend making a land fall soon As the wind has hauled around into the S.E. trades we are steering full & by & lay SW & SW by S most of the time

Wednesday Aug 31st 1859 "Continued"

Tuesday morning we got up our starbd cable & whitewashed it & its locker 10 A.M. Raised the Island of Ferdinand de Noronha & had it in sight the remainder of the day. It is in some places very pretty & green & in others barren & rocky especially the N. W. &

[209]

S. E. extremities. I should think it was about 25 miles long &
10 or 12 broad   in shape it is something like this

The Southern end is low & the Northern is high   the most striking
feature is the highest peak upon it, which I should call (if allowed
to name it) Finger Rock from its resemblance to a mans hand
with the index finger pointing towards the heavens. It may have
been created so to warn humans from coming there, for It was
formerly the "Brazilian Convict station" but as every one died
that went there, (from its sickly climate) they changed it to some
more healthy spot. I took a sketch (an indifferent one) of it as
we passed. At 4 oclock signalized a Yankee barque steering E.
During the night it came on squally & we had the royals in & out
once or twice. I have more to say but it is most 8 bells so I will
defer it till some other time although I have not had a better
opportunity to write since I have been aboard as every one is in
his bunk & asleep   the weather not being of the pleasantest
description

Thursday   Sept 1st 1859   Off Cape Blanco

Began by tacking ship at 4 o'clock, having shoaled our water
suddenly. Sounded & got 20 fathoms (white sand). Stood E by N.
2 hours & tacked again, laid S.S.W. & thought it would do. 8
oclock A.M. Sighted the Main land dist 20 or 25 miles. No royals
on, today   the breeze being quite stiff. Capt Gardner I guess feels
rather chagrined at having got to leward although it doesnt
amount to much after all   We cant be far from Pernambuco   I
wish he would call for a day or two   Still later. Were called out
at 10½ A. M. to tack ship, the land being distant only 4 miles
(Cape Blanco), steep part)   We are midway between Pernambuco & Paraiba. It is low & sandy   the highest part of the cape
being only 250 or 300 ft above the sea   It's face is yellow & red &
its top covered with trees which in one particular spot take the
appearance of a huge camel lying down. I heard nothing during
my watch below save the talk of an enthusiastic young man belonging to the port watch who was continually wondering if, &

wishing that some "*Catamarans*" might come off to us. Perhaps you dont know what a "Catamaran" is, so for your benefit I will explain. These natives being too poor to buy & not ingenious enough to make boats, they lash 5 logs to-gether & hew them sharp at one end, Put an enormous sail on them & perched high above the foundation on a sort of chair venture miles & miles out of sight of land in quest of fish. Ships not unfrequently meet fleets of them, when forced in shore as we have been

Friday SEPT 2ᵈ 1859 Lat   Long

Capt G. began this day *for us* by having us (Starboard watch) called at the very unseasonable hour of 5½ oclock to put the ship about. We lead a very pleasant life on the whole, not having a great deal to do. If I have the forenoon watch on deck I am not as a general thing set to work before one bell & the time (4 hours) slips along quite pleasantly in yarning & listening to Yarns spun by veteran "Yarners" then I have the Aftn below until 4 oclock when I again come on deck but only to put away the tools & work which may have been under way, which occupies us until 2 bells (5 o'clock) & then the other watch are all sitting about eating their suppers & talking & Yarning again with us. Then 4 bells strikes & I get my supper after which I take a hand at whist, Euchre or 7 up. Or else join the singers on the forcastle. They meet every night & commencing with soft melancholy & affecting songs continue until 6 bells when they take to a different kind sometimes touching on the operatic this continues until 7 bells when having but a half hour more they take to the noisy & laughable. Presently 8 bells strikes & then as a cap sheaf (or binder as D. calls it) all join in the chorus of "*Rink a chu link chu link chu la &c*" or "*Johnny stole a Ham*" and the echoes might be heard from Cape St Roque to Staten Land so loud do they come in with the last "*Down in Alabam*" We have French, Dutch, & swedish songs besides. It is most 7 bells, the watch will soon be called to breakfast, & then what with Chattering Frenchmen garrulous Scotchmen loquacious Dutchmen & Acquiesant Swedes I shall be unable to continue. "*So good morning*" C.A.A.

Saturday SEPT 3ᵈ 1859 Lat   Long

General washing & cleaning day but that never occupies us more than an hour & so we have the rest of the day to ourselves unless there is sail to trim.   Now let me see this is Friday the 9th & I cant think of anything of note that has happened & now that I am trying to write   that *"Jimmy Green"* is at me to play Euchre & he wont stop till I give in. We are very hard up for work & as a consequence are a great part of the time idle. The trades have flown (did so last night) & we are now steering S.S.E. full & by. I wonder what Dick thinks of it now. I remarked to him the other night that having got the trades north of the line they would not hold lower than 23° or 25°   He contradicted & wanted to bet me that we would have them down to 30°. and now they're gone and we are about 19° or 20° S. Two Cape Pigeons made their appearance this morning   a sure sign that we are getting towards cool weather.

S.   W

Tuesday Sept 20th 1859   Lat 37°. 30′   Long 6°. 00   Course S. W.

Seventeen days behind & no excuse to offer. We have had fair winds all the time (& plenty of it too) but have not had the fore topsail in *yet*, although it was rather doubtful a few nights since what we should do with it. The weather from hot, has changed to cold, & monkey jackets & mittens are in requisition. The only warm place aboard is at the wheel & there I tell you, it is warm enough work to keep her within two points of her course. Well, we are nearly two months out & everything prospers & goes as smooth & easy as *"rolling off a log"*   We have been put on allowance of water and have had to *see to* the cook lately as our water "began to have a habit of failing before 4 o'clock." We have also unshipped our spanker boom & bent a new spanker without any boom at all, which same spanker we had to alter twice before it would set well. Two of our 3 kittens have *"kicked the bucket"* & the remaining one is now over my head in my bunk singing out like a good fellow for me. This weather reminds one of *"Caphorn"*. Cold, dismal, dreary, ship covered with water continually, steering bad, fellows fishing for Albatross & Cape Pigeons, which abound in millions   By the way   we shipped one particular sea last night which comencing abaft the main rigging, deluged the decks all the way forward not forgetting the lookout whom it soaked, nor yet the galley door which it teetotally smashed without the least bit of ceremony. And yet it was no larger than the common run which board us. 3 bells   good aftⁿ

[212]

Monday S<small>EPT</small> 26th 1859   Lat 41°.00′   Long 18°.00′

Well according to my reckoning we are just about off the pitch
of the Cape.* The gale subsided some 4 days since, & we have had
the wind from the Northward, all the intervening time. The birds
will not bite, why we dont know but perhaps it is because it is almost breeding time   Today the sun is warming us up finely, & the
wind has just hauled around to the quarter. Our cards are all used
up & Euchre is at a Discount. Consequently we have taken to Qua-
drilles & Schottisches, for Amusement   And one infatuated individual has bought the carpenters fiddle to learn to play. He
knows about as much about Music as Music does about him, yet
you can at any time hear him scraping away on his "Cat's Entrails" Item. The last kitten died three days ago. And now we
are left with only two old cats that do incessantly fight & squall.

Friday S<small>EPT</small> 30th 1859   Well Around the Cape

One O'clock P. M. Very little wind, perhaps none at all, cloudy &
dreary, just cold enough to be uncomfortable. Reminds me of
many & many a December day I have experienced at home. The
watch on deck (port) are all fishing for birds, if my inclinations
tended that way I should be there too. Pafsed a large ship standing S. E. by E. The 2^d mate denominated him *an old Scheidam
loafer*" The carpenter is making a very pretty little cedar box
for the mate & for want of better amusement I have been watching
him. He showed me some pieces of Sandal Wood which he procured at Shanghae a year or so ago, four little pieces weighing
perhaps a pound & worth 3 or 4 dollars. I offered to buy them,
but he objected to selling as he wished to make a dressing case
of them, to be lined with Camphor wood. I shall try him again
however. I wish Capt Gardner would take it into his head to go
into warm weather again for I am decidedly tired of turning out
& going to the wheel in the cold, & there shivering for two hours,
(unless it is blowing & then 10 minutes will put you in a fever
heat)   Took the royals in last night & lost one man off the yard
(main) who luckily caught the royal backstay & thus saved himself. I was up at the fore & nothing but extreme caution saved me,
as the 2^d mate never trims a yard, with a free wind, & consequently

---

* Correct; but nearly 400 miles south of it.

the sail is rap full & ready to fight any one who attempts to master it. Sixty Seven days out to day   Course S.E.by.E.

Sunday OCT 9th 1859   Lat 42° or 43°   Long 56° or 57°

S.   E

The past 9 days have varied but little in semblance. The wind keeps hauling from S. E to N E (the long way around) & back again   The seas keep rolling & the birds fly the same. "Drive that dog away from the beef"   The mate's dog was stealing a march on the pan which has not been returned to the galley yet. Oh dear, I have thought seriously of giving up my journal altogether as I cant get a quiet moment half a dozen times per year, this is such a noisy watch. I have been up on the fore topsail yard this morning, shivering, & aiding to put a patch in the sail, alternately. Oh, pshaw" one is wrangling about a pipe & another is telling an anecdote 50 years old that every body knows, & yet another jolts against me in going out so I'm stopping.

Tuesday OCT 11th 1859   Lat 41° —   Long 71° or 72°

S   E

A fine clear day & cold. Wind from the S. W *"all the way from* "CAPH ORN." A very pleasant change from wet to dry. Am amused almost every night listening to the various anecdotes and twisters, spun by various garrulous "old shells," & *"Whoppers"* they are some times. One, *"Scottie"* is the most notorious for that description   Listen. "He is from somewhere in Scotland where "(as the sailors have it)" the *grace of God* never extends to. He says he served his time in a 1400 ton ship. Was in Ireland the time of the famine   Was in Australia Heavens knows how many years, (& if his statements are true) was of no inconsiderable note there. Was in the rifle brigade throughout the Indian War, (& dont say much about the interior) *conclusive evidence that he knows nothing more than anyone living in Calcutta a short length of time, would learn from hearing it spoken of.* Came home in one of the most extraordinary ships ever heard of, & making a quicker passage than ever has been made by *our own* clippers, & passing the burning steamship Austria. Was in a large building in London called the Globe, from its shape. When standing upon the floor you look out of a large skylight at the top & can see nothing but open space   ascend (per secret passage) to a certain height & you cant see the top or bottom (although a person on the floor can see

[214]

you), but a view of Paris "life size" is before you, a little higher
the Mediterranean Sea meets your gaze   higher, St Petersburgh,
higher, London, higher N. Y.,   higher Niagara Falls,   then you
can see out but not the floor,   descend & you can see nothing but
space,   he accounts for it through some necromancy in the atmosphere which is *a secret*, & says the building is owned by Albert
Smith gentleman & author. Was at Niagara & saw Blondin walk
across & wheel his barrow. Saw Wise Gager & La Mountain
descend in their Balloon. Saw all the wood burnt down at Rome
(N Y Central R. R.) Was Quarter Master of the Steamer Northern Light & a great chum of Capt Finklepaugh Saw Picolomini
on board the steamer & declares she is homely. Tells about seeing
150,000 houses burned down in Quebec Tells about his mothers
giving Lola Montes a sound rating at a time she was stopping at
her (his mothers) house. Tells of a 14 ton boat coming from England to Melbourne,   tells of an English nobleman's Yacht being
ballasted with Quicksilver. Denied my statement that the N. Y.
yachts trim with men, & in the same breath tells me of a pilot
trimming a 1400 ton ship with her crew in order to take her over
Mobile bar. Oh I could go on all the morning telling the Wonders
he has seen. He (according to his a/c) was brought up & educated
among noblemen &c, & had particular attention paid to his education Speaks knowingly of "*Logathrims*") has Read of "*Pompey
& Herculum*" Has one "*Dyagrotype*" Talks of the Allegahanys.
The English pronunciation of Edward Bulwer Lytton is Edward
Bulwer Littleton. Oh—it disgusts me to talk or think of him so I
will end by saying that he has not one friend in the ship, & is the
biggest growl & loafer or soger aboard

S.

Wednesday Oct 19th 1859   Lat 38°.00′   Long 102°. E

We have just finished washing decks, & as some of the hands are
below sail making & the rest outside I seize the opportunity to
fill a page. Since writing the last we have had fair winds & are
now heading E.N.E. (per compass) which with two points Westerly variation makes a NE. course *good*. The Capt⁵ policy is to
run to the Meridian of 100° E. upon the parallel of 40° S. or
thereabouts, which policy he has followed out. Now I presume we
shall steer two courses for *Timor* (which Island is our first landmark) as by reference to the Charts it will be seen that by going
direct, from our present position, we should in all probability

find ourselves upon the Barrier Reef Which encircles Australia some fine morning in the Month of Oct.* Now let me see, we have 3 pigs left of the 12 we started with, so I guess we will procure some more at the first opportunity Whether we will be able to get any curiosities among the islands or not is a hard thing to tell. But Mr Hurd (our Mate) says that when Capt G. (our Capt) took the Chinamen that brought the junk to N. Y. some 12 years ago,—home, that they went the same route as we go now, and traded with the natives for old iron &c And some of the Chinamen got for 3 small remnants of calico, 9 rolls or more of silver dollars that the natives took from a Dutch wreck some time before. Each roll contained 25 dollars. The Malays knew the value of it, but could not use it. I shall get what I can though I depend upon "Angier" ("Java Head) for the greater part. Mr Peterson gives her (When I say *her* I have reference to the ship) 4 months altogether, but if we take less than 140 days I shall be immensely surprised. If we had gone the usual route, up to Angier, & up the China sea we should have had head monsoons *and strong ones too* not to speak of a current of 4 knots or more in some places, (also ahead) and consequently 6 months would have been a good passage. Now we elude the currunts altogether, & the monsoons in a measure, by taking a broad sweep to leeward & up through the placid lukewarm Pacific & its corresponding climate. The atmosphere has cooled greatly during the last 3 days

Thursday Oct 20th 1859 Lat 35°. 18′ Long 105° 35
The finest day we have had since leaving cold latitudes. Have been all the forenoon on the main yard patching the sail. All hands sail making in the half deck. There is a sail in sight two points off the lee bow but what description she is of, I am at present unable to say. Boy John has been at the wheel all the forenoon watch (4½ hrs). A beautiful albatross is soaring about, but seems disinclined to bite. One *boy* sits near me cutting tobacco. Another hand is reading Harpers, another overhauling his "*Donkey*," (chest.) another darns his "*holy*" stockings. 2 more have just started for the carpenter shop to grind their knives &———I—am going to turn in, read 10 pages or more of Abbotts French Revolution, roll over &————dream if I can, until 4 o'clock awakes me to the realities of the ½ deck & that "*seive*" of a fore royal on which

* The Great Barrier Reefs fringe the NE coast only.

[246]

I am at present working. Halloa", who the mischief has been at that bobtail cat, her head is decked out in borrowed plumes (which will never be returned, by the way, to the poor "Mowry Mock" of whom we *took* them, (his beak & feet being hung up in the forward house) and her tail elongated by a single feather which she is laboring with feline pertinacity to rid herself of. Knowing that she cant displace those on her head, she, (unlike some animals who sport two less "*pedastals*)" does'nt trouble herself about them   Course N E ½ N

Friday Oct 21st 1859   Lat   Long

"Now stop talking Billy & let me write". Boy Bill sits opposite to me & seeing the name "*Surprise*" Written on my chest lid, wishes to know "if that was my first ship afishing" & upon being informed that it was, accedes to the above request & "*dries up*" & now what shall I write. The wind is light & completely aft, so we travel but slowly We signalized the sail which we raised yesterday but what country she hails from I have not heard Peter Miller from Scotland familiarly called "*Little Burgoo*" got a boatswains chair this morning & rigged it for the purpose of stopping the worming on the foretopmast stay. *And such a rig,*" *to be sure.* The first time he was hoisted up he discovered that the hank had no mousing & that he was in momentary danger of coming down in a manner more rapid than agreeable. So he got scared & must needs be lowered away Well, he *moused the hank* & hoisted the chair up to the masthead & entered it there. Upon getting in, the slings rendered through the hooks & the board slipped up on his back, & he sat on the bare rope, (very unpleasant indeed seeing that he couldn't releive himself) After struggling awhile & losing all his strength, he sat still & began slowly to recover himself, but he had at last, to go down the stay without changing his "*positch*", & he now sits by me complaining of stiff joints & cords, a pair of barked shins, & a general weaknefs, while his face is the color of the sky after sunset all this might have been prevented had he gone to work & rigged his chair properly

Sunday Oct 23d 1859   Lat   Long

A beautiful day & "Oh, joy," the S. E. trades. We were roused at 7 bells yesterday morning by the cry of "Starboard watch, Ahoy" 7 bells there below, & a request that we would come out & see the race. Upon looking to windward I discovered a Johnny Bull plunging & ploughing along in the act of taking in his fore & Mizzen royal probably thinking that we would do the same   but he found he was mistaken, as he began to fall astern, for we carry our three royals until everything turns blue   We were both sharp up (I. E. on the wind) & as WE brace sharper than the common run of ships he gradually fell off to leward until the wind hauled & we both steered a course, when he kept his bearings   This mornings daylight discovered him aw—a——y, on our weather quarter, & barely discernable. He proved by his signals to be the Potosi of & from Liverpool bound for Shanghae   84 days out.* Now see which gets there first

Wednesday OCT 26th 1859   In sight of the N. W. Cape of Australia

The watch are all asleep with two exceptions   W. S. B. who is making a pair of *"Shackle Beckets"* & myself. We raised the land this morning & are now running along parralel with it Last night while standing at the wheel, I saw Capt G. come up from below & catch Mr Peterson sitting upon the logchest. Now this having happened once before, & he having given the 2d officer warning not to do so again, he opened on him with, "This is the 2d time sir. I've suspected it often within the last six weeks while I have been sick & unable to come on deck. What do you mean by it, dont you intend to conform to the rules of the ship,   if not why did you come in her   I did not ask you to, I did not send for you. You know very well that it is against my rules. Now sir, if this happens again, you dont do another days duty aboard this ship. Here we are 10 miles off the land & you with your *head down,* a pretty example for the man at the wheel & the one on the lookout. *I suppose his head is down too"* Here he walked forward to the main mast & soon returned saying, "He's walking the forecastle,   I hope they have all got as much soul. The officer of the deck *Must* walk the poop, & the man on the lookout *Must* walk the forecastle. I like to see a man have the *soul of a man* as well as the body

Duff Day   OCT 27th   Off N. W. Cape

A beautiful day & almost a calm one. Quite an excitement occurred this morning occasioned by one of the men (the one reffered too on

---

* *Intrepid,* 88 days, but the eastbound run is more difficult from the United States than from England.

Page 20*) imposing on one of the boys. He slapped his mouth 3 or 4 times, whereupon I signalized the boy to "*sail into*" him, saying I would back him. So he ran out & got a belaying pin, & gave "*old Burgoo*" a whack over the brain pot with it. Burgoo then grabbed him by the throat to choke him, whereupon I thought it high time to "*assist*," & so made a rush but, "Bell was there before *me*" (Where he came from I did not know for I had not seen him previous to the fracas) but I now saw him take "*old burgoo*" by the throat & shake 7 bells out of him, & then give him a shove away, at the next instant slapping his hands together, "as if to rid himself of *dirt*" Mr Scottie did,nt know what to say hardly, so as he dare not tackle Bell, he gave vent to growls loud & deep, & finally told him that he would "get him yet in a place" where he would fix him. (He reffered to Shanghae) And so I told him that to tackle B. in any place with more than his match was to tackle me with him. Upon that he opened on me & talked "*Lamu*" very loud So, not to have any disturbance, I invited him out on deck to get licked & have the conceit taken out of him, immediately, this he durst not do & kept his jaws going until I told him to shut up or I'd demolish him where he sat, then he "*dried up*" And now the first jaw he gives me "*Down comes his house*" instanter Got the guns up, scraped & painted them & lashed them to the capstan. Steering N b E ½ E. & no land in sight. The wind is so light that it is doubtful whether we will reach Timor by Sunday or not. Jas. Green "*of Corsica*" is at presint on the flying jibboom trolling for Bonita, but the knowing rascals have a knack of discerning between a real flying fish & a lump of lead, bearing, not the slightest resemblance to any fish, with the exception that it is sometimes bright as it rolls & skips along the surface of the water

Sunday Oct 30th 1859 Lat 15°. 37.′ Long 113° about

Tis Sunday, a quiet, easy, sunny, Sunday in the Indian Ocean near that long settled island Timor.† And oh, it is so pleasant, just like the finest summer Sundays I ever enjoyed *at home.* Home,—I wonder what they are doing there now ah, they're all asleep, I fear, & dreaming of me, I hope!!, as I often dream of them—for there is 12 hrs & 35 or 40 minutes difference of time

* Page 214 in this book.
† *Nearing* Timor, rather; still about 700 sea miles away; little more than half this distance from Java, incidentally.

between here & there. (It is 3 bells (½ past 1 o'clock) in the aft^n.) Then too it is quite cool at home   perhaps they have fires lit; not so here,   I am in a cool shady place, with the breeze fanning me continually & apparulled in a shirt & trowsers of the lightest description & yet the perspiration rolls from me in large drops. It is Billy M.'s next wheel & he has been some time, drefs-ing, & endeavouring to ascertain, the coolest *"rig"*. He is now overhauling my till "seeking what he may devour," drefsed in dungaree trowsers   a calico shirt & a *"real"* Brigand hat in which the slouch is not artificial   Billy sees me writing about him & clea's. Now again. There's the carpenter with his moustache shaved off, how funny he looks. There was a great halabuloo this morning about some cake the cook lost last night   It was taken from his room right *over* his nose. Mr Hurd called the before mentioned Billy M. aft & *posed* him with "Billy do you like cake." Not knowing but that he was about to be the recipient of some of the aforesaid article Billy replied in the affirmative adding that he was very fond of it,   but on being interrogated regarding *"that"* cake denied all knowledge of the matter. The cook mean while swears vengeance on everybody & nobody   How blue the water is today, the carpenter is leaning over the rail & regarding —nothing with a thoughtful air. I wonder if he is thinking of home. Ah no! for he was left at the age of 9 to shift for himself in this wide world,   wide—its not so wide after all,   here we are at the antipodes & the elapsed time seems *so* short,   twas only a week or so ago (seemingly) that we bade good bye to the pilot & the highlands of Neversink, & here we are 13,000 miles from them; oh, I see with different eyes, the magnitude of things, to what I did in my school days. A Hundred dollars then was the height of my imagination   Now I spend more than that annually & consider it a very small sum indeed. Then I used to think that the upper end of Hicks st. Brooklyn, was the end of the world.— (*Ten blocks off*) (but I was not allowed at that time to roll my hoop beyond the corner), & to crofs a gutter was a far greater feat than, now, to crofs the ocean   Now the ends of the Earth are in a measure familiar to me. Thus, going to China, I had not heard of. Now, I have not only heard of it but have experienced the realities of such a trip. Then, a ship was a marine monster that I had seen pictures of. Now it is a sail boat with which I am familiar   Then all ideas of whales were associated with Jonah. Now the sight of one suggests lamp oil & Blubber hunters. Then a sailor was a sort of amphibious animal who wore a tail, drank *much* liquor, chewed inestimable quantities of tobacco, sang, danced, dam—d his eyes & was very merry *"When ashore"* Now I have them in numbers for companions but have always failed to find one of the above description. Not that they are all immaculate far from it, but that they have some redeeming traits They are for the most part generous to a fault, never *going back* on a shipmate. Allways help one another, especially if they get into any sort of a scrape. Crews often (nowadays) knock off duty & refuse to work until some shipmate who has been put in irons is free'd, & let a poor fellow board a ship in a foreign port & tell the men he is a sailor & has neither money, friends, or ship, if the captain wont ship him he is sure to turn up *"on board"* the day after sailing. There are exceptions to the rule but they are worthlefs fellows at best How beautiful the sea looks with its ever breaching waves. Theres the Steward looking at me from the galley door. I wonder if he thinks that I stole the cake. The mate is there also looking at some Chinese books. He comes around once a fortnight & distributes tracts & papers. At first he gave me Home Journals these failing, he gives me generally the best papers he has, today I got a New York Chronicle. They are all exchanges of *"Fowler & Wells," Bdwy* N. Y. Capt G. walks the poop swinging his arms & exercising himself as though he were handling a pair of dumb bells—but he isnt,—& from his frequent glances at the siezings of the main rigging which glances he has been throwing for 3 or 4 days, & from frequent examinations he makes in that direction we have all come to the conclusion that he intends having something done with those seizings.

Hurrah for our ships, our merchant ships
  Lets raise for them the song
That safely glide oer the foaming tide
  With timbers stout & strong
That to & fro on the waters go
  And borne on the rushing breeze
Like birds they fly 'neath every sky'
  From south to northern seas

    Hurrah for our ships our battle ships
      Our glory & our boast
    That carry death in their bellowing breath
      To invaders of our coast
    In glory & pride whatever betide
      May they sail around our shore
    But long be the day ere in battle fray
      We shall hear their cannons roar

Hurrah for our ships our stout steam ships
  That float in strength & grace
By fire & air their course they bear
  Like giants in the race
That bind the hands of kindred lands
  In close & friendly grasp
God grant no feud by death & blood
  May eer unloose the clasp!

    Hurrah for them all both great & small
      That float our waters free
    May they safely sail in calm or gale
      In home or foreign sea
    Hurrah again for our merchantmen
      Hurrah for our Men of war
    Ring out the shout for our steam ships stout
      Hurrah for them all—"Hurrah"——

              Copied from M^{c's} journal

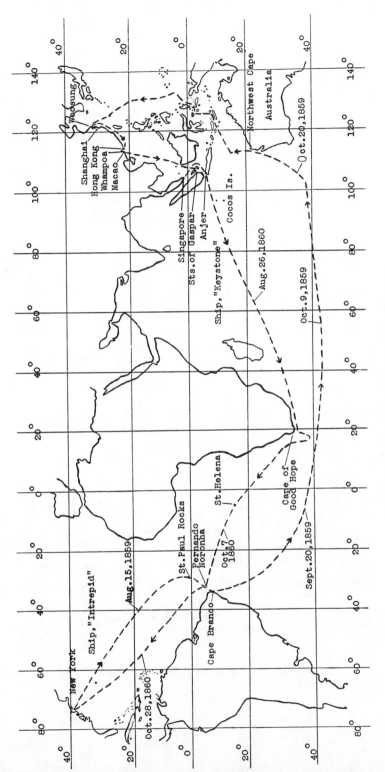

TRACK OF ABBEY'S SECOND VOYAGE TO CHINA AND BACK

TRACK OF ABBEY'S TRAVELS IN THE FAR EAST, 1859–60

CHAPTER XVII

ENCHANTED SEAS

Long 120 to 122 E

Thursday Nov 3ᵈ 1859 Off Sandal Wood Island Lat 9° to 10°S
Half past 3 o'clock. It is nearly time for me to go on deck. I have
succeeded in finding a comparatively cool retreat in the between
decks, where I have been lying since 12 o'clock reading *Lever's*
"Horace Templeton" which so engrossed my attention that it is
with difficulty that I relinquish it to pen these few lines. Land was
first seen Yesterday evening in the dog watch from 4 to 6. It was
so far distant as to be imperceptible to the unpractised eye, & one
there was & is who stoutly avers, that "It vash all nonsense" "I
hap youst so goot n'eyes sm you" "and I pe d——d for I can see
um" "no nor any pody else s'm says so." However this mornings
sun brought to our delighted visions, the *beautiful* shores of
"Jeendana" or "Sandal Wood Island" to which of all that I have
seen none can compare   with one exception—"("Pulo Penang" in
the Straits of Malacca".) Its Southwestern extremity is very high
bold & abrupt in its formation, and completely covered with
vegetation, while its eastern one is low, giving the whole the appearance of a dog swimming through the water,—an *immense*
dog. We have not approached nearer than 12 miles & have seen
no *prahus*. We are in momentary expectation of raising land on
our starboard bow but its name I do not know. It seems that we
shall not see Timor as our route lies more to the northward &
westward Through Flores Straits.*

Friday Nov 4ᵗʰ 1859

Between decks again, 10 o'clock A. M.   John is sleeping near me
& besides myself is the only one down here. The starboard watch
are, (with some noisy exceptions) over the side scraping the moſs
from the vessels sides. What a time I have had getting myself
fixed to write,   after meeting with numberleſs mishaps & de-
tentions I kicked my ink bottle slap into the hold & of course

* This route was not followed—as will be seen later.

smashed it, upon which I had a mind to let it go altogether & perhaps would, had it not already caused me so much pains to be relinquished without another trial. There is no land in sight at present but we are expecting to see some, hourly.

Sunday Nov 6th 1859 Off Ombay head

I have skipped one day & now must record what transpired. We raised Timor & several small Islands lying between it & Flores which looms up behind as large as the main land. Timor is at its South Western extremity (Rugged Peak) 5000 feet high. We passed along near the lesser islands with a very light breeze, indeed almost calm at intervals, & at such times the current, to all appearances, set us in shore, to the Westward & Northward. Toward evening however it freshened & we were enabled to proceed at the rate of 6 or 8 knots. Capt G. gave orders to be called at 12 o'clock but when that time came, it was a dead calm, & we were no nearer *"the narrows"* of the Straits than at 8. But the wind never steady, is also seldom idle, & ere 4 o'clock we were under brisk headway once more & when daylight broke could discern the *tree* which stands out on the most prominent point of Ombay (to the Southward & Eastward). The island is not so pretty as Jeendana but is nevertheless fine & has a splendid beach to land upon there being no surf of any magnitude. I have omitted to mention that I went in swimming with several others, although the mate remarked that blue sharks were plenty. The porpoises & thrashers of Flores St's had a grand field day yesterday or else they were engaged in a furious battle among themselves, for, from 4 o'clock until——now—I may say, they were gambolling & playing in all directions, & such playing They will at first roll along in rank & file 300 or 400 together, as peacably as could be & then with a rush spring out of the water slapping each other with their tails & fins & falling on one another as though bent on exterminating the school, but the appearance of a ½ dozen long lean wiry fellows of their species, known as thrashers, who would come upon them in the midst of the hubbub with the tails beating the water *"a la flail"* & themselves not at all particular if it struck the porpoises, would always create confusion, & an immediate & rapid stampede to some other place where the game or battle would be resumed, only to be interrupted again by their implacable foes the T's. It was during one of these stampedes when every one was laughing, & roaring at the terrified rapidity which

[224]

the porpoises assumed that some (I cant remember who,) cried out "Oh! look at that bird" I with the rest looked over my head about 10 feet, (I was seated on the knight heads) & saw a bird bearing a strong resemblance to a booby flying with a bewildered look & an undecided air directly towards the foretopmast stay, it was probably his intention to pass between the stay & the halyards but owing to his indecision & frightened condition he struck the stay itself & fell, within 6 inches of my finger ends, to the water I had no Idea that he was capable of so clumsy a feat or I should have been in readiness to seize him which I could easily have done had I been prepared to. The Island of Flores is about 300 miles long & contains a Volcano I know not how high* but of its power I have sufficient evidence for it destroyed over 7000 natives some 3 years previous. It is known as "LOBETOBIE" Indeed the whole of these islands with the exception of the oft mentioned & lovely Jeendana appear to be of volcanic formation & are comparatively barren. We have observed white rocks or cliffs which have been exposed by some portion having fallen off & I am inclined to believe they are chalk The beach is covered with palm trees with here & there a cocoanut. The landmark is a huge palm which we ran within 1½ miles of, when we had to stand out in order to clear a shoal which runs out about two miles. The wind headed off at 2 o'clock & we are now standing somewhere about East for the north end of Wetters island. Our Course is N. Capt G expressed a wish that we might get some refreshment, of some boats, & here he is holding off 5, 6, or 10 miles from the land & as a matter of course no native is fool enough to pull his prahu, so far.

Monday Nov. 7th 1859 Sea of Banda

It is 4 o'clock. (P. M.) The forcastle is quiet, as indeed it is all the while now, as the heat renders it to unpleasant to live in. The watch are on the topgallant forecastle watching the smoke of a steamer, which we discovered some two hours since, creeping along the West coast of Wetters island, that lies under our lee. It is a dead calm, & so still, the only noises heard, the click of the pump as the carpenter serves out the water, & the muttered voices of the crew as they converse, in the shady places The very air seems asleep, & yet with all this we had an excitement today. Some, wishing to go in swimming rigged a temporary ladder to put over

* 7,425 feet.

the side & while engaged at this one more presumptous than the rest, sprang in with the end of a rope. He had not been there two minutes when he was hailed by a voice from forward, "to, "get out of the water" He did so & was hardly clear of the surface ere a shark of the shovelnosed species shot around the bows as if he had been suddenly sent for & only relaxed his speed upon perceiving that his intended meal had eluded him

Wednesday Nov 9th 1859 Lat 3°. 25′ S. Long 125°. 36′ E
Calm at present, but there has been a fine breeze all day. Raised Bouro Island at 12 o'clock steering N. E. Quite a high island. We have crossed the Sea of Banda. Hot, hot weather, sweat rolling off me. I am tired of writing for I have been penning letters for the last two hours. We have been fortunate in getting thro the Straits ere this head wind, came up I am going up on the topgallant forcastle to see how the land looks now.

Friday Nov 11th 1859 North & West of "*Bouro*"
Daylight shewed us 5 sail within 10 miles of us. The Potosi (see page 26*) the "*Illumina*" (Eng) another barque (also Eng.) a vessel ahead whose colors are as yet indistinguishable, &, "The "*Live Yankee*"† a N. Y. Clipper for Shanghae. She left Aug 1st I suppose but we cant find out as she seems indisposed to signalize us more than to show her numbers & ensign. The Illumina is 130 days out from Liverpool bound also to Shanghae.‡ There is very little wind & that Little is ahead, so we have to beat, & it is fun to see us go around, one watching the other as jealously as can be, & vexed at every tak to "*get on*" I.E. if they cant have the same privilege. The little barque had a boat out yesterday and boarded a Prahus, of which we saw two engaged in fishing evidently, and this morning he put off for the Illumina She being a dull sailer,

* Page 218 in this book.
† The *Live Yankee* was considered by some to be as speedy as the *Red Jacket*, the holder of the principal transatlantic record (13 days, 1 hour, 25 minutes, New York to Liverpool, dock to dock). There is no question about her having been speedy. On her first voyage to San Francisco she was within one day of the record of 16 days from Cape St. Roque to 50° S. latitude in the Atlantic. Coming up the other side of South America she sailed from 50° S. to the equator in 16 days— within ½ day of the record. On this voyage the *Live Yankee* logged as much as 18 knots at times. Later, on a round trip from London to Calcutta, she ran from the equator in the Atlantic to her destination in less than 59 days. On her way home she was only 42 days from the Cape of Good Hope to London, another very fine performance.
‡ The *Intrepid* is 108 days out.

& also unable to brace as sharp as the rest of us, kept falling to leward, & at last a/c,s the little fellow had backed his main topsail and was waiting for the other to come up in order to regain his boat. Guess he'll know whom he boards again, & take care not to lose all he has gained the previous 24 hours as he *did* in this case. While wearing ship at 4 o'clock A. M. two of the men were talking of another who has ever been over officious. And one of them happened to remark "Oh, he dont know anything". Now Mr Peterson (2ᵈ officer) always gets excited when working ship & frequently executes the most absurd manouvres, so thinking that he was the subject of their conversation, he came up to Walter who had spoken and said "Yes he does know what he is about." W. then said "who is talking to or about you" "Not me Im sure" "oh" said P. I can hear & understand you at the same time laying hold of W's shirt, who threw his hand away saying "You had better keep your hands off me" then turned forward & W took hold the fore brace in order to pull. The next instant P. turned back and struck him unawares knocking him down & forcing the blood from his nose. W. is so small & was so stunned that he did not say or do anything more. Besides he is no fool, the quietest man in the ship, content to bide his time, knowing that he can obtain satisfaction at some future day, while *now,* he can do nothing as P. has the long end of the rope. I was at the wheel at the time, and believed it to be another person, whom he was having trouble with, all the time. Never was I more astonished than when I heard it was Blair Our China steward is sitting by me examining the pages, which he cant read, & asking me my age, & all manner of curious questions, original only in a Chinese brain. He says: "he hopes we go right back home to N. Y." & I join him in it. I guess I wont write any on my letters today

Saturday Nov. 12ᵗʰ 1859 5 miles north of yesterdays position
Spoke the *"Yankee"* last night, at 6 bells in the last dog watch. He was very short indeed, & continued his *"sweating up"* at which he was engaged when interrupted by *"Live Yankee Ahoy"* as soon as he possibly could. We took a squall at 8 o'clock in which, she by means of her studding sails ran ahead, but it soon after fell calm & we worked up to her, so fast that at 4 o'clock A. M. she was within 100 yds of our lee beam. We heard her men singing "Away, haul away, haul away my Rosa" this morning, as they again sweat home everything. She is a hard boat & I pity the poor

fellows that are in her Her last run was from Hong Kong to Havana with Coolies.* Their freight money amounted to $60,000 of which $50,000 was clear profit. She is again chartered for the same purpose. Our steward (a Chinaman) came on the topgallant forcastle this morning and spun a long yarn about Coolies. He appears to think that it is a blessing to them to take them away, for he says that thousands of them die annually of starvation. At present she is to leward & about abeam. The little barque is about 5 miles astern on the port quarter. The fellow that *was* ahead comes next, one mile farther off. Then the other Johnny Bull away under the land 7 miles distant, & last of all the "*Potosi*" with a topmast & lower studdingsail set, which however are not doing him much good. Its a race! four of us are bound to Shanghae. The Yankee left on the 3ᵈ instead of the first of Aug. as I had supposed, & is consequently 8 days ahead of us on the passage. Some of the port watch were in swimming again yesterday eve, they saw no sharks at the time, but twenty minutes after there was one of the Tiger species made his appearance, he was over 12 ft long. They are the most ferocious of their kind. Capt G. upon seeing him remarked, that he thought we had better leave off going overboard altogether, & I guess we will after that. Speaking of Tiger sharks reminds me of an anecdote of one, told to me by one of the men forward, whose veracity I do not doubt He was in a pepper trader on the west coast of Sumatra. Sharks are very numerous there &, there was over twenty huge ones, in the bay, with which they were in a manner familiar, because of their attendance on every boat that left the ship for the shore. They will go as far as the surf at the reef & there stop & await your return. The Malays are in no wise afraid of them when inside of that but will go in among & kill them right & left They had rather face Satan himself outside of it, however. They (the ships crew) caught them frequently & generally gave them to the malays who ate them. They had one one morning secured to the jib down haul & pulled half out of water which they meant to dispose of in the usual manner, one of the hands being forward, & happening to look for him could not find *him*, but found the down haul sustaining a heavy strain he raised a cry, & soon all hands laid hold & began to haul it in again. As it came to the surface judge of their surprise on finding that a huge tiger shark

* Out of 788 packed into her on this occasion, only 12 died, a remarkably small percentage for a voyage of this kind.

had swallowed their prize until ¾ of him was out of sight, but as they drew him up he let the small one slip until he was half out & then bit the tail portion off as clean as a knife would have done it, & disappeared. You can judge of his size when I tell you that the one which he swallowed was over 11 feet in length. If they can bite one of their kind in two as though done with a razor, what sort of an impression could they make on an hombre of my description. I dont think It likely that I shall ascertain by experience unless our *canoe* should sink amidst a school of them

How goes it about now Charley? (July 23ᵈ 1859)
Never better, though tis rather hot. Nov 12ᵗʰ 1859

Wednesday Nov. 16ᵗʰ 1859   off Pulo Pisang

It is morning, 6 o'clock. The sun is rising beautifully. I have slept all night, being laid up with a lame arm, & while the watch are washing off the decks I am sitting on the knight heads inditing this.—I have been trying to count the islands which are at present in sight, but they are too numerous for me, & we are continually raising & dropping them. Night before last two large sharks were privateering about us, but we could not catch them, and yesterday there was a still larger one under the stern, who also could not be *coaxed*". We were beset by a current, last night, which was loaded with drift wood, snags, shells, nuts, cuttle fish bone, fish of curious shapes & colors &c &c. We caught any amount of this stuff for curiosity's sake. The smell from Lookisong (or Landscape island as some one has most justly named it) is delightful, the perfume arising from the orange, lemon, lime, plantain bananna, & pineapple, groves is truly delicious and when assisted as it frequently is by an occasional tincture of nutmeg & spice, is above speaking about. Raised a sail ahead at daylight, which, we at first thought to be the *"Live Yankee"* (she having kept out clear of Lookisong & run ahead of us) At twelve o'clock however he was ahead of us about ½ a mile, & proved to be the *"Starr King"** of Boston, New York for Shanghae 123 days out. He sent a boat aboard us with her chief mate.

---

* This ship, with the apparently misspelled name, was christened in honor of the Rev. Thomas Starr King, one of the most brilliant speakers of his day. On one occasion she sailed in 36 days from 50° S. in the Pacific to a point very close to the Golden Gate—remarkably fast time. (She was detained outside by fog for 8 days.) At one time the *Starr King* held the record of 34 days from Melbourne to Hong Kong.

The crew came up out of the boat & informed us that they had been 38 days among the islands, had spent 3 days at Copang watering, had been aboard another ship for water the night before, That the Superior & Golden Rule were ahead a short distance, that the Superior had been so near going ashore 4 nights ago, that they had provisioned & watered all her boats & were ready to take to them at a moments notice, that, the Golden Rule narrowly escaped getting into a like predicament, & they themselves were not far from it also, that they had their Stewardess in irons for attempting to poison the 2^d mate & that they had easy times, but were *regularly starved*, (Which I believe is always a sailors complaint). In return we told them that we had a good ship no *"stunsails"* (at which they stared) were 11 days later than they from home, had plenty of water, & could beat any thing that we met   Asked them what we should tell the folks in Shanghae for them, at which they laughed and said they would risk our beating them. Put off with their boat for their own ship. ½ an hour afterwards she was struck aback by a squall & ran off to leeward. So were we but we *ran past him* instead of going off to leward & had the yards all braced & the ropes laid up, & were watching his manouvres, as he filled away again. To do him justice he did his best, But *good heavens*, how slow she moved in stays,   why we were ½ a mile ahead & to windward ere he got full headway on her. However he packed on his studding sails & favored by a squall was walking up to us again, when we were similarly accomodated & forced him to keep his distance. The wind however kept aft & as his best sailing point is, when his kites will draw,   he kept up with us all night

Thursday Nov 17th 1859   off some more islands)
At daylight we began to drop Mr Starr King, & raised 3 sail ahead. A stern chase neverthelefs is a long chase, & without we are favored with a squall we cannot ascertain their names. But if we *are* we will leave them all, for, few ships afloat can compete with the Intrepid in a strong breeze on the wind or abeam, she is so terrible square, & never takes in her royals until other ships furl their topgallant sails
Crofsed the Equator

Friday Nov 18th 1859   North of the line
There lay Walter S. Blair & Jimmy Green,   W. reading any old

number of Harpers, & Jimmy, unable to pursue the same occupation from his inability to read—tossing his arms & rolling his head about in vain endeavours to get asleep, and here sit I, on a fish davit, with the same old chicken coop for a desk, that I have dated all my letters from, trying to think of some thing that may interest a peruser of these pages We were steering N by W yesterday noon & had the Starr King astern 6 or 7 miles, when we raised Gilolo island (S point) & changed the course to N. E. which brought *him* nearly abeam. he kept the old course, running off to windward & northward from us, & I think must have experienced better winds for this morning he is on our weather bow steering the same course as we. I have no chart or map of these islands and so can give no reason for this change but suppose there are reefs to sound, & am willing to believe that Capt G. knows what he is about. No land in sight as we dropped the before mentioned island during the night. Oh how I do pray for an 8 knot breeze, for 12 days it would put us in Shanghae or off Woosung at the least. Kept a topgallant yard lookout, for a shoal that lies hereabouts somewhere but did not see it. Passed an innumerable quantity of logs. One hand picked up a beautiful Cuttlefish bone 9 in. long, with a beautiful pink tint on the back. He is at present very much attached to it but I guess, in course of time I shall be able to get it of him.

Saturday Nov 19th 1859 Lat 1°. 34′ N Long 128 or 9
Had a squall last night, which forced us to lower down our royals, but at the same time sent us ahead of the Starr King, as though she was at anchor. Oh these *stunsail* ships thats where we get to windward of them all, while they are lumbered & bothered taking them in, we merely stand by the braces, swing our yards, & dip our Ensign to them as we pass. Another struck us this morning at 8 o'clock, when we gained a little more, not letting go the royal halyards. Our antagonist is now 5 miles astern "*trying*" us "*on the wind*" but "*pshaw*" if he continues that game he'll be hull down by dusk, "*although* he is a clipper." No land in sight. Occupied this forenoon (although Sat.) setting up the Mizzen topgallant & royal stays & backstays. 12 days such wind as we have at present & we will be in Shanghae & receive our letters.

Tuesday Nov 22^{d} 1859 Lat   Long 119 (days out)
The past 3 days have produced nothing new, with the exception

of an island, which attains the tremendous altitude of 6 ft above the level of the sea. The weather is just as hot, the winds quite as *minus*, & we still keep the Starr King company. Hove to the other night in order that he should speak us, but the rascal, kept away, & passed out of hail, chagrined, no doubt, because we can beat him. Capt G. may possibly have wanted something of him, as we have but ½ a bbl. of rice aboard, & he was heard to remark that if that was the case we should have to resort to *first principles*. Cant understand; what does he mean: "*first principles*," why rice is *beneath everything*, & if they are any lower, what must they be. It is at present calm, we are "*sharp up*" on the port tack, with the bowlines hauled out, the ship rolls & goans, & the yards creak & jerk, the sails flap, belly, & collapse,—&—all is still for two seconds then follows a repetition, & thus we go. Perhaps there will a breeze spring up, if so, you hear the cry of "*Starboard Main brace*" or "Square the Crofs Jack yards" which done the men "*lay*" forward, move about listlessly wait for 8 bells" or something to turn up. This last seldom fails, & the yards frequently go round 5 or 6 times in as many hours But each consoles himself with the thought that it is only for 4 hours, & mayhap 2 of them are past. Every day is not alike though, for sometimes you lay 48 hours & never touch a rope, your sole care being to keep cool, a by no means easy matter just here. But we dont grumble for in lefs than 2 weeks we shall have to resort to monkey jackets again. Two winters a year is too bad, "*isnt it now*"

Thursday Nov 24th 1859 Lat   Long
121 days out from New York
"*Thanksgiving day*", & a holiday at home Now friends & families collect & have general jubilee, beginning with church service & Sunday clothes; flanked by a "*huge*" dinner, & the reserve brought up in the shape of music & dancing, when pretty girls, display their vocal powers & their pretty ancles, to the immense delight of—ahem. Oh.—h—h," dont I wish I was home, how I would carry on. Wonder if theres any snow. Visions of sleigh rides rise before me. Is the creek frozen—No; not the creek but the mill ponds. (Visions of skating, as before) But I'm here in a sharp wooden box, battling with calm, & squalls. They say, that "*this is the road to Shanghae.*" if it is, May I——Now I've only got *Duff* for dinner today while all at home will surfeit on turkey, goose, duck, veal, spare ribs, &c &c, &c *ad infinitum*. I have not been

with them for 2 years, on this occasion. The last time was in
—/57 I was sick, or rather just recovering from a 2 months ill-
nefs, they thought I was going to have the consumption, & this
idea was confirmed by me at the table, for I eat more than any one
in the crowd, & forced Uncle G. to remark, "he; consumption;"
"Yes consumption of *grub.*" Then there was one present, a dear
one, who will ne'er be present again, for he has gone to his long,
long, home. Poor little Ly; health personified, was he. But he's
gone gone, gone, and mourned as such as he was only, can be
mourned. In the choicest, & prettiest spot in all *"Montrepose"*
he's laid and I hope when I die that I may be laid there too. The
last 24th Nov. I spent at sea also. Twas in the Henry Brigham en
route for San Francisco, & I had Mc E. Ed. H. & Bill. A. for
company at dinner & a right good dinner we had, & jolly good
company they were too, all friends, one from R. another, an ac-
quaintance of almost as long standing, from B. & Allee as good
a fellow as N. Y. can produce. But today bids fair to be as sad &
lonely a one as e'er I experienced, for although I have a good ship
& some good fellows to talk to, there is no one from R. or with
whom I have been acquainted at home, so I have no one to converse with about the 24ths we have seen together or in the same
place. We have at last got a breeze, & are just laying our course,
on a bowline. The Starr King is said to be in sight from the topsail
yards, & is astern, so good bye to him, & you. I dont feel like
writing for I had but little sleep last night, got wet through &
its my next wheel, so I must prepare myself to *"take a shaving off
the wind"*

> Yours Truly
> Chas A Abbey
> Lat 4° 00′ N   Long 133°. E
> Near the Pelew *islds*

July 23d 1859 Dont you wish you had not gone?
Nov 24/59 This is hardly fair, did you know it would come on
Thanksgiving day?*

Friday Nov 25th 1859 Lat

Pen in hand again. How I thought & thought last night, on my
lookout from 2 to 4, about home. Between 3 & 4 bells they were

---

* A jest, as the pages in this ledger have no dates printed on them.

eating dinner, & likely thinking of me, & wondering where I would obtain a Thanksgiving meal. They suppose me to be in Shanghae for they knew not that we were coming this route. Quantities of drift wood & nuts &c, &c, (curio's) passed us last eve' in the dog watch. I obtained several, & have 3 or 4 cuttlefish bones among the rest. John" has come down, & says "his blanket would'nt be any the worse for a folding" so he is making it up preparatory to lieing down. Now some of the comicalities in Harpers tickle him, & he laughs, raises up, removes his pipe from his mouth, spits, resumes his "*Hubble Bubble*" lies down again & in two minutes is enveloped in a cloud of smoke, somewhat similar, I suppose, to the one which History reports to have so frightened Sir Walter Raleighs servant, that he deluged his Master with "*beer*", being under the impression that he was *on fire*". An epidemic has prevailed for the past two days, which for want of advice I will call the Hat & Cap fever, & so infectious is it that 10 out of 20 have made new caps   caps with high tops, caps with low tops round tops, square tops, & "*no tops*." Caps with short peaks, Caps with long peaks & as before, with "*no peaks*". Hat list, same formula. For my own part, being unwilling to have one like anybody else's, in shape or material, I have planned, modelled, built, & am wearing, a "white linen fatigue cap with a small black crown, (vizible only, from a perch over my head) & a very long very square, pasteboard peak. All I now need is a "*Pompon*" & I shall present quite a soldierly appearance. We're but a short ways from the Pelew Islands, & should we stand longer on this tack will sight the Carolines. That I SHOULD like. The natives have the best characters, of any of the inhabitants of the Pacific islands & are nearly white   quite a distinct race from any of the rest, & are very gentle kind & winning in there manners. Whalemen like to go *there*, best of any of the other islands*

Saturday Nov 26th 1859   Lat   Long

I sat on the house last night, talking with Billy M. until he went below, when I laid down with a blanket, & slept until two o'clock when I was awakined, by sensations of a squall, then I went below & the next thing I heard, was the 2d mate singing out for us to get on our oil clothes & stand by for a call. I sprung up & found that it was after 4 o'clock

* At this time the Carolines were a good distance due east of the *Intrepid*, Shanghai being to the west of north.

I was interrupted by the mate last Sat. & consequently did not finish. He came down to oversee some men who were pouring brine down the ventilators, an operation often gone through with in every ship for the purpose of keeping the timbers damp & unliable to crack or check, which might make them leak. We didnt get anything out of the squall Sat morning, but it looked like Cape Hatteras, & so we clewed up the royals & hauled down the flying jib until 6, o'clock when we again set them. Sunday our unremitting efforts were crowned with success & we caught a shark, a young one,—still a shark, and he would in time have been an old one, & a man eater. He was first seen forward, but made his way slowly aft, while some of the watch were busy *"porking"* the *shark hook* & bending a couple of towlines together   The bait had hardly been thrown over the taffrail, ere one of his pilot fish, seeing it, touched him on the port side of his snout, & thereby forced him to see it *also*. He made no more ado, but sauntered up & gobbled it in, & then *"Governor"* who had the line   giving it a slight jerk, hooked him just as nice as he possibly could have done, Round his jaw bone & out abaft his larboard eye. The next instant he was flying over the Intrepids taffrail, cabin & poop at the rate of knots with 5 or 6 *coons* a'hold of the line. He flapped thrashed   bit, tore, & flounced about, all to no purpose & finally *brought up* on the main deck abaft the starboard bilge pump, where he was soon dissected. As an instance of his power, he, after his tail & all his fins were cut off & his entrails taken out he snapped the blade off a sheath knife which one of the men playfully put into his mouth. His head was cut off & I took it for the purpose of getting out his jaws & while cutting about them he gave me several severe nips in the hand. He had 3 rows of teeth, (3 years old) but many of them were broken by his biting the hook   In his maw bag, was found a piece of meat which *"Britton"* had thrown over 15 minutes previous to his arrival & a beef bone of mine, thrown over, with a little meat on it ¾ of an hour before, & that was all, & it accounts for his hunger   There were several small Dolphins, travelling with him, which disappeared when he was hooked, & made there appearance again when I threw the remains of his head over board. They followed it down, down, as far as I could see it, (about 150 feet). So they feasted on their old companion, a thing which has been done by human beings not unfrequently.

Wednesday Nov 30th 1859   1,360 miles from Shanghae.

A great discussion on the respective merits of Corsica & Ireland, is going on over my head, on the combings of the fore hatch Corsica, being represented by the before alluded to Jimmy Green, contends that it is the *only place* in the world where good men & able, generate   "was'nt Napoleon born there?" Whilst Ireland argues that *it* is *the* place, to be sure,—"Daniel O'Connel," Ireland is backed by a tall, lean, lank, pock marked, specimen who hails from *"Bawstun"* (but who in all probability never sniffed air within 100 miles of Boston) and whom the mate, to use a slang phrase, is, *"dead nuts on"* & has nicknamed the *Sintimintil* Mick. Heres Billy M. come down to *devil* me a while, so I'll revenge myself by describing him. Height, about 4 ft 8 in. breadth about 2 ft thickness about—hum—well rather exceeding the medium. He's dressed in a blue shirt, light brown pants, with the knees & rear patched with black, and tucked in a pair of red topped boots. Black cap, & belt sheath & knife. He's looking over my Bowditch and seeing *"Sam Houston"* written on the fly leaf wants to know if it ever belonged to him. Of course it did! else how should his name appear in it. He is now arguing with me about the name of an island which, is Pulo Gasus in my Reference, & *"Pulo Bessy,"* *he swears in his"* it isnt though; I know. He's endeavouring to cultivate a moustache, Very feeble, Convex lens nescesary to find it. Now He's whistling a snatch of Opera. "When other scenes & other hearts." & writing a young ladies name on a slate. Of course the name is only imaginary. Change of music "Scenes that are brightest" now. I wonder what he's writing on the slate now. I have shown him what I have written. Effects rather ludicrous. First a laugh, arms *"a kimbo"* then another   arms slack. Number 3, down on deck, a roar, & not a gentle one, arms loose   Now he's gone up, to get me a sheet of paper to lay my pen arm upon so as not to dampen the page. The heat is great but not so oppressive as it has been. Music by Billy, (a series of waltzes)   I have a bet with him, that we will not get in, in 10 days, to be paid in New York. Guess I've got a *"sure thing"* on him too. He's just discovered that Shanghae is not down in the Epitome, & wants to know, what is in it's place. Chusan island I have told him is not far from it & now he's dropped the book & is ciphering away at

[236]

the rate of knots. Now for our Long 131° E. & how many miles
to the degree. Ah "ah" "skip those hard words." (hes made a mistake) Music "*Listen to the Mocking bird*" Hear him, only hear
him trill," he should be in the Opera (burlesque), (more hard
words) he cant find what he wants, now," he informs me. But that's
enough about him for once Grand finale, Music, "Thou art gone
from my gaze" &c. The weather is fine & the breeze fair. We have
nothing to do & are as contented a lot as you will find within a
week's sail of 4 months later news from home Our present course
is N by W. (no variation) I have the forenoon watch below, &
rice for, difference! then" thats Billys fault he is inquiring about
the difference of Long & so mixed my ideas. Please read dinner
instead Billy has read this & says Oh S'hugar

Thursday Dec 1st 1859   Lat 10°. 22′ N Long 131° E.

I have no Billy to bother me today, thanks be to Mr Hurd (1st
off.) who has him & all the rest of his watch, stretching ratlin stuff,
to be used in rattling down the mizzen rigging. There is no wind,
but a curious bobbing sea which so tumbles the Intrepid about
that it is sometimes nescesary to *hold on*, & prevent utensils from
pitching away "Oh My" after all my congratulations here comes
B. again. He at first sings out to me to send his love to R & then
seeing that I am writing my journal, says, "Oh I guess I'll keep
still today." He has'nt forgotten yesterdays experience. John has
just run up the steps, & sung out to me, "A shark " Abbey" "A
shark," "put that down" "with my name" So I have. Theres
considerable commotion over my head—Oh pshaw" John has just
returned & says it is only a Dolphin, after all. And now Monroe is
back, & adds, "Tell them that we just this moment saw a large
Dolphin off the starboard cat head, & that you would like to send
him home in this book, but cant, for he's gone & we hav'nt caught
him." So it goes one interruption after another, all day long.
Oh I wish it would Blow! blow! blow, a club topsail breeze from
the S. S. E. which would be right astern, & we would be in, within
a week, at least at Woosung where we shall in all probability
have to wait for the spring tides, to give us water enough to get
over the bars. Another cry of fish. I hope they catch some but it
is very improbable that they will for our bottom is covered with
pure copper, not composition, & consequently is very bright, a
quality which few fish but Dolphins admire & they are by no

[237]

means plenty. The shark the other night was very good, but that I suppose was oweing to his youth, & perhaps inexperience. We see no land now & I am quite glad of it, for we have had a plenty lately. "Why dont it blow," "why aint there a breeze" there ought to be, 10° 22′ N. today, made 25 miles during the last 24 hr's. it's scandalous but it cant be helped. "The more days, the more money", is all very fine, & would answer first rate if one could only get letters once per month or so. The first day of winter, & I have to stop every two lines, in order to wipe the perspiration from my face, while at home people are wearing overcoats. And yet a few days more & we will have it just as cold. These sudden changes never affect me in the least. Since leaving N. Y. Which was in July (26th) we have experienced *cold* & freezing weather, & again & at present weather to which the warmest days in N. Y. could not *begin* to compare. We have crofsed the line twice & the sun, twice, & we have been from 40°—N to 44°—S. & nearly back again, & this is the wide wide world that they talk about, a little round ball that men, *"cant handle"* but do play with & overrun in all directions   This rumor of the war in China is all that troubles me, for if it be confirmed *"we're stuck"* tea will command 5 or 6 dollars per ton a freight, & is consequently no object, *"rice droghing"* will most probably be our lot   if so God preserve us, for of all things I hate it is to load & discharge a ships cargo. We should in all probability go to Siam   Singapore Malacca *Penang* Aracan   Rangoon or Calcutta, than either of which I prefer a run to *Frisco"* with a load of *"Chink or Chong-foos"*

Friday Dec 2d 1859 Lat   Long.

8½ A. M. I have just finished my breakfast or rather, an apology for one   for today, being pork day, & the last barrel being *"Smelly,"* I have not dared to have a very voracious appetite. We have the N. E. trades, *perhaps,"* &, perhaps, have'nt   At least we have a breeze from N. N. E. which is light as yet (4 knots) but if the old Mother Goose rhyme be true that *"A mackerel sky,"* & *"mares tails" make a lofty ship carry low sails"* will soon be heavy enough. I hope mother Goose may prove a true prophet. The sunrise this morning was *beautiful.* For the first time in many days I was "on the pump," & consequently had ample opportunity for observing its splendor. If I was a poet I might describe it, but making no pretensions that way I shall let

the subject drop, with the observation that a painter should come
to sea, for truly beautiful colors. Some think that this spectacle
is insipid, at sea, from lack of scenery & contend that hills &
valleys, trees & houses, with mountains far in the distance, are
nescesary to make it magnificent. To all such I have but one
thing to say, *"Go & see, & judge for yourselves"* The next most
beautiful sight is Moonrise at sea, especially if the horizon is
flanked with clouds, when the moon bursting upon the vizion
through some opening in them, throwing a sheen across the sea,
which dances up & down, seemingly in welcome,—presents a
spectacle of rare grandeur. Oft times do I stand at the wheel,
in the dead of night with my helm down & the ship going off.* On
such occasions it is unnescesary to watch her & so I generally
"go off" in a reverie", with my eyes on Her Lunar Majesty, or
some of the stars, (these stars that look so big & beautiful in these
low latitudes,) may hap the Southern Cross, or if Low enough
down, the Magellan Clouds, sometimes interrupted by the
"G h f u u " of a Porpoise or two, (who when they find them
selves in the vicinity of a ship, disappear.) or the more monoto-
nous *"P, u, u a"* of some sullen, clumsy, blackfish. These however
seldom stop the currents of my thoughts, & I keep on stargazing
& musing, until brought to my senses by Mr Petersons question
of "Hows your helm Charlie" & then perhaps I find that there has
a breeze sprung up & the ship answering by a corresponding
manouvre has *come up* too. Then I shift my wheel from, Down,'
hard down" to "a turn & a half" to windward, & if the wind holds,
keep grinding water until 8 bells comes along & I am relieved of
my responsibility by either French Johnny, (who is better known
as *"Chaw"*) "Connor" the before mentioned Sintimintil *Mick"* or
"my shadow" "Billy Monroe." French Johnny is a *little* fellow
who can talk but *little* English. He is good natured & kind, & has
but one failing, he is continually mislaying his things, more
especially his pipe, this latter he seldom fails to loose once a
day & then he may be heard dancing about crying out "Who
got 'te my pipe," & quiet he will not be until someone says "Here,
J'ai votre pipe" for he knows his fault & seems to think that we
all ought to have an eye for him & his. He is a fine dancer, & a
passable singer & knows any quantity of French songs, which I

* I.e., with the helm hard down—in such a position as to bring the ship's head
nearer to the wind if possible—the ship still heads too far off from the wind due
to lightness of breeze.

would like to get the words of, but no, he dont understand English enough to make that plan feasable. However he learns me the music & on the whole is a very good fellow to pafs a leisure hour with. I am dead broke for reading matter, I have had several books from Mr Hurd, & I think I shall see him about another. Dick H. borrowed my "Love me little love me long" the other day, & was very much pleasd with it. That surprised me, the more, as he never reads anything, hardly, that is thoroughly, &, dont like Chaˢ Levers works, D,'Israilis or any of the popular novelists. Billy, has been down this forenoon as usual, but at my request has cleared out & is now deeply engaged, reading Littles living age. John lays over yonder conning an old Harper that has furnished him with amusement for 2 weeks or more. There is one old *"Matelot"* aboard who began the "Bankers Daughter" on the first of Aug. & finished it about the first of Oct. & he read steady too. This same old coon, came out of the forcastle the other night with his jackett & bag & observed "Im going to lie down right *in "the eyes of her"* under the bowsprit, so as to get the breeze through the hawse pipes. "Just give me a call if she strikes anywhere," will you" which he said so old fashioned & genuinely that *Bell* woke up all hands by his peals of laughter. His name is Bill. something but he is generally called *"Britton"* which with *"Governor" "Huster"* "Chaw" *"Bishop"* (his father is a minister) "Old woman" "Haul Taught" "Mᶜ Clusky" *"Copenhagen" "Matt" "Old Burgoo" "Little Burgoo" "Kreuzer"* &c, &c, are some of the misnomers applied to *"our Crowd"* Mr P. enquired of me the other day if I had been in the barque *"Yankee"* I told him no but in the *"Francis Palmer"* upon which he entered into conversation about San Francisco & the Honolulu & China trades & the vessels Engaged in them. He told me that he knew them all, as he had been boat keeper in the Pilot boat *"Dancing Feather"* out there for two years, & during that time had had many a long chase after them. The J. Faulconberg a Barquentine he said was the fastest vessel that side of the land, but I told him that she had given place to the *"Yankee"* although still ranking A. no 1 in regard to sailing qualities. The thing that used to bother him most, he said, was the Clipper Ship *"Sea Serpent,"* for Capt Whitmore* always had a crowd of friends aboard whom he took

* Captain Jacob D. Whitmore took command of the new *Tinqua* in 1852 and immediately set a "near record." On his first voyage he was within 150 miles of the equator in 13 days in spite of having been compelled to heave to on several

clear out to the *Farralones* & then delivered them over to the Dancing Feather drunk The Farralones are 30 miles off the heads & they not unfrequently had to keep the crowd aboard all night & part of the next day. But the Sea Serpent is coining money, out there she has not been home for nearly 4 years. Last Chinese New Years when I was in Frisco, Capt Whitmore had his ship drefsed out in flags, & no work going on, & he called on "Chy Lung" & all the leading merchants in town (Chinese) the consequence was that while a dozen or more ships were lying there trying to get a freight for Hong Kong & unable to do so from want of Tact on there Capts parts, The Sea Serpent loaded down to her scuppers, & cleared, with Chy Lung & Family on her pafsenger list. So much for Capt Billy Whitmore who is a great Chum of A. S. Lumus a friend of mine in San Francisco at the Bank of Exchange.

(P. S.) Blair says I have written ⎫
enough & Blair is a man of veracity ⎭ Yours Chas A Abbey

Tuesday Dec 6th 1859 Lat 20° $\overset{N}{—}$ Long 130° $\overset{E}{—}$

Four days have elapsed since I sat in this selfsame place & wrote the 4 preceding pages, & what a change has taken place We have run 10° of Lat. or so & the atmosphere from excessively hot, has become nice & comfortable. The trades took us as we thought on Friday, & increased in strength so much that it became evident that our togallant rigging & backstays wanted setting up so Saturday morning we did it & a very unpleasant job it was too, there being a head sea on & the ship under togallant sails. Sunday however, the breeze *"let up"* a little, & we set the royals & have had them on ever since. This morning we squared the yards as the wind is *"free"* once more. Split the flying jib Sunday morning & while mending it with Peter (a Swede who understands sail making a little) I noticed some fine No 12 duck in it which I observed I should like to have for pants. He said "Oh you can get yoost so much sm' you like in Shanghae" I

occasions in order to set up the rigging. The record from Sandy Hook to the equator is 15 days and 18 hours. The *Tinqua* required almost a week to cover those last 150 miles! Captain Whitmore took the *Sea Serpent* in 1855 after the *Tinqua* was wrecked off Hatteras. He retained command until his death at sea in 1860. Under him the *Sea Serpent* made a passage from Whampoa to New York in 79 days which has been bettered only three times. Her passage of 30 days from Newcastle, New South Wales, to Hong Kong also was very fast, as was her 17-day run from New York to the equator.

asked him if it was fine & would do to wear ashore, upon which he answered "Fine" oh yes! real nice, goot, stuff, I tell you sm' you get on a pair of them trowsers un a red shirt "*you shine*" I bet." Of course I thought so, "*to him*"; but pictured myself at home in a flaring red shirt & white pants, "*to myself*" & thought I would not drefs so." We are now engaged scraping down our spars & have almost done. Discovered yesterday that the main togallant mast was very poor indeed, being rotten for some 4 feet on the starboard forward part, & ditto at the heel. So perhaps during some of these *fancy* squalls which the old Intrepid so affects, it will get left behind. I hope not this voyage however Four days of a good breeze over the quarter would put us at Woosung Why dont it blow so; can you tell? Monroe & I sit on the house every night & talk as usual of every thing we know but we are nearly talked out & long for our letters "*like sixty*." I have a pair of satinet pants & a pair of duck pants, a Flannel shirt & a Cotton one which I have worn alternately for a long while & I have come to the conclusion to make them last home again. Not but that I have others but I dont need them I mean to see how little clothes I can get along with. Every other morning when we wash down I get one suit wet through & shift & dry them. The change I keep on two days & then get that wet, & put on the others again & dry these so it goes month in & month out in fine weather.

(Magico Simah group)
Friday Dec 9th 1859 Off the South end of the Loo Choos
Lat 20°. 40′ N Long 123° 30′ E *

The trades still hang on & strongly too Hove to last night at 11 o'clock having raised land directly ahead. Had the main topsail aback all the mid watch & the helm hard down. 4 o'clock filled away & stood for Sandy Island which presents a very singular appearance when seen, as it was by me at daybreak. Long low & black with one or two sandy spots of beach as white as snow, it was not unlike a Cape Horn porpoise on the leap. At 8 o'clock I relieved Bell on the fore topgallant yard looking out for land & shoals. I had a fine view of a large mass of rocks which we were passing to the southward of. It had the appearance on the South side of having once been frozen, & thawing out had

* From the context, the Long. seems more likely to be 125° 30′.

caved exactly as thawing dirt does in the spring, while to the northward it looked as though it had slid "A'la sand bank" into the sea, a reef stretched away from the western end of it which I was fearful we would strike. But we didnt. The Great island about 10 miles East from us, presented a fine appearance in general & looked as though it might be inhabitable, though *I* should prefer, almost any other place in the same lat N. or S. We are on the *qui vive* for Providence reef which lies in 125° 11′ E. Capt G. is rather haggard today & has been for the two past. It is rather dangerous navigating a ship through these rocks shoals & currents He remarked to the 2ᵈ mate when told that the wind was very unsteady, "Yes" Yes" You must watch her sharp" "thats" all you have to do from this to Shanghae" and to the man at the *"slue stick"* "Keep her close at it Walter we want every inch we can get" and he did keep her *close at it* indeed," so close that he nearly shook me from my lofty perch

Sunday Dᴇᴄ 11ᵗʰ 1859   Straits of Formosa*

10 o'clock. I have just come off the topgallant forcastle where I have been since 8 bells this morning looking out for some of the *"Leu Cheus"*. We have of a neccessity taken to short tacks, (8 to 10 hours) & are beating between the islands & the main land. We had 360 miles to make yesterday noon. The current is with us so long as we dont approach to near the coast of China, in which case it would be fearfully against us, for inside of Formosa it runs to the Southward at the rate of 5 knots while outside not 150 miles from it, It runs N. at the rate of 3 or 4. We have been about, 4 times since my last writing, & ere we have tacked as many times again hope to be at anchor at Woosung or the Saddle islands at least. Mr Peterson says the latter tho' he probably knows no more about the Capts intentions than I do. The weather is pleasant & just cool enough to enable one to work & sleep with comfort. The breeze is fine, though rather inclined to *bluster*, so sometimes we *sling* the flying jib & sometimes not. The Carpenter has just come in & caught me writing upon his bench, however he dont care as he is not busy Sundays.

Sunday Dᴇᴄ 18ᵗʰ 1859   Off the Saddle Islands

One week ago I *wrote up* in the carpenter shop. We were then off

---

* The Straits of Formosa are between Formosa and China; the *Intrepid* was considerably to the northeastward.

the North End of Formosa & ever since have been beating, tacking, & wearing, in order to reach that much desired end, Shanghae, & this morning our perseverance was rewarded by the raising of the Saddle group 55 miles S. E., or thereabouts from Woosung. At present we are surrounded by upwards of 600 fishing junks, the occupants of one of which, we *rather* startled, by ploughing along through their nets, which were spread precisely the same as a North River shad fisherman disposes his drifter. The islands are some 40 or 50 in number, high & bold, generally & frequently resembling a saddle. Please observe 5 minutes intermission." I have just been out to take a look at another celestial who was making for *his* net at the rate of knots, it being menaced by us at one end, & a school of porpoises at the other. Oh my" the other watch are sweating up everything forward, & our watch are as garrulous as monkeys, & as it is too cold to remove to some other & quieter place I will defer until we get a "*keel-ik*" down at Woosung, which will probably be tonight some time.

Thursday Dec 22d 1859 4 miles off Woosung

Well the anchor is *down* at *Woosung* & how did it come there. We endeavoured to paſs around outside of Great Saddle island but as the wind headed us off were obliged to run between them & amongst them. They are all barren, though a few feeble attempts at cultivation are evident to a close observer. The inhabitants are all fishermen & have a fine bay in which to anchor their fleet of boats which amounts, I should think to at least 2000, likely more. Overhauled & passed a Danish brig, which missed stays off *Pin Rock* & had the pleasure of being becalmed ourselves 3 miles from the same, where we lay until 9 o'clock in the evening when a fair wind took us out clear of all. The water changes here from clear to very muddy, very suddenly & continues so I am told all the way up to the Corea, thereby deriving its name of "the *Yellow Sea*" 4½ A.M. Raised the light ship (a brig painted red) distant 30 miles from Woosung 5 o'clock took a pilot (Am. Mr Ayr) & the tide having turned & the wind died away dropped anchor, at 11½ A.M. laid there idle, both ship & men, until 4 o'clock P. M. then up anchor & on a ways further until daylight failed & as the channel is not over wide & rather intricate, stopped again. 4 O'clock A. M. all hands up anchor again. 7 o'clock raised the Beacon (A Pagoda shaped tower) 10 miles south of Woosung. 10 o'clock A.M. Anchored at our present position. Now for remarks. We bought $1.25 worth of fish from one of the boats outside. The poor fellow doubtless had a fortune in that slight amount of money. One thing I notice in Particulur which is that the inhabitants of northern China are a larger, healthier, more rugged, set than those to the southward. Capt G. was very anxious to get up to town, but could not get a chance to go until we arrived here. We are the first boat of the Bouro fleet of Am. that has arrived, & we were on the watch for our chums all the while fearful that they would come up & pass us by hook & by crook. The pilot boats   junks & smacks are flying about us in all directions to say nothing of the sampans. As soon as the anchor was fast Mr Hurd got the boats adrift* & put one overboard. Capt G. then got in, & was pulled up to an Opium hulk, (of which there are plenty lying in the river)   the boat was then sent back but Bell, (coxswain) did not come direct   on the contrary, went foraging, for Grub. A white man at last stopped them & asked what ship they belonged to, & on hearing Intrepid at once invited them aboard his chop & ordered his hands to cook dinner for them, while he   saying that he knew Mr Hurd & our Capt went off to the opium hulk in search of the latter, so as to secure the privilege of *"Comprador"*   that being his businefs. Well; while all this was going on, our side, (the starboard watch) were furling sails, & squaring yards, getting out boats, & davits. During the melee subscriber enjoyed a fall, over the fore brace, which stiffened him out for a few minutes & knocked the flesh of the end of his thumb. The boat returned at noon & during the aft^n we laid on our oars. Mr Hurd told me that the letters would not be down until morning so I turned in. After a lapse of ½ an hour Billy M. came to our forcastle with a rush, saying as he punched me furiously Gus, Gus, turn out" the letters have come"   I went aft & there was the man who had entertained our boats crew, coming up the side. He shook hands with the Mate & to his interrogatory for letters, said that he had *a* letter for somebody on board, & produced it. The mate went to the light in the cabin to read the addrefs leaving us (5 or 6) shivering & waiting his return. He soon came & handed me the epistle without a word. Then there was a *"hurussh"* "What no more" &c, &c. "no! no more". Twas true   Capt G. himself has got none. Mine was from my Cousin G. N. at Rondout, dated Sept 13th Mr Hurd inquired

* "Adrift" not properly used here, as the lashings of the boats were removed and did not come off accidentally.

the date the next Morning, & said it was strange that I was the only one who received anything. But I took it quite naturally & told him that it was the 2ᵈ time it had happened to me   This Morning I turned out at 5 o'clock & went over to the other forcastle & was talking when I heard the steward singing out Gus" Gus" heres a letter for you. I soon secured them, (There was two) they were from Rondout & Watkins   Dave, Aunt S. Homer, Aunt L. & Willie, & contained nothing but good news, so all right. The Surprise (My Maiden ship) the Gamecock,* & the Skylark, are all loading for home at $5.00 per ton. The Surprise is almost full & will sail in about two weeks, where we will go is not yet talked about & wont be until we have the coal out. The stevadores all say "oh you go home too, I guess" but doubtlefs they have learned that sailors are always glad to go there, & as they are not sticklers for veracity, always tell you that. Yesterday Morning we saw 3 or 4 ships coming up & as we had nothing else to do, all hands gathered on the topgallant forcastle, & watched for our "compangons du voyage" whom we lost off *Gilolo*. Well heres the order of arrival   Superior first whom we were unacquainted with† beaten by 23 days††   Next Starr King second   whom we hailed with 3 cheers, which were returned heartily. beaten by 12 days†† Golden Rule 3ᵈ whom we were unacquainted with†   beaten 21 days††   We were all eager for Mr Live Yankee & had he made his appearance (which he has not done as yet) would have hissed & groaned at him everlastingly.‡ The scoundrel, he was so *short* off Bouro, perhaps he thought he would be in before us, taking it for granted that we could not sail any   however he will alter his opinion when he does come for we have beaten the *whole fleet*. The Judge Shaw & Mary Fetridge which sailed about the same time as we did have not yet arrived, & indeed they were not looking for us in 2 or 3 weeks yet. So my confidence in Capt G. is redoubled for he always has made good passages. All the

---

* The *Game Cock* was one of the very first "California clippers," being launched in 1850. She established and still holds the record of 19 days from Honolulu to Hong Kong. For this entire run she maintained the remarkable average of 261 miles a day. During the course of another voyage she averaged 306 miles a day for 7 consecutive days. See also picture facing page 113, and the text on that page, covering her race with the *Telegraph* (*Henry Brigham*).

† Reported, November 16, by the *Starr King* to be "a short distance ahead" of the *Intrepid*.

†† In length of passage.

‡ The *Live Yankee*, however, had sailed 8 days after the *Intrepid*, it will be remembered; and the *Intrepid* had been at anchor only two days at this time.

above mentioned ships rounded to under our stern where they are now anchored, with the exception of the Superior which hove up her anchor this noon & has gone up to Shanghae. There is not water enough on the bar yet to admit of our passing so here we lay until next Sunday (Christmas) when the water (spring tides) will be at its height. I am the more anxious to go up as I wish to visit the Surprise & perhaps send some letters home by her

Arrived at Shanghae   Dec 23ᵈ 1859*

Left Shanghae   Feb 4ᵗʰ 1860

Left Woosung   Feb 6ᵗʰ 1860

Left The Saddles (Gutslaugh) Feb 7ᵗʰ 1860†

Arrived at Hong Kong   Feb 10ᵗʰ 1860

Left Hong Kong   Feb 14ᵗʰ 1860

Arrived at Whampoa   Feb 15ᵗʰ 1860

Left Whampoa   Mch 10ᵗʰ 1860

Arrived at Hong Kong   Mch 11ᵗʰ 1860

Left Hong Kong   Mch 13ᵗʰ 1860

Arrived at Macao   Mch 13ᵗʰ 1860

* Three days after reaching Woosung.
† Off Gutzlaff Island the *Intrepid* started side by side with the *Yang Tsze*, the fast Shanghai–Hong Kong mail steamer, and beat her to port by two hours. Gutzlaff I. was named after the Reverend Charles Gutzlaff, a famous German missionary.

Early Recollections

When far away from those he loves
The sad & thoughtful wanderer roves
Bids to his home a long farewell
And goes in other Climes to dwell
Without one friend his thoughts to share
One heart that beats in kindnefs there
'Mid sicknefs, penury, & pain
What draws the sad heart home again?
Tis that the thought of early days
The memory of the past;
In tones more sweet than poets lays
Speaks to the lone outcast;
Mid gnawing want & sickening care
He hears a voice of blessing there
And by relentlefs fate undone
While all around look coldly on
Tells, blessed thought that still he shares
A mothers love, a mothers prayers

THE SHIP *SURPRISE*

From a painting by J. A. Wilson. Courtesy of N.Y., N.H. & H. R.R. Co.

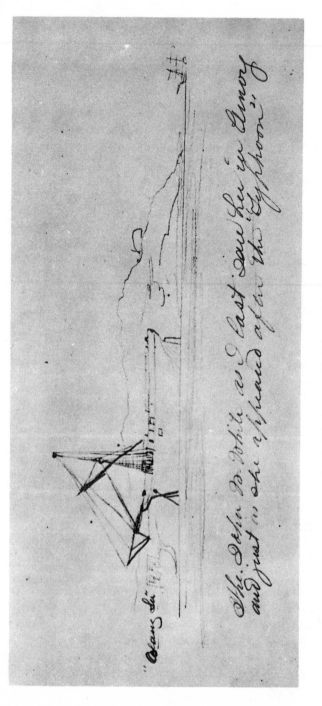

ONE OF ABBEY'S PENCIL SKETCHES

Left Macao MCH 17th 1860 for N. Y.

Monday MCH 19th 1860   Lat about 17° N.

As we are now again at sea & likely to be for some time I will resume my most uninteresting journal. I shall give no a/c of our port experiences with this one exception. On our short run from Hong Kong down to Typa Roads,—which was made in the evening,—we ran over a fishing boat,—We were just done supper & were deeply engaged in discussing the contents of a certain bottle, when, the 2ᵈ Mate who was on the forcastle inquired of the pilot if he saw that boat ahead, the reply was in the affirmative & we continued our conversation a moment when we heard *"Port"* & *"Starboard"* from two different voices alternately it was repeated twice by each, in 1/16 the time it has taken me to describe it, & then a sudden bunk, smash, crash, & falling of spars saluted our ears. I rushed up & out on the forcastle & looking over the side was just in time to see about 20 or 25 feet of a *"lorchas"* & 6 or 8 people struggling in the water directly under our fore Channels, it took but one glance to see that she was sinking, but ere I could have thrown a line to her she would have been far out of reach. Still not a sound was heard for two or 3 minutes & then began a series of shrieks & crys for assistance but what could we do for them, before we could have *"rounded to"* even, "Much lefs have beaten back to the scene of the accident," we should have been a mile or more to leeward. So we kept due on fully assured that all who were not killed outright by the smash would be picked up by their *chum* who was close to them or some other of the hundreds of their kind that was in sight It was not so much the Chinamen that we cared about but the poor women & children for the men are but pirates at best, though professedly fishing for a living, & would have made little of Wrecking our good ship & hamstringing her crew had they a good opportunity. We had our bowsprit lantern out & the phosphorescence of the water alone rendered any object of size visible at a miles distance, but they must have thought they could weather us & were deceived by the brilliancy of our light into believing us to be at a greater distance than we really were. At all events there they were 14 or 15 of them sitting on her rail & paying no attention to our repeated admonition to *"keep away"* & thereby go clear of us, & *there they sat* without making the slightest noise until, "our Martingale capsized them," "our prow cut them in to," (for we struck her amid ships & passed through her the bows going along the port side & the stern passing to starboard) & the waves were swallowing them up & then they began to sing out for assistance. We are two days out & have lost the Monsoons & got a head wind, however I am glad to be on salt provisions again for Ive eaten sufficiently of Chinese "*Caraboul.*"

Wednesday Mch 21st 1860   Lat 15° N.
The wind hauled last night at 12 M. & we tacked ship. Repeated the manouvre this morning at 6½. The weather is again excessively hot & flannels are at a discount Met two vessels of war last night, twas to dark to distinguish but we supposed them to be Transports. One was a steamer the other a ship the former towed the latter & both were under a prefs of sail. We are now engaged sail mending & are likely to be for some time to come. If we have no better luck than we have had we shall make but a poor passage, however, once in the S E trades we are as good as home.

Sunday Mch 26th 1860   Lat 5°. 30′ n   8 months out
This day 8 months we left Bedlows island New York bay, & since then what a road & distance we have travelled, what changes have taken place, what sights we have seen. How often on the outward passage did we wonder when we would arrive out, what our prospects would be, where we should be sent & oftenest of all when we should get home. Now that we are there bound, the wonder is, "What sort of a passage we will make." It is Sunday morning, one of those fine warm sunny tropical Sabbaths that could never be surpafsed if we could connect the enjoyments of home & friends with them, but that can never be, & though I've been in many places noted for beauty of scenery I find none to compare with home, & the Hudson river. Pulo Pinang "the gem of the Indies" is beautiful indeed, Sumatra, Malacca, Java, Sandal Wood Island, the same. Lookisong or Landscape Island is a paradise, but none of them are *home* Nothing about them reminds you of bygone days, & departed friends, you see none of the familiar haunts of your childhood. Spots to bathe in there are, but not the ones you took your first strokes in. Beautiful trees there are, & widespreading, but not the ones you were wont to resort to during the recesses in your schoolboy days. No marks

[250]

are on them such as your penknives were wont to make. Yet they are beautiful, far more so than any spot at home. Capt G. is walking the poop to leeward of the spanker boom & eyeing me & my book intently I wonder what he thinks I am about, he never saw it before. He has had his hair & whiskers trimmed & now looks a particle more like civilization than he formerly did, albeit he is by no means a savage, but a perfect gentleman, & would like to see everybody the same, though that is impossible to some of his *"bull dogs"* as he has facetiously termed us. And well he might for wherever we have been, we have had the reputation of being the smartest crew in port & indeed the ship is one a sailor can take pride in, for she is like a well broken faithful horse, that minds at touch of rein. For instance at Hong Kong when getting under way for Whampoa, whether it was that we were stimulated by the idea of going home, or not, we hove up the Anchor, loosed & set everything & were gone, within ½ an hour after we received our orders. And in taking in our canvaſs when it has been loosed to dry, other vessels would begin at 3 oclock & finish at 4½ may-hap we always waited for our countrymen the sloop of war Hartford* & raced with her & so proficient did we become that it was a hard matter for her to claim anything of a victory over us though of course she always beat us. But enough of bragadoccia. We are now in about 5° north & if this breeze (which we have the audacity to call the N. E. Monsoons) only holds as strong as it is at present even we shall paſs Angier by Wednesday next. There I must endeavour to procure a Monkey at All hazards, for that would tickle Willie, & he must be pleased even at the trouble of taking care of one.

Thursday Mᴄʜ 29th 1860   Lat 1° —′ n   Long 108° E
"We are nearly where we have been for the last two days" I.E. we have had so little wind that we have made scarcely any prog-reſs. We croſsed the sun day before yesterday, And if we could only procure a slight breeze would croſs the line by 2 or 3 this aftn. These days are most magnificent, the evenings cannot be sur-passed, & on the whole we are having a very pleasant time of it. It seems almost too bad that we cannot get on, but perhaps it is better to be *short of wind* here than in some place nearer home, which would make all hands *fidgety*. What wind we have is aft

---

* The brand new screw steamer, soon to become so famous as the flagship of Admiral Farragut.

& keeps quartering occasionally & then it is "Jibe the spanker boom," point the yards forward" & shortly after, "Jibe the spanker boom," & point the yards the other way, besides which we have nothing to do. Indeed it is too hot, & after working a few moments on the sail which has occupied our attention since leaving Macao, Capt G. ordered it below, until we got finer weather, (I. E. cooler). The water is covered with floating logs, feathers, nuts, Cuttle fish, & not a few snakes   long dull brown & yellow rascals that as they come alongside, turn their satanic features up, give one a devilish look & go—down—down—to the regions below for aught that I know. There are 9 small Islands on our Starboard bow, the names of which I do not know,   they are part of the chain which extends all along down from here to Angier. Saw a sail yesterday which Capt G. said was a topsail schooner, but it proved to be a barque. Oh what a lazy atmosphere,   the very deck buckets appear sleepy, & if one could only hear the singing of birds & buzzing of insects, one would imagine himself on a farm in the country, so loudly do our fowls cackle & squak. The main resort is the topgallant forcastle where both watch on deck & watch below congregate, the one to sew read or sleep, the other to sing, talk, & stand by for a call, which they often get & often will as long as such weather as this prevails. Now theres Dick H. sitting on a scuttle butt, with a book which he has been trying to peruse but has given up in despair & is trying to give *"Cho"* (a Frenchman) an insight to the mysteries of English Literature, a task which he will find fruitlefs I fear. Dick has been in the ship since she was built. Awhile since through some conversation I discovered that he was acquainted with an old schoolmate & friend of mine, & we have been *"laying pipes"* to surprise him upon our return, as he is unaware that we have been shipmates nearly two voyages. Now they are at Peter tormenting him. He is a Swede & besides being the biggest man in the ship he is the biggest fool, in fact I really think he is half crazy, for if a boy even says any thing to him he will talk & talk & jaw with him two hours. For instance, no sooner does the watch turn out than some one will say perhaps, "Now where are my shoes" "Peter youve hid my shoes"   of course being innocent he will deny having done so & while his head is turned the accuser will put the shoes (which he has had by him all the while) in Peters bunk & shortly after affect to find them there whereupon all will say to P. "Now there you go, "at your old tricks again, cant you break yourself of that habit" &c & Peter will get so crazy mad, that (being too much of a coward to "*go in*" & *clean* the *crowd out*) he will rush out of the forcastle cursing every body in general & some one or another in particular, thereby causing much merriment. Or maybe some one will declare (at supper time when all hands are collected together) that he has lost 4 or 5 biscuit or a piece of meat, & then, oh! hey" here," wheres Peter he's the man that took it & in spite of any evidence it will be proved on him & then he will declare war against all hands, but seldom goes farther than to smash his pipe on the deck or stamp up his hat & *clear the ranch*." Five minutes afterwards the chief instigator of the row might enter into conversation with him about anything, & he would forget all about his troubles

Singapore APL 19th 1860 (at the Sailors Home)

Look at this now," beautiful isnt it, laying here idle at the Consuls expense. But hold on," this is supposed to be a journal, though I fear it will prove a very uninteresting one. Well to recapitulate, on the 31st day of March at 10½ A.M. the Intrepid was running into the mouth of the straits of Gaspar (China Sea) with a fine breeze, & going about 6 knots per hour. Banca was in sight on the starboard bow & Gaspar on the port, & the rock on Belvidere shoal was nearly abeam, distant ¾ of a mile. The Capt was in the starboard quarter boat, the mate ½ way up the mizzen rigging with the glass, the port watch were all on the forcastle, I was in my bunk trying to get some *winks*" & one hand was singing "twenty five fathom" & "a white sandy bottom" when Crash," Smash," Bang," Thump," a ti Rump Bump Sug," went the ship & she was in her last resting place though no one thought so for a moment *"All hands lay everything aback"* work lively now boys" cried Capt G. *"Let go all the lee braces"* & in 3 minutes the sails which had filled so beautifully to the breeze were flat to the mast. *"Clear away the Larboard Quarter boat Mr Hurd & see what water we have"* I was in the boat for one, & saw the soundings taken, 2½ under the stem & Coral at that, 3 amidships, (blue rock) 4½ under the stern (same) On the port beam was a high pointed rock about the size of our long boat, nearly reaching the surface of the water, & had the ship struck half her length either side of her position she must inevitibly have knocked her spars out of her But no twas done easy thank Heaven. When we found that the wind would not back her off we got a kedge anchor out off the Port quarter took the fall to the main deck Capstan & found she would not budge. Then twas starboard watch forward, port watch aft & heave cargo overboard, & didnt it fly through the hatches!" Teas, silks matting, Cassia buds Annisseed & Annisseed oil, all mixed together, & spiced with Camphor, dunnage, & old fenders. Indiscriminately was it thrown, & I suppose it is floating around yet in want of an owner. We practised this for 4 hours occasionally trying the Capstan but twas futile No amount of persuasion could induce her to move, though we several times thought she started but twas only the Anchor "*Coming home*". All the while she was thumping on the rocks & tearing herself to pieces, & at 2½ P. M. she bilged & made water at the rate of 5 ft per hour. Of course we then knocked off & gave her up for lost & everyone began packing a few clothes that we absolutely needed & became resigned to leaving her, though it went hard. To think of leaving that splendid vessel, almost new, that never leaked or strained or jarred, at all, that splendid sea boat that weathered every gale so beautifully, that stately ship that carried her royals in almost any reasonable breeze. Oh! did she not look noble as seen from the boat with "*everything to the masts,*" those splendid spars that none in America could excel, & few, *very few*, equal. Well, at 8 bells (8 o'clock in the evening) a consultation was held on the Quarter deck, in which the Capt expressed himself highly gratified at the zeal & good behavior of everyone, & gave his opinions & advice in regard to our present situation, soliciting remarks. We left it all to him as our Capt yet & said we would obey him to the last & attend to his wishes, because he had always treated us like men & human beings & given us good times & an easy ship. He then thanked us for our Confidence, & requested that we should get a good nights rest, & be ready to take to the boats in the morning. But few slept however, for all were afraid of the spars falling & crashing through the forcastle deck, so heavily did she thump. But morning came at last & the boats were got out & veered clear of the ship. The axes were put in requisition & everything cut from taffrail to knight heads. The mizzen mast was a splendid spar, & refused to go even when left without any support but the Main took the mizzen with it when it fell, & the fore did not give us a chance to clear the last 3 Lanyards, but went by the board, & curious to relate rang the bell furiously in its descent, & proper it was that a knell should be tolled for such splendid spars, & rigging. This of course lightened her considerable, but the seas breached right over her neverthelefs. Oh it looked sad to see it to see them come curling & breaching, & run right up her side & over her deck & off the other, they never did so before but now she offered no resistance & lay firm & immovable on her bed of rock. The *mid ship* house was bent like a bow & the ship herself was in 3 pieces & going into more rapidly Well we began to provision the boats, but while doing so raised a sail. The 2^d mate with one quarter boat intercepted her & was told to hang up & come aboard. while he was away we began to fire our guns Mr Hurd & myself at one & the steward & John M. C. at the other. Said I to the mate "Pshaw this is all nonsense Mr Hurd she'll never hear us against this gale" (& neither did she as we afterwards discovered) "Oh never mind Charlie" says he "We may as well have our 4th of July here now" "since we cant have it at home" all right sir says I, Im agreeable, & at it we kept, firing wads at Beattie & Dick who were off in the long boat & trying to dodge them. The Mizzen mast went 25 ft above the deck & left a rope over the stump for us to run our ensign up *"Union Down"* & there it flies to this day mayhap. For we left it so when we went aboard the other vessel, which proved to be the French Coolie ship Galilei from Whampoa for Martinique The first thing *they* offered us was brandy, & we all accepted it readily. She filled away as soon as possible & very foolishly cast our boats adrift. He might far better have taken them in & thrown his own over-board for they were splendid ones, & worth at least $800.00. Well we staid on board of her for a week & then got to Angier There we fell in with the Beaver from Shanghae for N. Y. Capt G. tried to have some or all of us go home in her, but he had not enough provisions so we procured a Couple of Prahus & started for Batavia & the Am. Consul. We arrived there in 18 hours & went ashore. We all lived at a Tiffin house for two days & enjoyed ourselves hugely at Uncle Sams expense.* We left on the 11th of April for Singapore via Muntok & Riouw & arrived on the 15th Since then we have lived at the Sailors Home. The Consul has allowed us all nescesary clothing &c, & mails our letters for us. I have been looking out for a ship to come home in, but have not got one as yet Bell has this day gone on board the Samuel Appleton as 2^d Mate. Dick H is in expectancy of a sort of mates berth on board an Italian brig bound to Hong Kong. And old Capt Sherman of the Clipper ship

Hurricane was bound to have me go mate of a barque bound to Sarabang, yesterday but, I had no *"mates certificate"* & she flies the English flag, so her insurance would be insecure in case of disaster. Therefore I did not get it. If it had been an American vessel I should though. I live in style for I have a little money. Every evening sees me in my Curry driving out among the Nobility, & sometimes I condescend to grace the Esplanade with my gracious presence I suppose they all wonder who I am but I take care *"not to let that out."* All this costs me is 40 or 50 cents per day. This is a splendid place & very healthy too. I came acrofs one of my old shipmates in the Surprise, day before yesterday. He was extremely glad to see me, although he was *"3 sheets in the wind."*

* One of the duties of a consul—less important now than in the past—was to care for shipwrecked sailors.

CHAPTER XVIII

INTREPID'S NUMBERS 5490

"NOW NO MORE"

The preceding chapter gives the true story of the wreck of the *Intrepid*. About twenty years later a fiction writer read over these diaries and wrote a yarn based scantily on the wreck. It appeared in *The Youth's Companion* and included detailed descriptions of thrilling battles with pirates. These encounters started when the ship went on the rocks and lasted till the *Galilei* came along and saved the situation. This yarn has in some way been accepted as the truth and has found its way into some records as fact, instead of the fiction that it is.

Eventually about $2,000 worth of the *Intrepid's* $660,000 cargo was salvaged by a vessel from Singapore. In the general oriental freight of teas, silks, etc., there was a large consignment of firecrackers. It had been hoped to get these to the States before the Fourth of July. But the 1860 celebration of American Independence was doomed to get along without them.

The *Intrepid* had turned in one noteworthy sailing performance after leaving New York. After requiring 33 days to reach the equator—more than double the record time—she sailed from there to the Cape of Good Hope in 29 days. In fact she was considerably south of the Cape at the end of that time. This was very fast sailing. It gave her a New York–Good Hope time of 62 days, not much more above the record than was her New York–equator time. It is difficult to make many further comparisons since she sailed from the Cape to Ombay Pass rather than to Java Strait. This was because of the fact, it will be remembered, that she would have found the monsoon blowing against her in the China Sea if she had tried to go the shortest way. Of course, all fast times to China were set up by ships arriving there in the season of the southwest monsoon. The *Intrepid* ran from the Cape to Ombay Pass in 41 days, thus taking 103 days from New York. The record for the shorter distance of New York to Java Head is 70 days, 10 hours, made by the *Sea Witch*. The *Intrepid's* time from Ombay to Woosung was 44 days, and from Ombay to Shanghai, 47 days. Thus her total time from New York to Woosung was 147 days, and from New York to Shanghai, 150. Of course it was a slow passage but it could not have been improved upon greatly in that season of the year and under all the other existing circumstances. As a further indication of how long a pull it is to China (via Good Hope) when the wind is not right, it is of interest to consider here the extraordinary voyage of the *Flying Cloud*. She sailed from New York to Hong Kong, via Cape Horn *and San Francisco*, and made it in 137 days including a 10-day stop!

Southward bound toward her last resting place the *Intrepid* went from Woosung to Hong Kong in 4 days, requiring only 3 from Gutzlaff Island which is near the start. Probably no sailing vessel has ever surpassed this latter performance by many hours. Her time from Macao to the place of the wreck was 14 days. The record from Whampoa to Anjer is 7 days, 12 hours, made by the *Witch of the Wave* with the aid of a strong northeast monsoon, of course, which the *Intrepid* did not have. It is most unfortunate that the splendid ship did not have a longer life. She showed herself to be very speedy during her brief career. But, only an occasional ship can expect enough luck with the wind to set a record when her life is less than four years.

Captain Gardner and First Mate Hurd were not finished with the perils of the sea when the *Intrepid* went to pieces. Gardner got home from Anjer as a passenger on the *Beaver*, bound from Shanghai for New York. There he took command of the medium clipper ship *Asterion* and sailed her to Cardiff. The *Asterion* was owned by the same firm as the *Candace, Celestial, Comet* and *Intrepid*, Captain Gardner's earlier commands. She left Cardiff on December 4, 1860, reaching San Francisco in 139 days. From San Francisco she went to Baker Island in the South Seas where she loaded guano for Hampton Roads, Va. On the way home she came into the outer harbor of Pernambuco, Brazil, and Gardner sent this letter to the owners: "I arrived off this port the 15th, 75 days from Baker's Island, and came to the outer roads this morning. I think you had better insure, even at the extra expense, as the *Asterion* is not a clipper and will be a bon prize for the Southerners. I shall sail this evening and take a new route for Hampton Roads." The ship carrying the letter was captured 6 days out by the Confederate raider *Sumter.* Captain Semmes of the latter vessel got hold of the epistle and was much amused by it; but it did not enable him to capture the *Asterion.* She reached Hampton Roads safely whence she proceeded to New York in due time.

Here Captain Gardner was relieved by Hurd. The *Asterion* made a round trip to San Francisco and then sailed once more to the West Coast. This was her last voyage. Captain Hurd took her from San Francisco to Howland Island in the South Seas, where she took aboard 1,600 tons of guano. After covering only 50 miles of her journey home she was lost on one of the reefs of Baker Island. At this point began one more epic of the sea on which a volume could be written. Here, however, it is fitting to devote but a paragraph.

Though the crew got safely ashore it was only after a hard battle with the surf. The castaways made the best of it in huts built from the wreckage; but food was scarce and no ship put in an appearance to take them off. Except for gulls, about all they had to eat were snakes dug out of the ground. The chief mate and six men set out in a boat for Howland Island to obtain assistance. They failed to make their destination, and the best they could do was to reach one of the Gilbert Islands, hundreds of miles to the westward. The mate and three of the men finally ended up in Sydney, Australia. After being marooned on Baker Island for more than two months of misery, Captain Hurd and the seventeen men remaining with him were picked up by the *Herald of the Morning*—and this was a right famous clipper by which to be rescued. The shipwrecked mariners reached Honolulu on Christmas day, 1863, just three months after the wreck. And there we shall leave our friend the Mate of the *Intrepid.*

Abbey reached Singapore on April 15, 1860, 16 days after the wreck of the *Intrepid.* But his troubles resulting from the catastrophe were not yet over; for, at this stage of the proceedings, he came closer to departing this life than at any time prior to his final demise. Here he is, still at Singapore two months later:

"Sailors Home   Singapore   J<small>UNE</small> 11th 1860
How does that date suit you   reader.   Now I must tell you what has befallen me within the past 6 or 7 weeks. Soon after writing the last few pages I was engaged by the Capt of the Resolute to go

home. Well I joyfully went on board & to work I soon perceived a general debility coming over me, & got weaker, & weaker every day. I kept my feet (though with great difficulty,) for 6 days & then had to *give in* Capt Sheriff asked me what the matter was but I could not tell him. He then asked me if I wanted to go ashore. I said I did not but would if he wished it But he said no, he did not. However the next morning I received orders to get ready to go on shore, & wait for the Capt at the Consuls office. I did so & soon received an order to go to the Hospital. I got there as soon as I could & found that I had the Java fever I soon got worse & finally delirious in which state I remained several days I then came to my senses without an appitite & remained so for 12 days or more during the time the Hospital inmates were all removed to the new building. I recovered slowly & at last began to feel hungry. To make it short I lost my chance of getting home & laid 37 days among the sick & dying, when I was released at my own request. Out of a number that went down to the wreck Alexander Carstens & John —— a Swede, I hear, died of this same fever. Both were shipmates of mine. I am to go home in the ship St Louis as Consuls man if I am unable to ship & do duty as A. B. Previous to coming ashore I weighed 175 lbs & now I balance at 140, showing a loss of 35 lbs which my face confirms"

At last, however, the sun broke through the clouds and he got a chance to go home. It was not in the *St. Louis* but in the *Keystone*. She was not a flyer, but was scheduled to sail for New York anyway. The *Keystone* was a clipper ship hailing from Boston. Her career was not a notable one; little about her has come down to us. In 1855 she sailed from Boston to New York and thence to San Francisco, the passage from New York requiring exactly 150 days. At that time her master was Wm. McFarland. Now, in 1860, her officers included the following: Captain, Varina; First Mate, Pritchard; Second Mate, Burnham. It is in this ship and with these officers that our diarist keeps his last log.

CHAPTER XIX

THE LAST DIARY

Tuesday June 19th 1860   Singapore Harbor
This day I joined the ship Keystone, Varina Master, bound to
N. Y.

Wednesday July 4th 1860   Singapore Harbor   Ship Keystone
Opened the day with a grand Wash *"all over"* *"Hose"* conducted
by Mr Burnham 2^d officer, after which Mr Pritchard made a
cartridge for the little braſs gun which we have; (—said cartridge being about 1 foot long & containing nearly 2 lbs of
powder,) meaning, no doubt, not to be outdone by the loudneſs
of the report if he was by the number of them. At 8 bells up went
the colors, & *"bang"*, *"bang"* went the St Louis' carronades. We
were silent (saving our breath for 12 o'clock)   We then went to
breakfast, & while engaged discusing that, & where we should go
to spend our money & have a time, down came Sumatra   carried
away our fore signal halyards, split the burgee, & slatted the
awnings *"all to the mischief."* We rushed out   secured things
got wet & came below again. Well   the rain done   the main part
went ashore, & I called upon Dick. H. who is aboard the St
Louis. Came back & assisted to haul down the colors   numbers,
signals, pendants, jacks, &c &c, with which the vessel was be-
decked & at sundown *"Ker Whang"* went the little brass 6
pounder with a report that must have astonished all who knew
the size of the gun. The steam frigate Assaye of the Royal Indian
Navy did not recognize our rejoicings but an English Transport
in the offing, *"dressed ship"* with the *Stars & Stripes"* at the fore
in respect for the day. In honor of such a great occasion I could
not refrain from opening a pack of firecrackers, (which I bought
for Willie, in China,) & having a celebration. I shant recount the
surprise of *"Peche"* our bum boat man, when a cracker scorched
his bare legs, nor how quickly he made himself scarce

Thursday July 19th 1860   Singapore Harbor
The ship being ready for sea we signed the Articles & took our
advance.

Saturday July 21st 1860   ditto

Went on shore on liberty in order to get my sea stock of soap, cigars, matches, this, that, & the other thing, & had a very good time generally

Sunday July 22d 1860   same

Hired a "*Dingah*" & had 5 men to pull me around the harbor. Stopped on board the Liverpool ship "*Versailles*" & procured some books,   went on the St Louis & bade Dick. H. good bye, until New York   We both sail together, but as we have the smartest vessel of the two, will probably have our cargo all discharged ere she arrives home.

Wednesday 25th July   Singapore Straits

Got our anchor & made sail for New York. The Capt concluded to go through Riouw & Banca Straits, so the wind being ahead & the pilot not daring to run her through in the night, we anchored & furled everything but the topsails.

Thursday July 26th   One year from home   Riouw Straits

Up anchor at 4 o'clock A. M. & away again   during the day we made some 15 or 20 tacks & ran away from our two consorts (Eng.) the Versailles & William Stewart   They however kept under way some time later than we did & are now 4 or 5 miles to Leeward of us

Wednesday Aug 1st 1860   Mouth of Banca Straits

We have been tacking & wearing about since the last writing, with both plenty & no wind in vain endeavours to get to windward, but all to very little purpose as yet. Capt V. altered his mind & tried for Gaspar, but as if in defiance   old Boreas is coming direct from there, so this morning, finding himself almost on top of Banca head he bore up intending to try the other passage, (Banca Straits) but, himself fickle as the wind whose every shift he watches, he has again changed his mind & as I write   the starboard watch are staying her & I believe have her on the other tack once more.

Tuesday Aug 14th 1860   Lat 9°. 00′ S   Long 90°. 00′ or so E

about

No apologies to make, perhaps they are unnescesary   After our fruitlefs attempt at Banca we again kept up for Caremata pas-

[262]

sage (Billiton Straits) & after tacking & beating about with no regularity at all, & being called out at all hours day & night, got through & set studding sails in the Java Sea with our prow towards the Straits of Sunda, at Angier in which we anchored on the 10th inst, to find ourselves ahead of the rest anyhow. So I cant see Dick until he gets home I had one days boat duty there, got scorched by the sun, & diarheaed by the water, bought a monkey a pair of turtle doves, some cocoa nuts bananas & some Juggery, & then was happy to heave up the anchor & *"ylough"* out of it for home direct ever since we have had fine trades & would have a very nice time in any other ship, but,—go to sea on a log, & then you will have a slight Idea of this ships rolling propensities Here she is *"everlastingly dusting"* herself & going —*"Six Knots" "almost,"* & that with fuss enough for Sixteen. I am astounded Why I never saw a ship dive pitch & wallow about so, even in heavy weather & to sum it all up we have all de-nominated her a *"beastly brute"* & are anxious to get home more than ever. Bah she keeps rolling me off my seat, & I have to snatch my ink bottle & hold on all till she steadys herself a little.

Indian Ocean

Saturday AUG 18th 1860. Not many hundred miles off the Cocos islands*

Shadrack is dead. He committed suicide in the following manner. When I purchased him he was confined by a nasty dirty greasy bit of twisted calico, about the waist. I consequently got a new lanyard for him & spliced an eye around his neck at which he was much disgusted & endeavoured to show his dislike by pitching, tearing, bumping his head, biting his ropes &c, until finding no one would relieve him he (in a fit of temporary insanity I suppose) ran under, up, & over, down, the jib sheet whip took 5 turns around the standing part of his lanyard & *"Croaked"* (to use a phrase more striking than classic). Now I bewail Shadracks lofs greatly not because of his intrinsic value but because I know he would immensely tickle a certain little individual at the antipodes who labors under the Cognomen of William Chester Abbey Esq & I have partly promised to bring him one. But he must wait until next time when I will try again. I have now to look for my Turtle Doves of which I have the handsomest pair in the ship &

* Where the German raider, *Emden,* met her fate in 1914 at the hands of H. M. A. S. *Sydney.*

see that the poor little beauties dont follow in the track of their only too illustrious predecessor Shadrack. We are one week out from Angier & have made ordinary progress, we are always going though either fast or slow & have not been out of wind an instant so far

Sunday Aug 26th 1860   About 63° 00′ E. & 22°. 30′ S.

Once more am I experiencing a glorious sunny Sunday in the Indian Ocean, but tis not so pleasant as it would have been in the good old Intrepid. For here we have stunsails & staysails & cross-jack & plenty of work. Work they call it, but humbugging it is, to keep all hands on deck here just to get up 4 casks of water & mend a main topsail, which will never be bent again at least not this passage   Yet this is the famous *good* ship Keystone of Singapore renown. Our mate is a rascal & would demonstrate himself if it were not for Capt Varina, who admits of no brutality. But *this* does not prevent him from making us pump the ship out after 8 bells, & managing to keep us up 10 or 15 minutes over time at every opportunity. As late as last night he sung out to one hand, & asked him why he did not put the fore sheet in its becket as he told him to do (but did not give him a chance,) adding that if we didnt do a thing another time when he told us that he would *humbug* us the whole watch. To which I answered that I'd bet if he did he would'nt keep us up all day. He has struck none of this crew as yet, & if he does he wont go all around without catching a *Tartar*. We have run 25 or 2600 miles since leaving Angier (14 days) have split a crossjack a main topsail, & blown away a fore topgallant sail. The Capt bought some beef in Singapore for the best of Hamburg, but it proves to be the worst of h'Orse'. I have an idea, dont tell any body," "I'll get all I can & as I cant eat it I'll make snuff boxes out of it & realize a large profit on our arrival by selling them for Mahogany. No amateur could detect the counterfeit Walter is more unfortunate than I am, he has been laid up for 9 or 10 days with the dysentery & is generally weak. As for myself I am as large fat & as stout as I wish to be & can hardly believe that 2 months ago I only weighed 140 lbs The precursors of cool weather have made their appearance (Cape pigeons) & the nights are fine & chilly. I have the prettiest & best kept pair of pigeons aboard & seeing all the mates promenading the quarter deck trying to recruit their dirty & featherlefs persons I let mine out in the forecastle but one of them being dissatisfied with the contracted limits of the aforesaid place took one *swoop* & was out on deck. After taking a general survey of the accomodations which surrounded him, he concluded that the cabin was the place which suited him best & away he went aft through the door & up into the skylight amongst the *barometers* & *tell tales* therein hung. A little *forcible persuasion* at last got him into his cage again & out of it is not my intention to let him again before we get home unlefs indeed he *kicks the bucket*. Oh, they are such pretty little things its a pity to shut them up, but it cant be helped   Blow ye gentle zephyrs blow & let us get home once more

Thirteen months away today

	S.	E.
Sunday SEPT 2ᵈ 1860	30°. —	42°. or 43°. —

All our watch are combing   currying & brushing themselves up in honor of the day   Charley has his pigeons out & has let one pair go altogether   The he one has departed for parts unexplored while the she one is perched upon the fore topsail sheets taking a general survey   Peter has got George Welles hat on his head & is now endeavouring to shove his fist through a ninety year old coat. He is now promenading the decks, playing the boarding master   & wishing to ship all hands for Liverpool. Henry the mates brother in law is here collecting his Ledgers

Saturday SEPT 16ᵗʰ 1860   On the meridian of Cape Lagullas

Oh dear!! what shall I say   it is so long since I took a pen in my hand that I have almost forgotten how to begin. Lets see, it was a week ago last monday that we took our first gale & since, we have had awful weather. On that Monday eve at 7 o'clock twas blowing very fresh & we were taking in the mizzen topgallant sail, when both main topgallant sheets went together & we clewed all 3 up at once, & furled them, & well it was that we did so. The Capt has never been out here before, & is not posted, but the mate has, & is, so upon seeing the lightning & hearing the thunder he advised that at 8 o'clock our topsails should be double reefed but Capt V. thought he would hang on a little while & so our watch came on deck   I was on the lookout, & keeping my eye on the jib tack which I expected would part & let the sail go up the stay, when I heard something s—s—s—s—sr—ip bang!! & the fore topsail was in ribbons, & bound on ahead to report us perhaps   Then didnt I yell & get *all hands on deck* in no time, & we began

[265]

at once, first down came the fore topsail in a lump on the fore hatch where it couldnt fetch away, & then down came the mizzen topsail yard & we put 2 reefs in him quicker, then down & up at the main & double reefed him, then hauled up the courses & stowed them, in the melee the jib tack did go & the sail went clear up to the topmast head & gave us a job to get it down. We went aft to reef the spanker & while thus engaged it came down furious & we all stopped to look at each other in suspense. All at once the weather mizzen topsail sheet went & the rain began to pour down at once, the wind came in terrible gusts, like a typhoon, only quicker, every one was beaten down by the force of it & could not move, no one knew what to do. The Capt gave orders that the mizzen topsail should be clewed up but ere we could get at the clewlines it blew so strong that the ship was on her lee beam & trembling like an aspen leaf, but not moving at all. It was madness to clew up or start anything while this lasted for we should in-evetibly have lost all so Capt V. cried out in a voice rendered almost inaudible by the force of the gale *"Hang on everything"* "dont start an inch." but Mr Pritchard was roaring & cursing at us for not hauling up the mizzen topsail clewline & he was clearing away the main topsail halyards at the same time, so upon hearing the Capt sang out at the top of his lungs "You'll lose your crofsjack yard" clew up that mizzen topsail" "youll lose your crofsjack yard" *"Nary bit"* he wouldnt & didnt. Twas a terrible squall & the worst one we had. The main topsail is hemp & thick & hard as a board, but the force of the wind sent the rain right through it. We furled the mizzen topsail in the next lull, (which was a gale withal) & close reefed the main topsail set the main spencer & reefed spanker under this sail she hung to the wind & we were hove to, unable to run for two days. We opened every seam in the deck & made water like a basket

C. A. Abbey Esq

Sunday SEPT 23ᵈ 1860   Lat 30.20 S.   Long 14.00 E.
Once more after many privations and trials we are approaching the trade Lats & fine weather. Since writing Last we have ex-perienced two very severe gales the last one was a furious Nor-wester, or rather as Capt V. says a furious contradiction of na-ture, for, the causes of such a gale in this quarter he says he cant a/c for. (However he'll be obliged to account for some of its attendant consequences) such as split topsails & top gallantsails

(old rags at best) a strained ship & slightly damaged cargo. This aforesaid rascally Norwester, (which no old stager in these lats. would have risked an encounter with but have kept in close to land to avoid, or take the benefit of an opposite current in event of being unable to avoid,) blew us clean & clear out of our regular track, & current, into the track of the outward bounders 38°. S. We saw several, the first one of the Eng. Australian packets passed us as we lay *hove to*, scudding under a Close reefed Main topsail & reefed foresail. Whew? wasnt she going though. But we have now regained more than we lost & are clear for good no doubt, but our companions of a fortnight ago are past St Helena no doubt, all from superior management. We have but 12 hands out of which 3 are laid up & one is uselefs. So during the worst of the passage we have had 4 in a watch which with two at the wheel one on the lookout leaves 1, to answer the mates call. Oh, I wish the owner *"Old Butler"* (Old Hanks) was here to help us reef once. I wish he had to stand at that wheel with wet feet in a driving storm (cold weather) & hold on as all of us have done, & notwithstanding two releiving tackles get his entrails jerked out & perhaps his whole carcass *chucked* clean & clear over the spanker boom into a *"warm"* salt bath (gratis). Ill bet he'd allow the ship 20 instead of 12 hands, a screw wheel, double topsails, &c, for her next passage. Close fisted rascal that he is. But now for pleasanter topics. I've had my old Donkey out on the topgallant forecastle today for an airing & overhauled the wreck & remnants saved from the good old Intrepid. While thus engaged Capt Varina had me called aft, & in accordance with his promise gave me a quadrant & nautical almanac for practice, so now for navigation The theory I understand pretty well, now the practice I hope to have. Thus you see the Lat today at the head of this—a—article, not page. The instrument is one of the old Pigyoke stamp & rather unweildy, but neverthelefs true to an iota, mayhap truer. We will soon be in the trades & then for all hands & plenty of work until we lose them & also the N.E. ones, or get into cold weather but then who cares we're *"homeward bound"* & with good luck will be there in 45 days. We are all in a state of ruin, & are almost afraid to go aloft for fear the confounded halyards spars or rigging will give away & kill us the other night we commenced to make sail. the first that went was the mizzen topgallant halyards then the fore then the topgallant staysail down-haul. The next night the main & fore top-

[267]

gallant sails were coming in, we parted a clewline of each this morning the main was being hoisted up & the halyards went. Bob is looking on & coincides with me in my opinion that she is an unsafe brute, all around, & our lives are or have thus far been miraculously spared. During the late gale we parted the weather main topsail brace & the sail close reefed. There was a job & a dangerous one, the ship hove to, in a hurricane, & the yard going bang, bang, whack, jerk, & threatening to destroy all who ventured near. However, Bob & Ned started up with a preventer Ned went out & just had half a turn round the yard-arm when away he went, but luckily caught his leg on the *flemish horse* & kept his hold of the end of the brace, but that was all slack he got in & Bob went out & succeeded in knotting it though as he says his tongue was making buttons all the while. When we came on deck, another had to go & take the place of the first so away went Abbey with the end. Now look here, did you ever try to walk against a gale which withstood your efforts at progress. Well that was just my predicament as I tried to *get* OUT TO WIND*ward*. But by dint of perseverance & tugging away at the reef points I succeeded, & rove it, &—got down as fast as possible, *"You Bet"* (to use a San Francisco phrase) But when Mr P. came on deck he sent me up to take it off & put it out farther, clear the reef jig, shove the 2d reef clear of the topgallant backstay a job which resisted all my efforts. Only the other aftn as I had loosed the fore topgallant sail the 2d mate had both sheets hauled home previous to hoisting the yard up at all, the clews had turns in them & must be cleared, so up came a heaver to me & as I sat on the lee fore topsail yard arm, shoved the purchase into the clew iron & took one turn, away went the chains, the end nearly knocking my brains out let alone knocking me overboard. Well up comes the carpenter to shackle it on & while he was at work I noticed that the main was split from top to bottom. The mate was watching us from the deck & so I pointed towards it, he looked as though he thought me impudent & making fun of him, but, *"didnt"* look where I wanted him to, so, George roared out, *"Look at that Main top gallant sail"* Oh!! One glance was sufficient & away he rushed to have it taken in. I tell you I expect to get hurt or chucked overboard before reaching home & if this bridge should carry me safe I never could conscientiously praise it. Well go along old boat or as Peter says I'll get the pitch Kettle & crow bar & go on without you.

Thursday Oct 4th 1860   One day out of Saint Helena

Night before last at 11 o'clock we raised St Helena & at 9 a'm'. were abreast the town under the topsails. Capt V. prepared to go ashore, so we got a boat out, & "*Abbey*" by dextrous management inserted himself in it for the purpose of going ashore. Upon nearing the shipping a health officer stopped us & asked the Capt a string of questions one half of which he nor anybody else understood   told us that the American bark "*Starlight*" was in from the Coast of Africa & had Commander Mc Donough of the Am. Str. Sumpter as a pafsenger who would undoubtedly go home with us. We went to her & took Mc D. out & ashore with us. I saw a lot of Brooklyn & New York boys belonging to a Whaler then in port, & had some conversation with them. There is but one landing place & over that was an arch in red with "*The Watermans Welcome*" writ in yellow letters, & on the sides P. A. in large Capitals,   upon passing the gates, on every hand we saw "*Welcome Prince Alfred*" posted & wherever a flag could be hoisted a block was stuck. Then as a matter of course it was all explained. The Prince had left on Sat. previous. The town lies in a deep gut or chasm in the rocks & has a high wall on the sea side, which renders it as inaccessible as Gibraltar   As far as I could discern there is but one street the remainder being mere alleys. On passing the gates the first buildings are, the church, Hotel, Court House, as for the rest I believe every other one to be a Drug Store. We went to the market & got a lot of things for the sick ones on board, (who by the way are rather worse at present) & then after drinking sundry glafses of "*Henglish Porter*" at a big stone House down an alley, & labelled "*Tap*," Harry & I took our way down to the boat, with the spoils of our cruise leaving Bob & Henry to prosecute their researches in the direction of *Ladder Hill* which they ascended. It derives its name as you may suppose from a flight of 651 steps at an angle of about 15 to 20 deg. *from* the perpendicular. On the summit is an intermediate telegraph station. The principal one is on Mount Diana the pinnacle of St Helena, & so high that, well you can imagine, We were reported at Noor on the 2d & at that time although we were upon the lookout for the island, we could not see it, & did not until 12 hrs after, & it is distinctly visible at 90 miles distance. On coming down they proceeded to the Court House where some poor "*Matelots*" were on trial for stealing 10 pieces of beef & some bread. Poor hungry wretches. Upon going in their sheath knives were taken charge of until they came out, a proceeding which amused them much. Every other man one meets is a soldier ("*Regular Guffies*)" Prices are enormous. For instance we bought 2 lbs of the best butter for only 40 cts per lb. One coon facetiously proposed that it should be applied to the stem of our boat, adding that it was quite strong enough to pull her off to the ship, which was in the offing, standing off & on. There is a Dutch barque here 133 days out from Sunderland (Eng.) for Loando. (Coast) I doubt if she ever gets to her destination The Starlight leaves tomorrow or the next day, for Loando again, from there she goes to Boston. We have an old Whaling Capt. who has invalided himself home, he has the consumption I believe. As soon as we all got on board, (the Capt & pafsengers came in one of the Starlights boats) our own being so loaded that we had not room to pull her off hardly.) we filled away for New York, & I tell you the way we made sail was a caution to all lazy beholders when everything was on her she was going so fast that Com. Mᶜ Donough must needs have the log hove, so he hove it himself & found 5 knots in his hand when the glass was out which being multiplied by 2 make 10 miles per hr

N About
Sunday Ocᴛ 7ᵗʰ 1860 11° 26′ 14. 00. West

A beautiful day. Oh pshaw I cant write any more. We have all hands all the week & Sunday one has to do all his own work or else go ragged & dirty. She's not the old Intrepid with her Sat. holiday system & no work allowed on Sundays. I have a N Y. Herald of July 10ᵗʰ 1860 announcing the arrival home of the Beaver with Capt G. &c, &c.

S   W
Sunday Ocᴛ 14ᵗʰ 1860 Lat 5°. —′ Long 31° or thereabouts

Welles says he looks good enough in a tarry jumper & avers that he has no clothes. Poor fool he dont know that we overhauled his big black bag (besides which he has a chest full of something) & turned out 2 jumpers 3 light pants 5 pair of heavy ones &c &c ad infinitum, while he has been wearing one old pair ever since we left Singapore almost. But thats no news & had better have been left out perhaps, but then he stood close by me, & said it. The day is a magnificent one, a real S. E. trade sunday, but I fear the wind hitherto so lively is failing for we are going a bare 6, only. A little over a year ago we passed Ferdinand de Noronha in the Intrepid since then she has gone the way of all things & here I am in another ship expecting to make the same island tonight or tomorrow. "Oh," Dear" will Sandy Hook Barnegat or Fire Island or their lights never appear.!. We have our rigging work in a good state of progrefs & by next Sunday I hope it will be finished nearly. The other night at 4 o'clock (in the dark) as our watch was going below & the lookout was being reliveed a full rigged brig was discried almost *"on top ofus"* (to use a sea phrase) & the alarm given. Our course was N W by W. & the wind a little on the starboard quarter, his must have been S. S. W. or so We had *stun'sails* on both sides & I dont think he had any on. He was about 10 ships lengths off & coming down at the rate of 8 knots, for our beam. The mate took our binnacle light out (a bulls eye lantern) & shone it full at him at the same time putting our helm to starboard. Just then I heard 8 bells go aboard of her. Instead of bringing his vessel up to the wind he also put his helm up & a race began she sailed as well as we did & no one knows how it would have ended, had not Mr P. sung out "put your helm down you d——d fool what are you trying to do with her" which having no effect on him we shifted our own & at the risk of spars & booms gave the Keystone a *lively shake,* which luckily sent us clear. If that scoundrel had come aboard of us, blow me if I wouldnt have cracked some one of their heads. They had all the advantage* & by putting the helm the other way would have saved all the time & passed astern of us. Its my next wheel & I havent a single clean shirt to wear there, but I dont care, I'll go in a dirty one & give Capt V. a small decoction of my mind if he says anything, which, I dont think he will. Peter says I must put him down here too. A Norwegian, 22 or 3 years old. Been in American vessels about 5 years drefsed in nankeen, dungaree, a pair of Chinese shoes & an Angier hat, belt sheath, & knife, & the never failing pipe in his mouth. Blair is very sick indeed has fallen away to a complete skeleton & now the tables are turned, so that instead of washing me as he used to do in my helplefs days in Singapore, I wash him; but turn about is fair play, so I shant growl.

* Being somewhat behind.

Sunday Oct 21st 1860   Lat 7°. 05′ N.   Long 42°. 50′ W

Crofsed the line last Wednesday (35°. 20′ W.)   Yesterday morning spoke the Barque Golden Era, of Rockland from Callao for Hampton roads 74 days out. We have the ship almost all tarred down & more than half rattled. The Capt gives her 12 Days to the coast of America & he is an old S. American trader & ought to be an Oracle. Walter is very low it is very doubtful if he will get home with us but we are in hopes that as the weather cools he will stand it better but he is too far gone to recover completely The mate began to thunder night before last & tell how *"he'd knock h—ll out of any g—d d—n—d man in the ship if they did so & so any more* & so on. One said, *"you wont do it to me I know"* & the storm continued some time but like every cloud it had a silver lining & all is sunshine once more. He adjusted my quadrant for me today & said when he was done, "There; when she gets out of *"kelter"* again, just bring her along." Hes a smart man, knows his duty &c &c but he's a rascal, or to use a sea phrase ("a regular Horse")   Took two fancy squalls last night which sent us away towards N. Y. at the rate of 10 or 12 knots. about next Sunday I shall begin to overhaul preparatory to going ashore. Ah oo—o—o—hum Im sleepy good aftn

C.A.A.

Sunday Oct 28th 1860   Lat 17°. 27′ N.   Long 56°. 17′ W.

Walter, my only remaining shipmate in the Intrepid, died Last wednesday aftn & was buried almost immediately after, mortification having set in. Indeed that it was that eased his pain for his last twenty four hours. Charley & Ned sewed him up in canvass with an old capstan head (that was smashed the day I joined her in Singapore) for a weight. Poor fellow it didnt require much to sink him, for having eaten nothing for 3 weeks, he was hardly skin & bones. I was with him at 12 o'clock & he tried to say something to me but weaknefs & the approach of death rendered it inarticulate. I did not think him quite so near his end although not expecting him to live for 12 hrs John Butcher watching him & so I went to work. (He was delirious so it was uselefs to stay with him) I was in the main top & about 15 minutes after chancing to look on deck I saw them in the act of laying him out. As soon as he was turned the advance of mortification was plainly vizible through the skin of his back when all was ready & he was

[272]

placed upon the plank Capt Mayhew (paſs) read a chapter of Eccleseastics & said a prayer. The plank was raised, slid out, tipped up & poor Walters body plunged into the deep blue waters, which soon closed over him, the ship passed on & all Earthly traces of him were lost. He gave me his letters &c to send home in case he should die & told me to take all his things that I wanted, but they were few at best for he fared no better than the rest at the wreck, & a great deal worse since. The tar is all gone & the rigging work all done. Now we have to scrub the paint & maybe holystone the decks & all is finished for the Keystone.

Twenty Years Ago

Favor of Mr Walter S. Blair   Chelsea Maſs

Ive wandered to the village Tom ; Ive stood beneath the tree
Upon the school house playground that sheltered you & me
But none were left to greet me Tom ; & few were left to know
That played with us upon the green ; some twenty years ago

The grass is just as green Tom ; barefooted boys at play
Were sporting just as we did there with spirits just as gay
But the "master" sleeps upon the hill, which coated oer with snow
Afforded us a sledding place some twenty years ago

The old schoolhouse is altered now, the benches are replaced
By new ones very like the same our penknives had defaced
But the same old bricks are in the wall, the bell swings to & fro
Its music,s just the same dear Tom ; twas twenty years ago

The boys were playing some old game, beneath that same old tree
I have forgot the name just now, you,ve played it oft with me
On that same spot, twas played with knives by throwing so & so
The leader had a task to do—there, twenty years ago

The rivers running just as still, the willows on its side
Are larger than they were Tom ; the stream appears as wide
But the grapevine swing is ruined now, where once we played the beau
And swung our *sweet hearts* "pretty girls"—just twenty years ago

The spring that bubbled 'neath the hill close by the spreading beech
Is very low twas once so high that we could almost reach ;
And, kneeling down to get a drink, dear Tom, I started so ;
To see how sadly I am changed ; since twenty years ago

Near by the spring, upon an elm, you know I cut your name
Your "sweetheart's" just beneath it Tom; and you did mine the same
Some heartlefs wretch has peeled the bark, twas dying sure but slow
Just as that one whose name you cut died twenty years ago

My lids have long been dry, Tom; but tears came in my eyes
I thought of her I loved so well—those early broken ties;
I visited the old church-yard, & took some flowers to strow
Upon the graves of those we loved, just twenty years ago

Some in the church-yard laid, some sleep beneath the tree
But few are left of that old class, excepting you & me;
And when our time shall come, Tom; and we are called to go
I hope they'll lay us where we played, just twenty years ago

Sunday Nov 4th 1860   Lat 24. 47^{N.}   Long 64. 30^W

The paint is scrubbed, but the decks are not Holystoned, (nor
are they to be this passage,) & all are anxious for home. One
Year ago yesterday I was off N. W. Cape (Aus.) racing with
the Eng. ship Potosi, (myself in the Intrepid)   Then I was
contented & happy in a good ship with agreeable companions
(some of whom are no more in this world) & expecting a pleasant
voyage up through the handsomest & most beautiful islands on
the face of the globe, to Shanghae, & from thence a speedy return
home, which expectation was realized up to the 1st day of April
1860. Now I am in a ship very good in herself, with an excellent
captain but one who has had trouble with his mate ever since
leaving home, which makes it unpleasant all around. Next there
is no one in the forcastle with whom I have any thoughts in
common. They being all very good fellows, to tell the truth, but
belonging to the lower clafs of mortals (or more properly perhaps) to a class with whom I cannot sympathize. Consequently
while I bear an appearance of joviality & laugh & sing & tell
stories with the best of them & am liked by them all (for without
bragging I can say there is not one in the ship with whom I have
had the least difficulty) I am secretly the most anxious, for home,
the most eager for a breeze, of any of them   For we have now
been nearly becalmed for 4 days & many & vociferous are the
supplications to St Antonio to *"Blow" "Blow" "but no breakee
de masts"*. I find St Antonio to be the sailors favorite God during
a spell of calm weather & have heard many an affirmation that it

is he that holds Boreas in leading strings. But the more super-stitious are worried out, & for the past 12 hrs have stuck to it that his reverence is on a *Bust*, & has consequently forgotton his poor devotees. Our distance from New York or Sandy Hook rather, yesterday, was 1084 miles NNW ¼ W. But a little distance if we only had a breeze, 5 days easy sail. Yesterday we bent our storm suit for the thunder squalls have been threatening us ever since we have been becalmed. And we may get a *Norwester* or so ere we have done. A heavy swell from the Northward has been prevalent for some time. I will now lay down my pen hoping that when I take it up again I will not be subject to the summons of "*Port Watch Aho-o-oy 8 bells there below*" "*Do you hear the news* "*Come show a leg or a Pursers stocking*" *Theres a steam-boat waiting for your chest*" "*Your Ice Cream is getting all cold*" accompanied with a punch in the ribs & an inquiry as to whether its "*Your wheel or not*" & "*Whos got the lookout*" or to the frequent command of, "*Lee Main Brace*" or "*Jibe the spanker boom over.*"

Yours Truly
Chas A. Abbey

New York Dec 19th 1860   119 Nassau St

Well, I have been ashore nearly a month & now begin to want to go away again. The Keystone Arrived on the 21st of Nov making a 114 day passage in the clear. Dick Huston arrived 4 days since in the St Louis after a long & tedious bumping passage.

Journal of a Voyage in the Ship Intrepid

from New York towards Shanghae China thence To Hong Kong thence to Whampoa Thence to Hong Kong thence to Macao thence towards New York as far as the Belvidere shoal, Straits of Gaspar where she struck & proved a total loss. Took the French ship Galilei to Angier, thence via two Prahus to Batavia, thence via Steamer Macassar to Singapore thence via ship Keystone of Boston to New York where we arrived Nov 21st 1860

Aug	28th	1859	Sighted the Rock of St Pauls
Aug	30 "	"	" Ferdinand de Noronha
Sept	1 "	"	" Cape Blanco & coast of Brazil
Oct	26th	"	" N. W. Cape, Australia

[275]

Nov	3d 1859	Sighted	Jeendana or Sandalwood island
"	"th "	"	Ombay, Timor, & middle islands*
"	6 " "	"	Pulo Cambing & Wetters island
"	9th "	"	Bouro island
"	10 " "	"	Kalla Bessy
"	16 " "	"	Pulo Pisang, Ceram, Lookisong & Pulo Gassus
"	17 " "	"	Gillolo island
"	28 " "	"	one of the (Egoi group,) a part of the Caroline islands†
Dec	9 " "	"	3 of the Magjico Simah group
"	18 " "	"	Saddle islands
"	20 " "	⎰ Anchored off Woosung there not being water ⎱ enough to allow us to pafs the bar
"	23 "	Anchored at Shanghae
Feb	4 " 1860	Left Shanghae
"	7 " "	" Woosung
"	10 " "	Arrived at Hong Kong
"	14 " "	Left " "
"	15 " "	Arrived at Whampoa
Mch	12 " "	Left "
"	13 " "	Arrived " Hong Kong
"	" " "	Left " "
"	" " "	Arrived " Macao (Typa Roads)
"	17 " "	Left " for New York
Mch	31st "	Struck Belvidere shoal
Apl	1 " "	Abandoned the wreck
"	8th "	Arrived at Angier
"	9 " "	" " Batavia
"	11 " "	Left "
Apl	15 " "	Arrived " Singapore
July	25 " "	Left that "*confounded*" Singapore
Aug	10 " "	Arrived at Angier
Aug	11 " "	Left "
Oct	3 d "	Made St Helena
"	" " "	Left " "

* Actually sighted Timor, then Ombay, on November 4 and/or 5.
† The *Intrepid* was never very close to the Egoi Islands or any of the other Caroline groups. Probably one of the Pelew Islands was sighted.

CHAPTER XX

LATER YEARS

ABBEY reports the *Keystone* as "making a 114 day passage in the clear." It is not certain from what point this time is measured. Possibly the *Keystone* was 114 days to New York from the last time the anchor was weighed during the protracted effort to get away from the general vicinity of Singapore.

There follows here a tabulation in which the *Keystone's* passage is divided into sections and compared with that of the *Charmer* when Abbey came home in her four years before.

	Keystone	Charmer	Record passage of the Sea Witch
Singapore to Anjer	16		
Whampoa to Anjer		27	10
At Anjer	1	0	0
Anjer to Cape of Good Hope	36	34	26
Cape of Good Hope to St. Helena 17 ⎫			
Cape of Good Hope to Equator ⎬ 31		22	19
St. Helena to Equator 14 ⎭			
Equator to New York	35	33	22
Anjer to New York	102	89	67
Singapore to New York	119		
Whampoa to New York		116	77

Thus the *Keystone* made just about an average clipper ship passage from the Far East to New York, surpassed by the *Charmer* primarily as a result of the latter's fast work from the Cape to the equator.

A great deal had indeed happened in the past four years with regard to Abbey's views on going to sea. Those grievous times in the *Surprise*, back in 1856, were merely the first of many days to be spent by him in ships. This voyage which ended in the *Key-*

stone was the last one, unfortunately, of which Abbey kept any kind of a record—at least none has yet come to light.

Abbey spent three more years in the clippers, and his travels during this period consisted of two more voyages to the Far East. Although they were long they were not without interest. After four months at home, following the *Keystone* passage, he went as A. B. in the clipper ship *Daylight* from New York to Hong Kong. Thence he started for Shanghai in the ship *John White*, and ran into a typhoon, August 8, 1861. The blow was so terrific that the vessel was dismasted and barely reached Amoy a week later in a sinking condition. This place is just 300 miles up the China coast from Hong Kong which the *John White* had left 16 days before. During Abbey's brief service in this ship some of the crew mutinied. Abbey was one of those instrumental in suppressing the outbreak. This incident must have been fraught with interest; unfortunately, however, no details of the event have come down to us.

For five months Abbey had charge of one of the gangs of a wrecking crew at Amoy that was engaged in wrecking the French steamer *Isere*. During this employment he had a finger partly crushed; twenty-three long years later it was amputated. After the wrecking job he got a berth as Third Mate of the ship *Kate Howe* in which he finally reached New York again. Thus he became an officer at the age of twenty. This was the second successive voyage to the Far East in which he was virtually shipwrecked, and each voyage consumed more than a year.

Abbey was home only a month this time and then sailed from New York for Hong Kong in the 5-year-old clipper ship *Hotspur*. It was the year 1862 and not much more than a dozen American clippers altogether were built later than the *Hotspur*. As her career was short, her reputation for speed is not so high as it deserves. She broke no records but defeated several ships with great reputations, while sailing over the same routes at the same times. Each voyage of the *Hotspur* was from New York to China. On her maiden trip she required only 90 days from New York to Hong Kong—very fast. Returning home on her third voyage she sailed from the Cape of Good Hope to St. Helena in 8 days, and from the Cape to New York in 45, despite 5 days of northerly gales toward the end. On her next trip home she passed the big, speedy *Sea Serpent* in Sunda Strait and beat her to New York by 9 days. On her fifth return passage she beat our old friend the *Surprise* from Batavia to New York by 5 days; and this in spite of the fact that the *Hotspur* was within 2 days' sail of Sandy Hook for 6 days.

The next voyage of the *Hotspur*, her sixth, was the one in which Abbey sailed in her as Second Mate from New York to Hong Kong. It is a good thing that he left her at the eastern end of her journey, or he might well have acquired the reputation of a Jonah. For on the way home the *Hotspur*, with a million dollar cargo aboard, was wrecked and became a total loss. On February 17, 1863, she piled up on one of the Paracel reefs, which form one of the many groups of shoals and island dots lying between the Philippine Islands and the mainland. The shipwrecked mariners piled into three boats which soon became separated. One made the mainland, whereupon its occupants were captured by natives. After being held prisoner for a week, they escaped to an English vessel. One boatload was picked up by a Chinese junk and landed safely. The third boat got to shore all right but a passenger died on the way. By a strange coincidence her name was Mrs. Abbe.

After leaving the *Hotspur* at Hong Kong, Abbey made Shanghai in 4 days on the steamer *Yang Tsze*. When Abbey was in the *Intrepid* back in 1860, he encountered this very steamer off Gutzlaff Island, it will be remembered, and the *Intrepid* won the ensuing race to Hong Kong. Abbey's next ship after the *Hotspur* was a small clipper called the *Fruiter* which was engaged in trade along the coats of China and Japan. He was in her for over a year, starting as Second Mate and ending up as First or Chief Mate. After that he shipped at Shanghai as First Mate of the Danish bark *Hermine* bound for New York with a cargo of coolies. He reached home on May 3, 1864; his last voyage in the clippers had lasted nearly two years. In these last three years in sail, it is seen that Abbey rose from A. B. to Chief Mate, first attaining the latter rank at the age of 23.

At this point two major events of Abbey's life transpired. Less than three weeks after he got home he married his childhood sweetheart, Pamela C. Hjortsberg, of Brooklyn, N. Y. She was the sister of Edward Hjortsberg who had been one of Abbey's shipmates in the *Henry Brigham*, it will be remembered. And earlier, he had been a schoolmate of Abbey at the Columbia Institute presided over by Abbey's father. About the time of his sister's marriage Edward became one of the first and one of the ablest pilots of western ships in Far Eastern waters; and he made some of the earliest charts of those seas. When the U. S. Navy undertook its punitive expedition against the Korean river forts in 1871, the piloting of the gunboat *Monocacy* fell to the lot of Hjortsberg; this was one of the most important jobs in the whole operation.

Abbey's other big step upon his return home was his taking leave of the clippers and entering the U. S. Revenue Marine in July, 1864. This is the Treasury Department organization better known as the Revenue Cutter Service and now called the Coast Guard. Abbey obtained a commission at the outset—Third Lieutenant, the lowest rank of course. His commission bears the signature of Abraham Lincoln. The Civil War was still very much in progress, and as usual the Revenue Cutters were serving along with the regular Navy ships. Abbey's most important wartime service was in the *Forward*, operating in the waters around Beaufort and Wilmington, N. C. His duties on that station ended in March, 1865, when he was made prize master of the captured schooner *Emmaline Johnson*. She is said to have been the only prize brought in to New York City during the War. He was promoted to Second Lieutenant just after this occurrence, and to First Lieutenant two years later.

In 1870, when 29 years of age, Abbey obtained his first command, the *Rescue*. The following year the personnel of the Revenue Marine was overhauled and numerous competitive examinations were held. As a result of the examination given to the first lieutenants Abbey jumped from No. 36 to No. 2 in his grade. Continuing up the ladder he was commissioned Captain in 1877, the youngest captain in the Revenue Marine. At this point he began to suffer from the stagnation which was so prevalent in all branches of the Service in the latter part of the last century— the stagnation caused by the lack of vacancies in the higher commissioned grades. All of his service until 1889 was at sea, and almost all was along the Atlantic Coast. A thrilling book could be written about almost any quarter century of routine sea duty that falls to the lot of a Revenue Cutter officer—the storms, the ice, the shipwrecks, the rescues and salvage, the hardships and dangers. We cannot undertake to examine them in this volume. As an indication of the activity of the Revenue Marine there is included here a table of statistics covering the operations from 1871–9.

Number of vessels boarded and examined	218,479
Number of vessels seized or reported for violation of law	14,192
Number of vessels in distress assisted	1,578
Number of miles sailed and steamed	1,600,679
Number of lives saved	555

While serving in and about Newbern, N. C., shortly after the Civil War, Abbey had the unusual distinction, for a Yankee, of winning the favor of the Southerners. They requested and obtained his return to that station on two later occasions for additional tours of duty. Perhaps the most important single assignment that Captain Abbey had in all these years was that in connection with the sealing situation in Alaskan waters and the Bering Sea in 1886. The principal job was to stamp out the illegal killing that was being carried on in non-territorial waters by outlaw sealers of various nationalities. The orders included the performance of a great many acts and the procurement of many kinds of information about many islands and waters. The *Corwin* was Captain Abbey's ship on this duty. Here again many interesting chapters could be written, but they cannot be included in this volume.

In 1889 Captain Abbey was made Inspector General of the Life Saving Service and Superintendent of Construction for all the coasts of the United States excluding Alaska. He served in this capacity for six years, maintaining his headquarters in New York City whence he sallied forth on his many long trips to various stations. This position, of course, is an extremely important one in the Coast Guard organization. When sea duty came around again the Spanish War was drawing nigh. The latest and last Cuban revolt was in progress against Spain, and Captain Abbey's duties included the supression of filibusters operating from the United States. When war did come, the Revenue Cutter *Gresham* was ordered from the Great Lakes to the scene of action and Captain Abbey was ordered to Milwaukee to bring her around. On reaching the St. Lawrence River above Montreal the *Gresham* had to be cut in two in order to get her through the canal locks. This was done at Ogdensburg, N. Y., and she was put together again successfully below the last shallow water. By the time she was ready for action, however, the fighting was over.

After completing his three-year tour of sea duty Captain Abbey was ordered back to his desk at New York as Inspector

General of the Life Saving Service once more. This was a fitting tribute to the manner in which he had carried out his duties on the earlier occasion. He reached the age of 64 in 1905 and so was retired. The following year he was made Senior Captain when that new rank was created. He had served the Government continuously for 41 years, more than two thirds of them at sea. In all that time he had never been incapacitated for duty nor had he ever been laid off, "waiting orders." Of great value was his work of inventing and perfecting devices for increasing the efficiency of the Life Saving Service and its material. Some of his inventions bear his name. In retirement at Northport, L. I., a heart ailment curtailed the vigorous activity which he longed to continue in his chosen field.

He was the father of eight children and his heritage appears in many of them. Two followed in his footsteps in the Coast Guard. One of the tasks in which these two officers engaged was the raising of the battleship *Maine* from the bottom of Havana harbor. Treasures of the family now include a flower that was salvaged from Captain Sigsbee's table 13 years after the disaster. Another one of Captain Abbey's sons, an Alaska mine operator, was named for the ship commanded by the father at the time the child was born. One son was unable to undergo the discipline which held sway in Captain Abbey's household, and ran away from home in his youth. He found his way to China and is reliably reported to have sold the first bicycles in that country. One of Captain Abbey's daughters survives and she has to her credit the successful passing of the technical examinations for master of a ship.

A very large man of splendid physique, Captain Abbey survived until 1919, thus living 78 years of a very full life. Until the end his interest in both national and international affairs was intense and he was an untiring reader. He was an early member of the Cosmos Club of Washington and spent many winters in the Capital. He numbered many of the great men of the world among his friends. A stern but kindly man he was a believer in plain living and high thinking; and with Chesterfieldian manners, he was indeed "a gentleman of the old school." In a heartfelt manner he was interested in humanity, in nature, and in the universe, and truly "hearkened to the music of the spheres."

Captain Abbey was always quite reticent about his experiences, though they compassed such a wide and varied field. It was difficult to draw him out. And so it is not surprising that his family never learned from him even of the existence of the diaries which comprise the body of this book. They were not discovered until a few years ago. After reading them, and after hearing of his subsequent attainments, it is fair to assume that young Abbey received a splendid foundation for his life when he spent the years of his boyhood before the mast in the clippers.